# CLASS, LANGUAGE, AND AMERICAN FILM COMEDY

This book examines the evolution of American film comedy through the lens of language and the portrayal of social class. Christopher Beach argues that class has been an important element in the development of sound comedy as a cinematic form. With the advent of sound in the late 1920s and early 1930s, filmmakers recognized that sound and narrative enlarged the semiotic and ideological potential of film. Analyzing the use of language in the films of the Marx Brothers, Frank Capra, Woody Allen, and the Coen brothers, among others, *Class, Language, and American Film Comedy* traces the history of Hollywood from the 1930s to the present, while offering a new approach to the study of class and social relationships through linguistic analysis.

Christopher Beach teaches at the University of California, Irvine and the Claremont Graduate University. He is the author of three books on various aspects of American poetry.

# CLASS, LANGUAGE, AND AMERICAN FILM COMEDY

CHRISTOPHER BEACH

CAMBRIDGE
UNIVERSITY PRESS

PUBLISHED BY THE PRESS SYNDICATE OF THE UNIVERSITY OF CAMBRIDGE
The Pitt Building, Trumpington Street, Cambridge, United Kingdom

CAMBRIDGE UNIVERSITY PRESS
The Edinburgh Building, Cambridge CB2 2RU, UK
40 West 20th Street, New York, NY 10011-4211, USA
477 Williamstown Road, Port Melbourne, VIC 3207, Australia
Ruiz de Alarcón 13, 28014 Madrid, Spain
Dock House, The Waterfront, Cape Town 8001, South Africa

http://www.cambridge.org

First published 2002

Printed in the United Kingdom at the University Press, Cambridge

*Typeface* Adobe Garamond 11/14 pt.   *System* QuarkXPress   [HT]

*A catalog record for this book is available from the British Library*

*Library of Congress Cataloging-in-Publication Data*
Beach, Christopher.
Class, language, and American film comedy / Christopher Beach.
p.   cm
Includes bibliographical references and index.
ISBN 0521 80749 2 – ISBN 0 521 00209 (pb.)
1. Comedy films – United States – History and criticism.   2. Speech and social
status – United States.   I. Title.

PN1995.9.C55 B43 2001
791.43 617 – dc21       2001025935

ISBN  0 521 80749 2  hardback
ISBN  0 521 00209 5  paperback

# CONTENTS

# ACKNOWLEDGMENTS

I owe a great debt to Linda Williams, who helped point me in the right direction in the early stages of this project. I also owe thanks to Alice Fahs and Lee Medovoi, both of whom made valuable suggestions about individual chapters, and to the various members of the UC Irvine community who discussed the evolving book with me. Finally, thanks to Carrie Noland for all her support and encouragement, without which none of it would have been possible.

# INTRODUCTION

Of all the genres of Hollywood film that underwent the transition from silent to sound production in the late 1920s and early 1930s, it was the comedy, along with the musical, that most obviously benefited from the arrival of the "talkies." Screen comedies of the silent era – though they had included sophisticated social comedies by directors such as Cecil B. DeMille and Ernst Lubitsch – had been dominated by the physical, slapstick, or clown comedy popularized by such actors as Charlie Chaplin, Buster Keaton, Harold Lloyd, and Harry Langdon. The sound era brought to the fore an essentially new genre of dialogue-based romantic comedy, a genre that foregrounded both the art of spoken language and the nuances of class-based relationships.

In silent comedy, class divisions tended to be depicted in terms of crude dichotomies. The characters created by comedians like Chaplin, Mack Sennett, Mabel Normand, and the Keystone Kops represented working-class types and situations that were immediately familiar to their audiences and that would allow the filmmakers to parody conventional middle-class standards of behavior. In Chaplin's films, for example, the tramp figure stands as a universally recognizable icon of lower-class status rather than as a fully delineated social individual. The tramp was already well established as a stock figure in American popular culture, from music hall and vaudeville to pulp literature, newspapers, comic strips, and nickelodeon pictures. Chaplin's tramp, as a particularized variant of the familiar character type, remains a constant throughout his films, prompting some critics to question the social relevance of the tramp figure or even its basis in real life. "The tramp character," as Theodore Huff remarks, "could be of any country and of any time."[1] Chaplin's tramp is, in fact, more an "eternal clown" than a well-defined individual operating within realistic social structures.

It was not until the early sound era, when the highly specific social codes involving speech were added to more general codes governing behavior and dress, that comedies moved beyond slapstick caricatures of middle-class and upper-class society and began to reflect more nuanced social distinctions. The advent of spoken language in film permitted a much more intimate relation between cinema and the specifics of social reality, including class. While a silent filmmaker like Chaplin could explore class relationships quite effectively through such elements as plot, setting, character, costume, and physical movement, sound films could use the additional dimension of speech to register more subtle differences in social class, ethnicity, and educational or geographical background. In addition to the use of gesture and physical appearance, filmmakers could now convey social distinctions through such linguistic signs as accent, diction, vocabulary, grammar, and verbal proficiency, as well as the sound of the voice itself (rough vs. smooth, raw vs. refined). In the work of early sound comedians such as the Marx Brothers, W. C. Fields, and Mae West, the new combination of spoken text and visual image became a coherent mode of semiosis. The movies could now unify speech and image in presenting more coherent and complex characterizations. Films like the Marx Brothers' *Animal Crackers,* Mae West's *She Done Him Wrong,* and Frank Capra's *It Happened One Night* – all made within the first few years of sound cinema – were in large part the products of a new social semiosis made possible by the introduction of spoken language to the filmic medium.

In this book I am concerned with the representation of social class in American film comedy from the beginning of the sound era to the present. I use the analysis of a variety of comedies from different points in the development of Hollywood film and from different subgenres within the larger genre of film comedy to explore the representation of social class and social mobility. I argue that the issue of social class was crucially important to the development of sound comedy, and I propose two reasons for this importance. The first of these is the historical fact that the origins of sound film coincide almost exactly with the beginnings of the Great Depression. Given this historical coincidence, it is only logical that the formative early history of sound comedy would trace the social upheaval and increased class consciousness that characterized the 1930s. The second reason for the importance of class relations in Hollywood comedy has to do with the medium of sound film itself. As an intensely *verbal* genre, comedy was the form that best exploited the possibilities of spoken language, including the potential of spoken discourse to articulate differences based on class and on related social formations such as gender, race, ethnicity, educational background, and geographical origin. With the advent of sound in the late 1920s and early 1930s, the enlargement of the semiotic possibilities available to filmmakers had important narrative, aesthetic, and ideological consequences. The presence of spoken language in film made possible the representation of the many forms of symbolic power and linguistic capital with which speech is invested. My understanding of comedy as a genre deeply concerned with both class and speech is not new. Comedy has traditionally been a mode that uses language to examine and critique existing social structures, including those governing the construction of class. What this study does provide, however, is a closer analysis of the complex reconfiguration of social relationships within a wide range of Hollywood sound comedies, and of the different ways in which the verbal dimension of these films contributes to their representation of class issues.

Finally, the book makes a larger argument about the status of film comedy within American culture as a whole. As one of the most popular genres of American film production, and one of the most widely disseminated forms of cultural representation during the past seventy years, film comedy is an intriguing instance of a popular form that provides moments of genuine social critique while also fulfilling its primary function as a source of mass entertainment. As a genre, comedy examines and critiques social structures – including those of class – and at certain points in history it has served as an important facilitator or mediator of society's attempts at self-critique. Yet at the same time, as an important component of the culture industry, film comedy responds to the need for what Richard Dyer has described as a "utopian" form of entertainment, an escapist and often ideologically conservative response to the social conditions operative at different historical moments.

Given these dual and often conflicting tendencies within American film comedy, the representation of class also possesses an important historical dimension. The diachronic study of American comedies undertaken in this book allows us to see how Hollywood has negotiated class relations in the genre of comedy and to ask how films of different eras have addressed issues of class and their relation to other kinds of social issues. In the films of the early 1930s like those of the Marx Brothers, we find a more overt representation of class antagonisms, as Hollywood cinema played out the tensions inherent in a period characterized by profound socioeconomic disruption. By the late 1930s – with the more restrictive post–Production Code limitations on social content – class tensions are largely displaced onto gender tensions. Although class antagonisms are still apparent, the dominant forms of romantic or "screwball" comedy are more concerned with the fantasy of a cross-class romance enacted by its male and female leads. In the postwar era, comedies become even less concerned with class relations per se, but they continue to examine questions of social status and the relations between forms of sociocultural distinction and forms of gender and sexual difference. Finally, within what I will designate as the "postmodern" era of American film comedy (the 1970s, 1980s, and 1990s), the treatment of social class takes a wide variety of forms, from the critique of mainstream middle-class values in the work of Woody Allen or Albert Brooks to the parodic vision of certain class fragments in the work of filmmakers such as the Coen brothers, John Waters, and Whit Stillman.

Steven Ross's highly informative study *Working-Class Hollywood* has provided a comprehensive treatment of class issues as they pertain to films of the silent era.[2] My work on class in *sound* comedy should provide at least a partial complement to Ross's book, though my approach is in important ways different from his. Unlike Ross, I am not a film historian seeking to document the impact of changing class attitudes and class relations on American film, or to explain the impact of political radicalism and labor movements on film production. Instead, I am interested in analyzing through "close viewings" of a number of Hollywood films the representations of class relationships within the genre of American film comedy. Although I have tried to contextualize these representations within the broader history of class definitions and attitudes during the period in question, my interest is less thematic and sociohistorical than rhetorical and aesthetic. I ask: How does class function within the particular genre of comedy in a way that is both socially provocative and aesthetically challenging?

For the purposes of this study, I define class as the system by which social divisions are created, delineated, and maintained. In a culture where class boundaries and relationships are less historically determined and less rigidly imposed than in many other societies, the definition of class becomes a highly flexible rubric providing limitless possibilities for both narrative and comic treatment. In the United States, class is interwoven in a dense social fabric with such determining factors as gender, ethnicity, race, religion, education, and geography. As Amy Schrager Lang puts it, "class, race, and gender appear not as self-sufficient categories, much less independent ones, but as vocabularies from which the language of identity is drawn."[3] In the history of American film, therefore – as in the much longer history of American literature – the representation of class cannot be isolated from other kinds of representation. Instead, class must be evaluated in a dialogue with other factors that emerge in particular films: ethnicity in the case of the Marx Brothers or Woody Allen, gender and sexuality in the screwball comedy, or race in the films of Richard Pryor and Eddie Murphy.

Chapter 1 of this book examines the beginning of the sound era, contrasting the sophisticated social comedy of Ernst Lubitsch with the first five films of the Marx Brothers and arguing for a reading of early sound comedy as a highly transgressive genre. I proceed in the second and third chapters to a discussion of the emergent screwball comedy of the middle and late 1930s. I focus Chapter 2 on the evolution of the screwball genre and its more typical manifestation in films like Gregory La Cava's *My Man Godfrey* and Mitchell Leisen's *Easy Living;* Chapter 3 is a more sustained reading of the mid-1930s comedies of Frank Capra. In the fourth chapter, I look closely at representative films by two of the most important directors of classical Hollywood film comedy in the early 1940s – Preston Sturges and Howard Hawks – in order to examine the increasingly parodic (and even self-parodic) nature of the screwball format. The fifth chapter takes up the Hollywood comedies of the 1950s – in particular films by Vincente Minnelli, Frank Tashlin, and Jerry Lewis – focusing on their attempts to negotiate a postwar American obsession with social status. Chapter 6 looks at the mode of "postmodern" comedy as exemplified by the films of Woody Allen. In the final chapter I turn to contemporary social satire, focusing on both mainstream Hollywood comedies and films by independent filmmakers that offer strikingly different views of postmodern American social existence.

It has often been argued that the United States is a nation with no meaningful language of class. Nevertheless, it is important to acknowledge and analyze the ways in which the medium of film has not only reflected but also helped to shape Americans' ideas of class, class identity, class distinction, and class conflict. Steven Ross has usefully delineated the way the movies of the silent era "taught audiences, especially newly arrived immigrants, what it meant to dress, to think, and to act like a member of a particular class," presenting "competing visions of what the working class, middle class, and upper class looked like" at a time when traditional class identities were in flux (xiii). By the late 1920s and early 1930s, when the first of the sound films I examine in this book were being made, the social function of film had changed considerably, as had the social composition of its audience. The audience for these films was largely middle-class and educated, unlike the audiences Ross describes for the early silent era. The romantic comedies of the 1930s continue to deal with class issues, but they are concerned less often with presenting overt class conflicts between highly polarized groups (i.e., wage-earners and capitalists) than with exploring the possibilities of various kinds of interaction between members of different classes.

The subject of class was a particular preoccupation of filmmakers throughout the period between the world wars: Lary May identifies seventy-five films made during the 1920s with the explicit theme of "success up [the] class ladder," and many more of these films were made during the 1930s.[4] That social mobility was a focal point of interest during these years was hardly surprising, given both the personal trajectories of many who worked within the film industry and the institutional history of the cinema itself. Virtually all of the Hollywood "moguls" running the major film studios during this period were from ethnic (Jewish) backgrounds, either immigrants themselves or second-generation immigrants. Most of them grew up in working-class families – their fathers being tailors, cobblers, waiters, and shoe salesmen – and they embody in their own personal histories the kind of upwardly mobile trajectories plotted in many of the Hollywood productions for which they were responsible.

In fact, the importance of class issues in the films of the period, and especially the theme of class ascension, can be related to the overall drive to gentrify the film industry and its products. Both executives like Adolph Zukor and directors like D. W. Griffith had sought to move Hollywood film up the social scale from the decidedly working-class nickelodeons of the early 1900s to a form more commensurate with the ideals of cultivated audiences.[5] As of 1908, the high point of the nickelodeon, the majority of the audience had been working-class; by the late 1910s and early 1920s, according to Lary May, "the core of the new audience was made of precisely those people who would have not appeared in the neighborhood of a nickelodeon" (164). The films made by Griffith and other directors were increasingly geared toward middle-class tastes, and they were shown not in the nickelodeons but in luxurious picture palaces and socially integrated movie theaters that were in safer neighborhoods and supplied more luxurious amenities. As Ross notes, "studio moguls realized they could make big money by turning moviegoing into a 'respectable' entertainment that catered to the rapidly expanding and amorphous ranks of the middle class" (9).

For immigrant and working-class audiences, the cinema became increasingly a means of assimilation into mainstream American life. At the same time, for middle-class spectators, the social stigma attached to the movies all but disappeared during the late 1910s and early 1920s. By the late 1920s, film had become completely respectable, and its audience largely bourgeois. In an effort to promote visions of class harmony that would cater to a middle-class audience, films of the 1920s shifted attention away from the problems of the workplace and toward the pleasures of the new consumer society. These films often depicted cross-class fantasies, stories of interactions and romantic involvements between an upper-class and either working-class or middle-class protagonist that conveyed an underlying ideology of class harmony and reconciliation. These cross-class films, as Ross argues, "shifted attention away from the deadening world of production and toward the pleasures of consumption," teaching their audiences that "participation in a modern consumer society made class differences irrelevant" (195).[6]

This role of film as a promoter of social harmony was not entirely new. As Miriam Hansen suggests, film was from an early point in its development marketed as a "democratic art," a form of popular culture that could "submerge all class distinctions in an ostensibly homogeneous culture of consumption" (65). By the 1930s, commentators were already well aware of the power of the movies as a socializing and homogenizing influence. As early as 1939, Margaret Thorp pointed to the role of Hollywood in "furnishing the nation with a common body of knowledge": "The movies span geographic frontiers; they give the old something to talk about with the young; they crumble the barriers between people of different educations and different economic backgrounds."[7] According to social historian Richard Pells, the movies fulfilled not simply a democratizing function, but a fundamentally conservative purpose of "educating people to the accepted fashions and norms of behavior"; Hollywood films inspired not simply community but "conformity."[8] This tension between the vision of American film as a democratic and socially unifying medium and that of Hollywood as a reactionary manifestation of the American culture industry is often played out in the films themselves. In the comedies of Capra, for example, it is through the treatment of class relations among the film's characters that more general sociocultural relations both within Hollywood and within American society as a whole can be viewed and (re)interpreted. As a highly flexible cultural medium (unlike the opera or Broadway theater, for example), film was uniquely positioned to negotiate such sociocultural issues. Film was a prerecorded mass medium that could be packaged and sold to very different class constituencies with no change in the fundamental product being offered. As Thorp points out, admission charges in the late 1930s ran "all the way from $2.20, and even more, for first showings in big urban theaters to 10 cents in the farm districts and the third- and fourth-run city houses," with an average price of 25 to 35 cents (10). Seen by every part of the socioeconomic spectrum, Hollywood films were among the cultural commodities that contributed to the breakdown of class barriers and to America's view of itself as a relatively classless society.

The expanding audience for film – the most widely disseminated form of mass culture after the First World War – was in part a result of the blurring of class boundaries in American society from the turn of the century into the 1920s. This is not to say that American film neglects or deemphasizes class issues, but that it presents them in a context which may not always accurately reflect social realities as they exist at a particular historical moment. Read as a subset of Hollywood films in general, Hollywood comedies are not merely reflecting in some unmediated sense the class dynamics of the era in which they are made. Instead, they represent a reciprocal relationship between audiences and filmmakers, and an even more complex configuration of relationships between those who make films (writers, directors, producers), those who finance and distribute them (the studios and their parent corporations), those who control or censor them (the Hays Office), and those who watch them (an extremely diversified audience).

A better understanding of these relationships will help us to answer the question that this book begins to address: To what extent did sound comedy of the studio era function as social critique, and to what extent did it function – in the terms of Richard Dyer – as pure "entertainment," as an escapist fantasy or a utopian alternative to the everyday situation of Depression-era Americans? In his influential essay "Entertainment and Utopia," Dyer deals with the genre of musicals and not with nonmusical comedies. Nevertheless, it would seem that much of his definition of entertainment as a utopian form of escape or wish-fulfillment and a response to "specific inadequacies of society" would apply to comedy as well, particularly during a period like the 1930s:

> Entertainment offers the image of "something better" to escape into, or something we want deeply that our day-to-day lives don't provide. Alternatives, hopes, wishes – these are the stuff of utopia, the sense that things could be better, that something other than what is can be imagined and maybe realized.[9]

That Hollywood films fulfilled some form of utopian or escapist fantasy for moviegoers was the view of many commentators of the Depression era, who pointed among other factors to the tremendous popularity of Walt Disney's extravagant and nostalgic productions, to the lavish musicals of Busby Berkeley, and to the luxurious settings of Hollywood films which allowed women viewers in particular to escape from their hum-drum lives into utopian dreams of elegant cars, streamlined penthouses, and sable coats. It is overly reductive, however, to read film comedy as an essentially utopian genre. While many comedies do involve some form of wish-fulfillment or liberation from authority or oppression, there are numerous exceptions to these tendencies, as in the more satirical films of comedians like the Marx Brothers and W. C. Fields, and more recently in the films of

Woody Allen, John Waters, and the Coen brothers, to take only a few examples.[10] I would argue that even within many comedies that appear to offer utopian solutions, there are elements that work against such simplified resolutions of social or ideological conflicts. Although comedies by definition involve some sort of "happy ending" for the central characters, it is important to remember that even though a film's resolution may represent a movement toward the society's dominant ideology, the nature and articulation of the dramatic conflicts within the film should not and indeed cannot be ignored. Perhaps more than utopia, what the most interesting comedies provide is a means of envisioning potentially liberating forms of transgression. The kinds of social transgression permitted within the films made by Hollywood in the 1930s – whether in gangster films or screwball comedies, two of the most popular genres of the decade – were, despite the efforts of the censors, the best release valve for Americans whose average lives were increasingly limited in both economic and sociocultural terms. Because of the nature of comedy as a genre that is perceived as "lighter" and thus as less threatening to society, the kinds of transgression permitted (often in the form of satire or parody rather than in the form of explicit statement) tend to be greater than in other genres. As Steve Neale and Frank Krutnik suggest, comedy is often allowed a considerable latitude, since "subversion" and "transgression" are to at least some degree "institutionalized generic requirements" of comedy.[11] We need only think of the fact that in 1940 and 1941, during one of the tensest periods of World War II, American comedies ridiculing Hitler and the Nazis were made by both Charlie Chaplin *(The Great Dictator)* and Ernst Lubitsch *(To Be Or Not To Be)*. What these comedies offered audiences was not a utopian vision of the world, but the opportunity to laugh at a very serious and very threatening issue.

Throughout the history of sound film, American comedies have enacted transgressions against a wide range of societal, institutional, and historical forces: against systems of law and order *(Trouble in Paradise, The Lady Eve, Take the Money and Run, Serial Mom)*; against a rationalistic, bureaucratic, and repressive society *(Bringing Up Baby, Holiday, You Can't Take It with You, The Bellboy, Sleeper)*; against prescribed forms of feminine behavior and sexual conduct *(She Done Him Wrong, I'm No Angel, Design for Living, Desperately Seeking Susan)*; against excessive forms of consumerism and commodification *(Easy Living, The Long, Long Trailer,*

*Bananas);* against ideals of domestic and family life *(It's a Gift, Polyester, Raising Arizona, Real Life);* against the small-town American ideal *(Nothing Sacred, The Miracle of Morgan's Creek, Hail the Conquering Hero, The Trouble with Harry);* against wars and the governmental policies that support them *(Duck Soup, M\*A\*S\*H, Dr. Strangelove);* against bourgeois conformity *(The Seven Year Itch, The Graduate, Something Wild, Hairspray);* and against American business and the corporate ethos *(Christmas in July, The Sin of Harold Diddlebock, Will Success Spoil Rock Hunter, The Apartment, Annie Hall).*

Yet the element of transgression in these films – while it may suggest an implicit or even an explicit critique of social and political structures – does not always succeed in articulating a clear critical vision. The transgressive moment in film comedy cannot be subsumed either under its function as entertainment and spectacle, or under its antithetical function as social critique. This ambivalence is particularly true of those films that present social transgression in terms of crossing class boundaries. In many of these comedies, a tension exists between an acute awareness of class differences on the one hand, and a desire to smooth over such differences on the other. The prevalence of this tension can be explained both by the generic structure of comedy – which encourages a certain degree of social critique but ultimately relies on a more affirmative outcome – and by the unique structure of American ideology. The democratic or populist ideology defining America as a classless society – and the closely related ideologies of the American Dream or American success story – is often seen in American literature and film as coming into conflict with real-life situations in which class distinction represents an impediment to social mobility. These situations can be depicted in tragic terms – as in Theodore Dreiser's novel *The American Tragedy,* a story of a cross-class romance gone sour – or they can be treated in comic terms, where class discrepancy becomes a source of humor, satire, or farce. In American sound comedies, the transgression of class boundaries is often the source of plots and narrative situations. Moreover, the tensions created by the transgression of such boundaries are negotiated through spoken language and its interaction with the visual image.

The transgression of class borders that takes place in American film comedies, and the way in which language functions as an agent of such transgression or subversion, has received only limited attention in previous discussions of the genre. I do not intend to provide an exhaustive theoretical treatment of these complex issues, but I hope that this book can serve as a useful opening to further work in this area.

The two theorists whose ideas have informed my work on film comedy are the Russian literary critic Mikhail Bakhtin and the French social anthropologist Pierre Bourdieu. The case for Bakhtin's importance to film studies has been persuasively made by Robert Stam in his book *Subversive Pleasures*. Stam points to the relevance of Bakhtin's work on language, and especially to his notion of "speech tact," the organizing force within everyday language and the "basic meter" of spoken utterance.[12] In Bakhtin's lexicon, "speech tact" is the ensemble of codes governing the genre and style of speech; these codes are in turn determined by the aggregate of social relationships and ideological horizons at a given moment and in a given social situation. Bakhtin rejects the notion of language as a static system: for him, language is always subject to individual and social variation, a dynamic process constantly generating new norms or challenging the official norm. The mode in which language exhibits this generative and subversive potential is most often referred to as "dialogism" (language as a dialogue rather than a monolithic utterance) or, even more radically, as "heteroglossia" (language as a polyphonic mix of different styles, genres, and voices). Stam applies Bakhtinian literary analysis to film study; he proposes that, like literature, film can be read within its "generating ideological environment and . . . the generating socioeconomic environment which permeates it" (33).

Bakhtin's theory clearly provides a means of articulating the connection between class and language. His theories of dialogism and heteroglossia provide a means of understanding the production of different speech genres and performance styles as they occur in sound film. Furthermore, Bakhtin's idea of the "carnivalesque" – a form of linguistic or social interaction that emphasizes the creativity of the common people (the speech of the marketplace as opposed to that of the official culture or ruling classes) – suggests a way of reading film as a subversive and democratizing form that can incorporate marginalized or repressed elements of society. The carnival can be evoked by film in a number of ways: as part of its own history as a form of popular entertainment (vaudeville, the nickelodeon, the peepshow); as a setting or locale within the film (the fairground, the sideshow, the circus, the amusement park, the red-light district); through any number of metonymic references (laughter, clowns, masks, the use of stock comic characters); or, more generally, through a spirit of hyperbole, excess, anarchy, or manic behavior. The carnivalesque mode of social discourse as it operates in either film or literature uses language, among other forms of behavior, to liberate the characters (and potentially the audience) from the restraints imposed by good taste and etiquette, from all that represents the official culture. Stam includes in the carnivalesque tradition the films of the Marx Brothers and Preston Sturges, certain films of Stanley Kubrick and Mel Brooks, and the films of such stand-up comics as John Cleese, John Belushi, Robin Williams, and Richard Pryor. I would also include in this list many of the screwball comedies of the 1930s, certain films of Howard Hawks and Billy Wilder, the films of Jerry Lewis and Frank Tashlin in the 1950s, the early films of Woody Allen, and, more recently, the films of Jim Carrey.

As useful as Bakhtin's theories are for an understanding of screen comedy, I would supplement them with the sociocultural theories of Bourdieu. Bourdieu's model of "social habitus" provides a more nuanced index of class relations than the somewhat crude polarizations of the official culture and the marginal or subaltern culture offered by Bakhtin. In addition, Bourdieu's work on language in *Language and Symbolic Power* provides a more detailed analysis of the relations between linguistic practice and cultural power. As Bourdieu has persuasively argued, spoken language is one of the primary means of articulating the history of a given speaker. The style of speech adopted by a speaker – for example, a character in a film – is always marked by a certain class disposition ("habitus") that informs every aspect of spoken language, from pronunciation to the use of a particular vocabulary or slang, from the telling of jokes to the use of class-based references. Speech is, in fact, one of the most deeply rooted of bodily dispositions. As Bourdieu observes, "linguistic, especially phonetic, competence is a dimension of bodily hexis in which one's whole relation to the social world, and one's whole socially-informed relation to the world, are expressed."[13] Through language, class difference and class conflict are articulated as linguistic difference and linguistic conflict:

> Communication between classes . . . always represents a critical situation for the language that is used, whichever it may be. It tends to provoke a return to the sense that is most overtly charged with social

connotations. . . . This objective effect of unveiling destroys the apparent unity of ordinary language. Each word, each expression, threatens to take on two antagonistic senses, reflecting the way in which it is understood by the sender and the receiver. (40)

Bourdieu's theory of "linguistic habitus" – the system of sociocultural dispositions that governs linguistic practice – is highly relevant to the study of a verbal medium such as sound film. The conditions of existence of a particular class within a class-divided society are reflected in the linguistic habitus of a character or set of characters, a habitus that can be represented very effectively within the filmic medium. Regional, ethnic, and class-based accents and manners of speech are frequently used to mark cultural differences and boundaries in film. In the Marx Brothers' films, for example, Chico's exaggerated imitation of a stereotypical lower-class Italian accent, and his propensity to misinterpret standard English, combined with Groucho's constant gagging, abrasive voice, and rapid-fire speech patterns, mark the Brothers' class and ethnicity, both of which are played against the upper-class and nonethnic speech of characters such as those portrayed by Margaret Dumont. The relationship between Groucho and Dumont, or between Chico and the respectably middle- and upper-class characters with whom he interacts, constitutes a form of class warfare carried out on a linguistic plane.

Along with class habitus, other social factors such as gender and ethnicity can also function as markers of difference that can parallel or intensify class relationships. As Kathleen Rowe has argued, gender functions within the Hollywood film as a social disposition that determines aspects of a woman's class position: "In the romantic comedies of the 1930s and 1940s, which invariably invoke class differences, the unruly woman's class primarily identifies her as 'other,' outside the middle class and free from its conventionality."[14]

Rowe traces the representation of "female unruliness" in comic heroines from this era, including the characters played by Mae West in her 1930s comedies, as well as the characters of Susan Vance (Katharine Hepburn) in *Bringing Up Baby* (1938), Sugarpuss O'Shea (Barbara Stanwyck) in *Ball of Fire* (1941), and Jean Harrington (Stanwyck) in *The Lady Eve* (1941). We can easily supplement Rowe's list with such examples as the characters of Lily Garland (Carole Lombard) in *Twentieth Century* (1934),

Ellen Andrews (Claudette Colbert) in *It Happened One Night* (1934), Eadie (Jean Harlow) in *The Girl from Missouri* (1934), Theodora Lynn (Irene Dunne) in *Theodora Goes Wild* (1936), Wanda Nash (Lombard) in *The Princess Comes Across* (1936), Linda Seton (Hepburn) in *Holiday* (1937), Lucy Warriner (Dunne) in *The Awful Truth* (1937), Melsa Manton (Stanwyck) in *The Mad Miss Manton* (1938), Eve Peabody (Colbert) in *Midnight* (1939), Tracy Lord (Hepburn) in *The Philadelphia Story* (1940), Polly Parrish (Ginger Rogers) in *Bachelor Mother* (1940), and Gerry Jeffers (Colbert) in *The Palm Beach Story* (1942). The "unruliness" of these comic heroines does not always involve an attack on middle-class propriety from an inferior class position, but it usually involves some disruption of class categories. In *The Awful Truth,* for example, Lucy Warriner feigns a lower-class status in order to upset the plans of her estranged husband Jerry to marry a society woman; in *Bringing Up Baby,* the upper-class heiress Susan Vance takes on the persona of a gangster's moll, "Swinging Door Susie," in order to effect an escape from jail.

In different ways, each of these women uses language and the voice to disrupt masculine and middle-class forms of control, thus defining a different linguistic habitus from that of the middle-class male characters who surround her. Female characters can effectuate such social and linguistic disruptions either from a higher position on the class scale, like that of Susan Vance, or from a more subordinate position like that of Jean Harrington or Polly Parrish. Given the highly limiting moral code for the social and especially the sexual behavior of women characters in films of the period (at least in part the result of the stringent Production Code imposed in the early 1930s), the disruptive social force of these characters is usually exemplified most forcefully in their use of language, often their most effective modality for exerting social power. In the case of women characters – and also in the case of ethnic characters like the Marx Brothers – language is a place of relative freedom from the constraints that apply in other arenas of life. In screen comedy, female characters can use various kinds of wordplay and verbal manipulation of men in order to challenge or avoid the rules of middle-class decorum.[15] In fact, the linguistic and social transgressions of these screwball heroines are not so far removed from the forms of social disruptiveness exemplified by the anarchistic performances of the Marx Brothers. Both kinds of performance were reactions against an oppressive and unequal social order; both were characteristic of a genre in which systems of class, gender, and ethnic privilege could be worked through, tested, revised, or rejected. Finally, both kinds of comedy relied on the power of language to effect social critique. As we shall see in the first chapter, the Marx Brothers' films represent some of the most brilliant examples in American film comedy of the use of linguistic conflicts to represent conflicts within the social order.

# 1

# A TROUBLED PARADISE

## Utopia and Transgression in Comedies of the Early 1930s

I

Although Hollywood films of the Depression era would never take the vanguard of social critique, they exerted a powerful influence on the way Americans perceived their place within an increasingly divided society. Social commentators of the late 1920s and early 1930s saw film as a way of exposing class disparities. The movies were a potential means of "undermin[ing] the ideological structure of the middle," of "consolidat[ing] the working class," and of bringing the artist and intellectual into direct contact with the masses.[1]

Among the genres of Hollywood film, comedy was to prove one of the most effective in reflecting the social crises of the Depression era. Although Depression comedies may not have satisfied the desires of critics like Dwight MacDonald and Robert Gessner for a socially engaged cinema, they did provide a commentary on wealth, power, and class privilege that functioned as a popular indicator of current social perspectives. Hollywood responded to the ideologically charged early years of the Depression with two very different kinds of comedy, each of which exploited the possibilities of cinematic speech but which used spoken language for very different purposes.

The first of these comic modes was exemplified by two films made by Ernst Lubitsch in the early 1930s: *Trouble in Paradise* (1932) and *Design for Living* (1933). In these films, a smooth, effortless, and highly stylized use of language becomes an end in itself, as the brilliantly witty dialogue of the central characters displaces the need for any direct treatment of social issues. The second direction taken by sound comedies in the early 1930s is exemplified by the Marx Brothers' Paramount comedies. In these films language becomes a medium in which difference – whether defined in terms of ethnicity or class – is actively foregrounded. To use the terms of Bakhtin, language in Lubitsch's comedies is relatively monologic – remaining within a fairly narrow sociolinguistic spectrum – whereas language in the Marx Brothers' films erupts in a continual play of dialogic or heteroglossic difference, a disruption of linguistic similarity and continuity.[2] This disruption, or negation, of normative social discourse takes its most extreme form in Harpo's completely silent performance, but it can also be heard in the ethnic accent and continual malapropisms of Chico, and in the ad-libbing and associational free play of Groucho.

Both the Lubitsch comedies and the Marx Brothers' films can be inserted into comedic subgenres, which have been called "sophisticated comedy" and "anarchistic comedy," respectively. These in turn are the source of what have been to this day the two dominant modes of Hollywood sound comedy: romantic comedy and comedian comedy.[3] *Trouble in Paradise* epitomizes the trend in early 1930s romantic comedies, marking a high point in the genre of sophisticated comedies that included films such as *Design for Living,* as well as *Private Lives* (1931), *Tonight Is Ours* (1933), and *Reunion in Vienna* (1933). All of these films were adapted from stage plays, and all involve characters who are either wealthy or sophisticated, or both. In "anarchistic comedy," on the other hand, as represented by the early 1930s films of the Marx Brothers, Eddie Cantor, Joe Cook, W. C. Fields, and the comedy team of Wheeler and Woolsey, the comedy emphasizes not the narrative coherence of the plot or the stylistic coherence of the film itself, but the performances and personalities of individual comedians. Stylistically, these films do not foreground the seamless continuity of plot, dialogue, and characterization typical of a Lubitsch comedy. Instead, they seek an expressive anarchy that places the comic performer on a different level from the film's other characters and that at times allows the performer to break character and confront the audience directly. In one example of this form of linguistic spontaneity, Groucho Marx moves in the course of one scene in

*Monkey Business* through the rhetorical styles of a patriotic stump speaker, a dance instructor, a gangster, a quiz show host, a little boy, and a flirtatious woman.

## II

On the surface, at least, these stylistic differences would appear to have sociopolitical implications that might lead us to read them in terms of the changing class dynamics of the early 1930s. A film like *Trouble in Paradise* is most easily read as socially reactionary. As Gerald Mast suggests, it is on the most overt level a "slick, shiny, escapist comedy about rich people in Europe."[4] Although Lubitsch can be seen to problematize this reading by subtly satirizing the very class he appears to celebrate ("carefully sticking a pin into the pretensions of high society," as Mast puts it [218]), the film's overall sense of stylistic decorum, and the fact that it fails to challenge the social order in any profound sense, lead us to read it as ideologically conservative, especially within the context of Depression-era America. In the relationship between Gaston Monescu (Herbert Marshall) and Mariette Collet (Kay Francis), the sociological reality of Gaston's less elevated class status is subjugated to the need for a romantic plot. Within the intensely verbal medium of Lubitsch's film, their relationship is developed on a linguistic plane that leaves little room for social codes based on class habitus. Although the film hints at Gaston's social background, his character in the film is in no sense defined by any sociohistorical reality other than that which is conveyed through his elegant and witty speech. In one speech to Mariette, Gaston refers to "the crash" and "the market," and he characterizes himself as a member of the "nouveau poor." The reference remains vague, however, and it is impossible to make any definite assumption about his class or social background.

If the film is a satire, as Mast suggests, it is a very gentle one. Lubitsch may enjoy poking fun at certain members of the upper class – the "genteel nincompoops" who populate the world of the film and who serve as foils for the sophisticated crooks Gaston and Lily, but there is no overriding indictment of the rich, and the filmgoer has no sense that Lubitsch would trade this rarified world of wealth, beauty, and luxury for any other. In fact, the developing romance between Gaston (the crook) and Mariette (the

millionairess) is intended to be sincere, and his betrayal of her at the end is
too poignant to be read as entirely satirical. That the romance of Gaston
and Mariette is meant to be both genuine and aesthetically appealing is
made clear in both the film and the screenplay. After the passionate scene
between them in Mariette's bedroom toward the end of the film, Gaston is
described as "a man in love, completely shaken," and his decision to leave
with Lily at the end of the film is extremely difficult. Gaston later tells
Mariette, in what we must take as an honest avowal: "I came to rob you,
but unfortunately I fell in love with you."

Mast misreads the film in injecting it with a more cynical social attitude and a more trenchant social critique than it in fact contains:
"Although the social-realist milieu never intrudes into the film . . . it always
hovers alongside it – even further ridiculing the wasteful emptiness of Paradise" (219). But the "paradise" of the title is not simply a "clockwork toy"
to be played at will by Gaston; it is a momentary glimpse of a potential
utopia in which beauty, love, wealth, and social privilege are combined.
The utopia appealed as much to Lubitsch (who was also the director of a
number of operettas more unequivocally celebrating a similar upper-class
milieu) as it does to Gaston and Mariette, and, presumably, to the audience. That the film's paradise falls apart is not of Gaston's own choosing
(never in the film does he "beat the toy" of society by "knock[ing] the
workings out of it," as Mast suggests). Instead, the "trouble" is caused by
the actions of others who for their own reasons want to derail the seemingly too perfect relationship. Lubitsch's film, with its brilliant screenplay
by Samuel Raphaelson, is at its best when it combines in bittersweet fashion the sense of a real passion with an ironic awareness of its ultimate
impossibility. This dual sense is conveyed by the language of the final dialogue between Gaston and Mariette:

GASTON: Goodbye . . .

MARIETTE: Goodbye . . .

GASTON: It could have been marvelous . . .

MARIETTE: Divine . . .

GASTON: Wonderful . . . But tomorrow morning, if you should
wake out of your dreams and hear a knock, and the door opens,
and there, instead of a maid with a breakfast tray, stands a policeman with a warrant – *then* you'll be glad you're alone.

MARIETTE: But it could have been glorious.

GASTON: Lovely.

MARIETTE: Divine . . . But that terrible policeman!

GASTON: Goodbye . . .

While on the page such dialogue can appear overstylized and even stilted, it is very effective on screen, especially since its distinctive rhythm has been set up by earlier dialogues in the film. The synchronization of the two characters' speech, emphasized by the repetitions of phrasing and the alternating use of the single adjective, framed by the "goodbyes," and interrupted by the intrusion of a level of reality (the policeman) which Mariette only partly acknowledges, represents the perfect concordance of the characters, a linguistic harmony that seemingly overcomes any class boundaries. While earlier in the film Gaston used language to deceive Mariette (as in the scene where he convinced her to leave more money in her home safe with the argument that "every conservative person should have a substantial part of his fortune within arm's reach"), now he uses it out of respect for her as an equal in love.

If there is any cynicism in the film, it is directed equally at everyone, including the audience. As Pauline Kael remarks: "The cynicism . . . isn't disillusioning – the cynicism intensifies the lovers' feelings of helplessness. We're all in the same gondola."[5] While the film's final "joke" may in a sense be played by the two thieves on the wealthy Mariette – who loses her pearl necklace, her handbag, and 100,000 francs along with Gaston – it is significant that she retains her dignity even at the end. When Gaston shows her the necklace he has taken (her "gift" to Lily), Mariette graciously offers it "with the compliments of Colet and Company," thus making clever reference both to her own wealth and magnanimity, and to Lily's scornful exit line of the previous scene – "Goodbye, Madame Colet and Company."

The language of the film, while it is used in certain scenes for clearly satirical effect (as in the dialogues between Gaston and Giron), more often functions as a link between mutually sympathetic characters: Gaston and Lily, and later Gaston and Mariette. In another scene near the end of the film, the symmetry of dialogue between Mariette and Gaston is used to suggest through *double entendre* a sexual liaison that could not have been directly expressed:

MARIETTE: What are you going to do with my day tomorrow, M'sieu Laval?

GASTON: Well, we'll have breakfast in the garden.

MARIETTE: Um-hum . . .

GASTON: Then riding together.

MARIETTE: Um-hum . . .

GASTON: Then lunch in the Bois –

MARIETTE: Together.

GASTON: Then a little nap –

MARIETTE *(restraining an automatic "together"):* How do you like my dress?

GASTON: Beautiful.

The success of this kind of dialogue depends on the audience being pulled along with it, seduced along with Mariette into the inevitable idea of "a little nap . . . together." Such artificially stylized dialogue draws us further into the utopian vision rendered in the film, a vision reinforced by the striking Art Deco decor, the gorgeous costumes, and the elegant cinematography of Victor Milner.[6] Furthermore, the dialogue illustrates Pierre Bourdieu's point that "[l]inguistic exchange . . . is also an economic exchange which is established within a particular symbolic relation."[7] It is Gaston's linguistic competence, the "expressive style" of his discourse, which seduces Mariette and which gradually establishes the terms of their economic, as well as their romantic, relationship. If, as Bourdieu suggests, "the whole social structure is present in each [linguistic] interaction" (67), then we can read the linguistic economy of this film as one in which Gaston's linguistic superiority balances Mariette's social and economic superiority, allowing them to occupy a temporarily equal footing. Yet by relying so much on the seamless flow and perfect balance of language, the film also covers up the social and ideological dimension of linguistic exchange, providing, in Richard Dyer's terms, a utopian form of entertainment rather than a form of meaningful social critique.

If the film's box-office success was any indication, contemporary audiences wanted (or needed) to be entertained in exactly that way.[8] James Harvey calls the film "an idyll," a utopian form that establishes a complicity between the film and its audience. If the film creates a "community of cleverness," as Harvey suggests, by projecting a dream of "supreme, effortless, omnipotent authority and self-possession," it is a dream that unconsciously assumes an identification with the kind of upper-class environment that could make such authority and self-possession possible.[9] As the Depression deepened, the urbanity and wit of *Trouble in Paradise* came to represent a stylistic perfection that was also a dead end in the development of sound comedy. As the Depression continued, such idyllic visions of society and romance would disappear from the screen, yielding to the streetwise comedy of the screwball genre.

## III

The Marx Brothers' Paramount films, appearing concurrently with Lubitsch's comedies and made by the same studio, represent in many respects their polar opposite, the only evident similarity being the brilliant quality of the comic writing.[10] If Lubitsch's film deemphasizes the function of language as a marker of social status, the Marx Brothers' films offer a cinematic space for the continual contestation of "the linguistic relation of power" described by Bourdieu. Although they may not constitute the "hymn to anarchy and whole-hearted revolt" which Antonin Artaud found in them, the Marx Brothers' first five sound films certainly use plot, physical action, and language to disrupt social norms and conventions, to challenge the habits and the rules of society, and at times to challenge even its cultural and political institutions.[11] It is always dangerous, as Henry Jenkins suggests, to elide form and content in such a way as to "blur the boundaries between thematic anarchy and a set of aesthetic practices that can be labelled anarchist" (8), but it is equally important to recognize, as Jenkins also does, that the anarchistic comedies of the early 1930s do contain "elements of political satire," and that several of them "use a political setting as a backdrop for their star comedian's gags and performances."[12] Among the Marx Brothers' films, the clearest example of a film with direct historical and political relevance is the 1933 *Duck Soup,* which takes place in the mythical kingdom of Freedonia, a state that is far from utopian and that actually ends up in a brutal war with its neighbor Sylvania. As Joe Adamson has pointed out, it does not require a great deal of imagination to derive a sociopolitical context for this film:

*Duck Soup* was prepared amid an atmosphere of ruin, disruption, and veritable collapse. Not only was Hitler taking over Germany, but Roosevelt was closing the banks in America, Paramount was tottering near bankruptcy, and financiers were flitting in and out of the picture like moths. Groucho was spearheading a movement to form a Screen Actors' Guild, which was only going to benefit the majority of Hollywood actors who were not movie stars, and was only going to alienate everyone else.[13]

Although I agree with Adamson about the importance of placing the film in its social context, I am less interested in tracing the direct political or social reference of the Marx Brothers' films than in looking at the ways in which their use of language and imagetext contributes to their more general critique of social norms, and in particular of class distinctions and hierarchies. The Marx Brothers' films offer an extreme case of destabilizing the "normal" laws of social discourse; in these films, linguistic competence often bears little relationship to the social or class structures that might under normal circumstances produce it. The comic antiheroes represented by the Marx Brothers do not use and misuse language simply for the purpose of seducing others or ingratiating themselves with society. Even in his dialogues with Margaret Dumont, in which his ostensible object is seduction or ingratiation, Groucho nearly always manages to offend her. Throughout their films, Groucho and the other brothers use language in order to frustrate the normal rules of society and puncture its pretensions. Groucho's linguistic skills allow him to disarm a murderous gangster (in *Monkey Business*) and to run a college *(Horse Feathers),* a sanitarium *(A Day at the Races),* and an entire country *(Duck Soup).* At the same time, Groucho is continually frustrated by the linguistic incompetence of his brothers Harpo and Chico. Harpo frustrates Groucho by silently undermining his authority, as when he responds to Groucho's admonition in *Horse Feathers* that "you can't burn the candle at both ends" by pulling from his pocket a candle doing just that. Chico, on the other hand, uses his misunderstanding of the English language to his own advantage, frustrating Groucho with strings of bad puns. Unlike the world of Lubitsch's *Trouble in Paradise,* where Gaston's intelligence allows him to triumph over the stupidity of his upper-class dupes, the world of the Marx Brothers is one in which, to quote Allen Eyles, "stupidity defeats intelligence every time."[14]

might begin by analyzing the most basic level of speech in these films: the quality of the voice and vocal mannerisms of the Marx Brothers themselves. As Amy Lawrence has suggested, "it is the voice in sound film that makes dialogue *matter,* that takes it out of its narrative function and makes it sound, that invokes a psychological, imaginary system of spectacle as opposed to the purely representational association of title and image in silent film."[15] A written transcription of dialogue conveys only a part of the meaning of filmic speech and fails to capture the tone of voice, intensity, and timbre of the spoken utterance.[16] The Marx Brothers' films are a perfect illustration of the need to *hear* filmic speech in order to understand fully the use of language. The dialogue is often humorous on the page but many times funnier as delivered in the films themselves. The contrast with the suave, sophisticated, imperturbable, socially refined speech of Hollywood actors of the early 1930s – represented by Herbert Marshall and Kay Francis in *Trouble in Paradise,* for example, or William Powell and Myrna Loy in *The Thin Man* – could not be more pointed than in the case of the Marx Brothers. Groucho's grating voice, his constant "gagging," and the barrage of language he inflicts on his interlocutors form one set of antitheses to Herbert Marshall's normative Hollywood speech and decorum; Chico's non sequiturs, fragments, and malapropisms constitute another. Whereas Gaston's speech is always to the point, Chico's speech is hilariously pointless. Whereas Gaston always observes the social pretense of seeming to respect his interlocutor (even while subtly making fun of him), Groucho overtly parodies and frustrates anyone who attempts to engage him in conversation.

Although both Gaston and Groucho survive by the use of their verbal intelligence to manipulate others, they go about that manipulation in completely different ways. As Gerald Weales suggests, "the Ernst Lubitsch touch is rather far removed from the Marx bludgeon."[17] Groucho, whether as Mr. Hammer, Captain Spaulding, Professor Wagstaff, or Rufus T. Firefly, is a relatively harmless and ineffectual grifter/shyster figure impersonating a nonethnic (presumably WASP) character but clearly identified with an ethnic background. In class terms, he would appear to be self-educated (whereas the Chico and Harpo characters, despite their intelligence and musical talents, are marked as uneducated and illiterate) and from lower-middle-class origins. In most of the films, however, Groucho has managed to gain some temporary position in society: he is, as

Allen Eyles observes, a social parasite who has reached that position not by talent or hard work, but by some form of trickery or misunderstanding.[18] Since he cannot successfully disguise his true class or ethnic background for long by assimilating into the dominant (upper- or upper-middle-class WASP) society represented by the Margaret Dumont character, his attempts at manipulation and graft usually fail. But while he will never triumph over upper-class society in the overt way a more elegant trickster like Gaston Monescu can, his ability to deflate the pretensions of high society is far greater than Gaston's, and the resulting satire is far more radical in its undercutting of bourgeois speech and manners.

The status of language in these films is itself significant, since language as it is used in society appears to be constantly devalued, or at least revalued, by the linguistic creativity of the Brothers. Harpo is the most extreme example of the devaluation of language, since he manages to get along perfectly well without using it at all, substituting various objects and physical mannerisms for speech. He whistles, plays his harp, honks his horn, pulls endless objects out of his coat, and does his annoying leg routine in what amounts to a constant gag on the very superfluity of speech (in contrast to Groucho, in whom speech becomes superfluous by its abundance). *Written* language is almost nonexistent in the films, and when it does exist it usually ends up being destroyed by Harpo (books in *Horse Feathers,* the mail of the hotel guests in *The Cocoanuts,* the telegram in *Duck Soup,* the immigration papers in *Monkey Business)* or becoming inconsequential, as when Zeppo leaves out the "body of the letter" dictated by Groucho to his lawyers in *Animal Crackers.* This destruction or effacement of written text, which reaches its comic high point in *A Night at the Opera* in the scene where Groucho and Chico systematically tear apart their contracts for signing an opera singer, also has class implications. The illiterate Harpo and Chico and the literate but socially anarchic Groucho have no use for contracts, letters, and official papers, all of which are documents serving the interests of the dominant class and perpetuating an unequal social order. They also seem to have little use for the telephone, mocking its use as an aural transmitter of "important" social messages. In *The Cocoanuts* Harpo eats the desk telephone, and in *Duck Soup* Harpo and Chico thwart the efforts of Groucho (Freedonian president Rufus T. Firefly) to answer the phone, prompting Groucho to quip sarcastically, "You know, I'd be lost without a telephone." In *Horse Feathers*, a telephone is used as a nutcracker, and in *Duck Soup*, Harpo attempts to use one to light a cigar.

Furthermore, nearly every possible kind of speech act and discourse is parodied in the films: the land auction in *The Cocoanuts*, the pretentious "I-have-returned-from-darkest-Africa" speech in *Animal Crackers*, the opening convocation and biology class in *Horse Feathers*, and the trial scene, political speeches, and cabinet meeting of *Duck Soup*. Usually, these parodies are attacks on some more general form of linguistic and social pretension: of high society and the art world *(Animal Crackers)*, of academia *(Horse Feathers)*, of government and international politics *(Duck Soup)*, of real estate investments *(The Cocoanuts)*, and of the bureaucracy of passport and customs authorities *(Monkey Business)*. Parodies also take the form of allusions to other films, film genres, plays, and books: O'Neill's *Strange Interlude* in *Animal Crackers;* Dreiser's *American Tragedy* in *Horse Feathers;* Maurice Chevalier vehicles, Westerns, and gangster films in *Monkey Business;* and the "mythical kingdom" film in *Duck Soup*.

The carnivalesque settings of the Marx Brothers' films, both at Paramount and MGM, lend themselves to a heteroglossic play with linguistic differences that deregulate the status of the discourse being parodied, allowing the Marx Brothers to upset the presumed class system of each environment. Such settings as a resort hotel, a weekend house party, an ocean liner, and a college campus, and in later films the opera, the racetrack, the sanatorium, the circus, and the department store, allow the Brothers to engage in certain forms of broader cultural parody. The climactic opera scene in *A Night at the Opera*, for example, burlesques the high cultural pretensions of the opera, a class-identified form of entertainment that seems to have inspired the particular scorn of the Marx Brothers. Here various forms taken from popular or mass culture – such as a baseball game, a sword fight, a circus (with Harpo on the flying trapeze), and a popular film (Groucho as Tarzan) – interrupt and make fun of the "serious" opera (Verdi's *Il Trovatore*), as the appropriate scenery is replaced by backdrops of streetcars and battleships. Ultimately, however, the opera itself is not undermined as other cultural forms are in the earlier films. At the end, order is restored to the opera company as the "good" singers triumph and Groucho and Chico both get commissions. We might compare this treatment of the opera in the MGM film with the more subversive trial scene in *Duck Soup*, its Paramount counterpart, in which Rufus T. Firefly's declaration of war causes the entire assembly, including generals, ministers, and guards, to break into song. The song ("Freedonia's Going to War") turns into something between a vaudeville theater and a revivalist meeting, as the Brothers and the rest of the cast perform versions of "Hi-De-Hi-De-Ho," the parodic "All God's Chillun Got Guns," and a folksy rendition of "Comin' Round the Mountain."[19]

Another means of disrupting linguistic and cultural conventions in the Marx Brothers' films is the use of what Michel Chion has called "relativized speech."[20] When cinematic speech is "relativized," it is taken out of the strict linear continuum of the theatrical model. Such "relativizing" can be accomplished in a number of ways, several of which occur in the Marx Brothers films: by the rarefaction of speech or dialogue, for example, in the alternation of silent and spoken sequences (Harpo's scenes vs. those of the other Brothers) or the insertion of silent sequences into a sound film (the mirror scene in *Duck Soup*); by the overproliferation or superimposition of speech, as when characters interrupt each other or speak over each others' lines, or in Groucho's rapid-fire speech; by the submersion of speech beneath other sounds (Margaret Dumont's speech to Groucho at the beginning of *The Big Store* is completely drowned out by Harpo's furious typewriting); by having a character speak directly into the camera as an aside for the theater audience (Groucho in most of the films); or by the use of non sequiturs and irrelevant digressions (i.e., the famous "Why a duck?" scene in *The Cocoanuts,* the O'Neillesque soliloquies by Groucho in *Animal Crackers,* the impromptu geography lesson in *Monkey Business,* and the biology lecture in *Horse Feathers*). In each of these cases, the disruption of cinematic convention becomes the formal equivalent for the flouting of social caste and tradition.

Like Gaston in *Trouble in Paradise,* Groucho and Chico are defined by their use of language, but whereas Gaston's transgression is against the society he robs and the woman he loves and leaves, in the case of the Marx Brothers the transgression is also against language itself, against the class-based codes of language use. This transgression is, in the words of Mark Winokur, "the most visibly resentful action allowed the anti-heroes," a form of "contained anarchy, more effective than the gangster's because motivated by the desire to replace power structures not with other structures but with critiques of power."[21] Although this form of barely contained anarchy can be found in the work of various comics of the early sound era—from Laurel and Hardy to W. C. Fields to Eddie Cantor—it is in the Marx Brothers' films that it reaches its most dizzying proportions.

The comic imagetext also plays a particularly important role in the Marx Brothers' films, figuring their indebtedness to traditions of both vaudeville (with its emphasis on verbal play and song) and silent film. Each of the Brothers is associated with a highly iconographic physical appearance that finds its verbal accompaniment in a particularized style of speech (or, in the case of Harpo, the absence of speech). Thus Harpo's lack of speech is paralleled on a visual or imagistic level by his curly blond wig, battered top hat, oversized raincoat, and bug-eyed, puff-cheeked stare. The imagetext created by Harpo denotes the "transcendent fool," suggesting an impoverishment that is socioeconomic as well as mental. Chico's dunce-cap hat, ill-fitting jacket, and generally vacuous expression, along with his ethnic accent and truncated speech, signal the wise fool immigrant, a step above Harpo's position on the social scale, and an intermediary link between Harpo and Groucho in most of the films.[22] Groucho's greasepaint eyebrows and mustache, cigar and glasses, oversized tuxedo, bent-over lope, and lecherous leer, are all commensurate with the verbal overabundance, the unquenchable appetite (for money, sex, power, or whatever he can hope to get), and the impulsive, antisocial, obnoxious behavior that mark him as an obvious *arriviste.*

Groucho's imagetext is more difficult to place on the social scale than those of Chico and Harpo, but he often appears as a parodic version of the self-made man, whose dubious origins have not quite caught up with him. This status takes its most extreme form in the character of Rufus T. Firefly, who at the start of *Duck Soup* has just been named president of the tiny republic of Freedonia. It is clear that his appointment has nothing to do with his own qualifications but is entirely due to the influence of the wealthy Mrs. Teasdale, who for some unknown reason has developed a tremendous admiration for him. As his name suggests, Firefly has appeared from nowhere and will disappear again just as quickly. Firefly's ephemeral nature is literalized in the brilliant gag of the opening scene. While the assembled guests await Firefly's arrival as the country's new leader, Mrs. Teasdale leads them in repeated choruses of the national anthem, "Hail, hail Freedonia, Land of the Brave and Free!" as we see Firefly waking up and getting out of bed, sliding down a fireman's pole, and, arriving from the rear of the hall rather than through the door everyone is expectantly watching, taking his place among the guards and holding up his cigar in place of a sword.

Other examples of such parodic roles are the college president Quincy Adams Wagstaff in *Horse Feathers,* with a name that manages to be both high WASP and somewhat ridiculous at the same time, and Captain Jeffrey T. Spaulding, the African Explorer, a parody of the big-game hunter from *Animal Crackers* who is so self-important that the minute he arrives (to the chorus of "At last, the Captain has arrived") he sings "Hello, I Must Be Going."[23] The parody of respectability and social importance in all these films also functions as a parody of the typical Hollywood lead: Groucho is always paired romantically with a taller woman, either Margaret Dumont or Thelma Todd.

Although Winokur focuses more on the Marx Brothers' ethnicity than on their class identification, he indicates that the Marx Brothers' accents "define them regionally and economically": the Brothers are "ethnic and poor, no matter their financial position within the story" (138–39).[24] The persistence of this poverty and ethnicity in the Marx Brothers' films acts as a subversion of the American ideal of ethnic assimilation and the classless society. Groucho is also often paired with another male character who is higher on the social scale but who is an even greater, if better disguised, phony than Groucho himself. In *The Cocoanuts* there is Harvey Yates, a fortune hunter and jewel thief who poses as a real estate investor; in *Animal Crackers,* there is Roscoe Chandler, whose current position as a wealthy patron of the arts disguises a former identity as a fish peddler from Czechoslovakia, Abe Kabibble ("Ab-ie the Fish Man"); and in *Duck Soup,* there is Ambassador Trentino from the neighboring republic of Sylvania, a shady character who, despite his aristocratic pretensions, is just as interested in marrying Mrs. Teasdale for her money as Groucho is.[25] The Marx Brothers' films never permit the kind of refined gentility Gaston and Mariette represent in *Trouble in Paradise.*[26] In all their films, the Marx Brothers attempt to reverse the process of class distinction by undermining the class privilege of those above them in the social scale. As Groucho most succinctly phrases it in *Monkey Business,* "the stockholder of yesteryear is the stowaway of today." These films, released during the early years of the Depression, recognize more fully than any others made in Hollywood during those years the grotesque nature of social and class pretensions – and the social inequalities they are based on – during a period marked by intense economic hardship and social dislocation for many Americans.

As performers and creative collaborators in their films, the Marx Brothers were acutely aware of such class discrepancies. The Marx Brothers' parents on both sides were Jewish immigrants. Their father Sam Marx (born Simon Marrix) had arrived in New York from the contested region of Alsace and went by the nickname "Frenchie"; their mother Minnie had immigrated from Germany. Sam Marx was an unsuccessful tailor whose income, according to Groucho, hovered "between eighteen dollars a week and nothing."[27] Sam's limited command of the English language may have been at least a partial influence on the representation of immigrants in the Marx Brothers' films as either silent (Harpo) or linguistically backward (Chico).

Throughout most of their childhoods, the Brothers lived in a three-bedroom apartment in Yorkville, where the four older boys shared one room, and for a time even one double bed. One coal stove in the parlor provided heat for the apartment, and a single bathroom for eight people meant long lines and few baths. The deep mistrust and resentment of authority and socioeconomic privilege featured in the Marx Brothers' films certainly had roots in their early childhood, a time when they were taught to fear the visits of the rent collector. As Groucho recalled, "We were so poor that when somebody knocked on the door we all hid."[28]

Also typical of their working-class immigrant experience was the Marxes' lack of formal education. Chico was the only brother to finish high school; Groucho left school before his thirteenth birthday; and Harpo only completed the second grade. While Groucho, and to a lesser extent Harpo, were avid readers who became authors in their own right, the Marx Brothers treat higher education with relative contempt, as is most clear in the college satire *Horse Feathers*. This satiric attitude toward the institutional aspects of higher learning has clear class origins, as is evident both in the spoof on the WASPy Huxley College in *Horse Feathers* and in the claim by Dr. Hugo Z. Hackenbush (Groucho) in *A Day at the Races* to have attended the exclusive Vassar College. When informed that Vassar is a women's college, he says that he only discovered that fact in his junior year. The satire on academia, and on "experts" of all kinds, is a motif throughout the Marx

Brothers' films. In *Animal Crackers,* Harpo is incongruously identified as "The Professor." In *Horse Feathers,* Groucho plays Professor Wagstaff, the new president of the college, who goes on a mission to recruit football players for the college team in a local speakeasy. He also recommends doing away with the academic curriculum altogether in order to promote the chances of the football team. Wagstaff's anatomy lecture, which he delivers after having the real biology professor removed from the classroom, breaks down into a spitball fight between Chico, Harpo, and himself. In another scene, all the books in Wagstaff's office are destroyed by Harpo, who throws them on the fire. In the scene intended for the finale of the original film, now extant only in stills, the Brothers contribute to the literal destruction of the college itself. Harpo accidentally sets fire to the college, and the Marxes sit playing cards, apparently unaware of the conflagration as the college burns down around them.

Of the Marx parents, Minnie was the more socially and economically ambitious. She put her sons on the vaudeville stage starting with Julius (Groucho) in 1905, and in 1910 she moved the entire family to Chicago in order to improve the Brothers' chances for a career in small-time vaudeville. Vaudeville may have been the lower-class alternative to the "legitimate" theater, but it still offered significant opportunities for financial reward, especially for its top-billed performers. Even as early as 1906, the fifteen-year-old Groucho (billed as "Master Julius Marx") was earning more on the International Circuit than his father was as a tailor. Over the next seventeen years, Groucho was joined by Gummo, Harpo, Chico, and finally Zeppo; the Brothers worked their way slowly up the ranks of vaudeville until in 1923 they were able to perform their first "legitimate" musical comedy *I'll Say She Is!* on the Broadway stage. The move from vaudeville to Broadway represented not so much an opportunity to rise in social status as a change necessitated by their current economic situation and by the gradual decline of vaudeville as a viable career option. By this time, in the words of Glenn Mitchell, the Marxes were "blacklisted, broke, and very close to abandoning show-business altogether."[29] The show went on a lengthy national tour before finally opening in a minor Broadway theater, the Casino, where it had a highly successful run of 304 performances, thus propelling the Brothers to a new career in legitimate theater and eventually in the movies.

The poverty experienced by the Marxes in their early years is a clear motif throughout their autobiographical writings. In one anecdote told by Groucho to his son Arthur and later recounted in *Life with Groucho*, Groucho nearly lost an arm in a disagreement over who was to get the last sweet roll at dinner.[30] Whether the story is real or apocryphal, it clearly reflects the kind of socially inflected humor characteristic of the Marx Brothers' filmic interactions. It is a brand of humor involving situations that could equally well have been treated as tragic rather than comic. Chico's legendary addiction to gambling, and Groucho's penchant for stock market investing and his famously tightfisted nature, can also be traced to an obsession with money brought on by a childhood marked by poverty and material deprivation.

From their early vaudeville acts to their later screen personas, the Marx Brothers' performances were strongly marked by their class and ethnic status. This fact in itself accounts for much of the difference between the Marx Brothers' early films and other comedies of the period. As Charles Musser points out, "in the period through 1930 and beyond, American film comedians seldom played overtly with both [the immigrant experience and the working-class experience] at the same time."[31] It is in fact the juxtaposition of the permanently lower-class identification represented by the Marxes as performers with the often very disparate class positions occupied by their characters within the films (presidents and cabinet members, professors, wealthy African explorers, hotel owner-managers) that provides much of the humor and contributes to the deflation of class pretension. Furthermore, the occupations the Marx Brothers (and their screenwriters and directors) chose to satirize are often strongly identified with a very different ethnic type. As of 1930, there were in all probability no Jewish "African explorers," very few Jewish college presidents (especially not on campuses with names like Huxley College), and no Jewish presidents of European republics. The idea of presenting a character identified with lower-class Jewish New York as leader of a European "magical kingdom" at a time of growing nationalistic and antisemitic sentiment was an even more radical transposition of class and ethnic roles than in Groucho's other films.[32] Perhaps, given the disappointing reception of *Duck Soup* in the fall of 1933, it was *too* radical a gesture for contemporary audiences. It is significant that Groucho never portrayed a character with a similarly exalted social status in the MGM comedies, where he is given more conventionally comic roles.[33] The social marginalization and downward mobility of Groucho and the other Brothers in the MGM films of the late 1930s can be read as indicative of a greater social conservativism of Hollywood and perhaps of the nation as a whole. It represents a retreat from the more progressive forms of social and cultural critique and the more probing analysis of class and ethnicity found in at least some comedies of the early part of the decade.

## IV

Before turning to more detailed analysis of an exemplary film from the Paramount period—the 1930 *Animal Crackers*—I will provide a brief anatomy of the forms of class-based humor in the Paramount films, drawing primarily on examples from *Duck Soup*.

First, and perhaps most common, are actions that flaunt the social code, usually calling attention to the pretentiousness and rigidity of upper-class social convention. At the beginning of *Duck Soup*, for example, Groucho as newly appointed president Rufus T. Firefly is greeted rather pompously by Margaret Dumont as Mrs. Teasdale: "As chairwoman of the reception committee, I extend the good wishes of every man, woman, and child of Freedonia." Firefly responds by pulling out a deck of cards and offering her one: "Never mind that stuff," he tells her, "take a card." When she inquires what she might do with a card, Firefly replies: "You can keep it, I've got fifty-one left." Here, Groucho's action is marked as socially inappropriate on two levels: it is irrelevant and silly, thus puncturing the high seriousness of the social occasion; and it is also a class-based reference to a cultural practice (card tricks) that would presumably fall beneath the dignity of an upper-class matron like Mrs. Teasdale. This class-based reading is confirmed by the string of insulting remarks that follow. Firefly compares Teasdale to a saloon or dance hall ("How late do you stay open?") and to a decaying building ("I hear they're going to tear you down and put up an office building where you're standing"). Of course, the humor of such scenes depends on the obtuseness or self-seriousness of the insulted party. In this case, Dumont as Mrs. Teasdale never misses a beat, ignoring Firefly's insults and telling him pompously that "the future of Freedonia rests on you." The implication of this exchange is clear: the social conventions guiding the behavior of a Mrs. Teasdale – or that of any of the other characters Dumont plays – are informed by such deeply embedded class dispositions as to be undisturbed by anything Groucho or the other Brothers can do to shake them. The humor comes in the discrepancy between Groucho/Firefly's exalted social status as a character within the film and his inability as a persona (Groucho as Groucho playing Firefly) to cause even a minor disturbance in the social order through his words and actions.

Other actions in *Duck Soup* convey the same disregard for social propriety. When he arrives at a party at the house of Mrs. Teasdale – greeted by another round of "Hail Freedonia!" by the assembled guests – Firefly takes a doughnut off one guest's plate and dips it in the coffee of another as he walks by, all with perfect nonchalance. (In this case, one wonders whether a high-society woman like Mrs. Teasdale would really be serving doughnuts at her garden party, but the success of the gag outweighs the requirement of social realism). The dipping of doughnuts, as we also know from the roughly contemporary *It Happened One Night,* is an act coded with important class implications.

As a sign of the carnivalesque reversal of social propriety, food and eating (or drinking) are involved in many of these scenes. At the beginning of the court-martial trial for the spy Chicolini, Firefly takes out his lunch and pours himself a glass of milk. He then turns to his assistant Bob Roland (Zeppo) and asks him why the original indictment papers were not placed in his portfolio. When Bob replies that he didn't think they were important, Firefly responds: "You didn't think they were important? You realize I had my dessert wrapped in those papers?" He then proceeds to hand the empty milk bottle to one of his generals: "Here, take this bottle back and get two cents for it." Here, the joke centers not only on food, but on a decidedly working-class concern for thrift within a totally inappropriate context.

The second type of jokes are those that mock the linguistic and social pretensions of the more educated or socially elevated classes. One exchange between Firefly and Mrs. Teasdale in *Duck Soup* illustrates the phenomenon:

MRS. TEASDALE: Your Excellency!

FIREFLY: What's on your mind, babe?

MRS. TEASDALE: On behalf of the women of Freedonia, I have taken it upon myself to make one final effort to prevent war.

FIREFLY: No kidding!

MRS. TEASDALE: I've talked to Ambassador Trentino and he says Sylvania doesn't want war either.

FIREFLY: Eether.

MRS. TEASDALE: Doesn't want war eether.

FIREFLY: Either.

*(Mrs. Teasdale sighs.)*

FIREFLY: Skip it.

Groucho continually undermines the speech acts of his interlocutor, whether by using inappropriately familiar or colloquial language ("Babe," "No kidding," "Skip it") or by interrupting the flow of overly pompous speech by correcting her pronunciation. The more inflated another character's speech becomes, the more opportunities Groucho has to ironize it. Throughout the film, the repeated use of the title "Your Excellency" to address Firefly, along with the general formality with which he is addressed, is mocked by Groucho's very presence and mannerisms. Such titles take on the absurdity of a formal language that has lost touch with the social reality of the situation. Similarly, in the scene in which Trentino tries to obtain information about Firefly from Chico and Harpo (the spies Chicolini and Pinky), he continues to address them as "gentlemen," ignoring the fact that they are acting less like gentlemen than like hyperactive five-year-olds.

The third type of class-based humor is one involving ironic allusions to elevated social origins. In *Duck Soup*, for example, Firefly remains relatively unperturbed when Trentino calls him a "swine" and a "worm," but appears to take deep offense when called an "upstart." Firefly slaps Trentino's face with his glove and hands him his card, which Trentino promptly tears up, declaring that "this regrettable occurrence may plunge our countries into war." After Trentino leaves (having been told by Firefly to "scram"), Firefly turns to Mrs. Teasdale:

FIREFLY: The man doesn't live who can call a Firefly an upstart. Why, the Mayflower was full of Fireflys, and a few horseflies, too. The Fireflys were on the upper deck and the horseflies were on the Fireflys.

In the next scene, when Trentino says he is willing to forget the incident, Firefly once again protests:

FIREFLY: Forget? You ask me to forget? A Firefly never forgets. Why, my ancestors would rise from their graves and I would only have to bury them again. Nothing doing.

Jokes about family origins, especially involving the *Mayflower,* contain a clear autobiographical reference to the Marx Brothers' own status as the sons of immigrants with little or no known ancestry. None of the brothers even knew the name of their father's parents. In fact, their father's family background, like that of so many other immigrants, was erased from history. Even his Alsatian homeland was historically erased when it was annexed by Germany after the Franco-Prussian War. In the scene from *Duck Soup,* Firefly's speech deflates the pretensions of those who use their Puritan ancestry to make a claim for social superiority. Even those who came over on the *Mayflower,* he reminds us, were once ordinary immigrants who had to deal with flies and other inconveniences.

The last, most transgressive, and perhaps most disturbing form of joke or gag involves actual physical violence against wealthy or upper-class characters. One fairly innocuous example of this is the fruit that is thrown at both Trentino and Mrs. Teasdale at the end of *Duck Soup.* Bombarding Trentino with fruit while he is stuck in the door during an intended assault on Freedonian headquarters is justified on both narrative and comic levels, but the gratuitous attack on Mrs. Teasdale, provoked only by her singing a triumphant "Hail Freedonia" (albeit in annoyingly operatic fashion), suggests a deeper motive. The humor here is based on differences of both class and gender, pitting the anarchic lower-class male energy of the four Marx Brothers against the "refined" upper-class female persona of Dumont, an actress who seems particularly out of her element in this playroom atmosphere. An even more distressing example is from *Animal Crackers,* where, in a scene often cited for its seemingly misogynist hostility, Harpo uses the character played by Dumont (Mrs. Rittenhouse) as a human punching bag.

In 1930, such a scene was not only a distasteful gag, but also a powerful visual metaphor for the large-scale social conflicts that were just below the surface. In these isolated examples, the class antagonism characteristic of the Marx Brothers' films is transposed from the linguistic plane to a physical manifestation of class struggle.[34]

## V

Of all the Paramount films, *Animal Crackers* is most clearly a satire of high society. At the time the film was made, the Brothers had been financially wiped out by the stock market crash of October 1929, each losing his entire personal fortune. Groucho, who had scrimped and saved all his life, lost the $250,000 he had invested in the market; Harpo was even harder hit, temporarily going into debt as a result. The original stage version of *Animal Crackers* opened in October 1928 and ran until April 1930; thus the crash and its immediate aftermath were concurrent with its performances. The film was released in September 1930, by which time the prolonged effects of the crash were relatively clear, despite denials by President Hoover and others. Although we can only guess at the psychological effect of the crash on the Brothers and on their subsequent work, it is clear that their resentment toward those with inherited wealth and the kind of social standing that such "old money" made possible was a motivating factor in the creation of *Animal Crackers*.

As Charles Musser suggests, the film portrays the Marx Brothers as "Jewish hustlers insinuating themselves into WASP high society, itself shown to be a model of corruption and doubtful respectability"(63).[35] The comic premise of the film – that the elitist society of Mrs. Rittenhouse (Margaret Dumont) and her friends remains unaware of (or at least unconcerned with) such an ethnic and socioeconomic invasion – is among other things "an aggressive assault on the exclusionary policies being applied to Jews by WASP-dominated universities, country clubs, and other public and private institutions"(63). The satire on the pseudo-aristocratic pretensions of the Rittenhouse household is made even clearer in the stage version, where one scene omitted from the film involves a costume party with figures from the court of "Louis 57th."

The film contains not one but two upper-class matrons – Mrs. Ritten-house and Mrs. Whitehead – whose world of house parties and art col-lecting is contrasted not only with the Marx Brothers but also with the penniless artist John Parker, the fiancé of Mrs. Rittenhouse's daughter Arabella. Parker, who has no connections in high society, is judged socially unworthy of Arabella, who is encouraged to pay less attention to him and more to wealthy men like Roscoe Chandler, the New York art collector and owner of the famous painting by Beaugard, "After the Hunt," which is to be displayed in the Rittenhouse home and unveiled at the party. For Mrs. Rittenhouse, such parties are primarily an opportunity to gain social capital, not to enjoy oneself: "The trouble with you is, you don't take these social affairs seriously," she tells Arabella. But Arabella and John represent the decent and honest young couple, uncorrupted as yet by the social world in which they move. They also retain a sense of humor, which allies them with the carnivalesque world represented by the Marx Brothers. When Mrs. Whitehead, assuming Parker to be on the social register, asks whether he comes from the Massachusetts Parkers or the Southern Parkers, Arabella replies that he comes from the "Central Parkers," a witty allusion to the bums who inhabit the park's benches.

When Mrs. Whitehead and her sister Grace find the original Beau-gard hanging in the Rittenhouse home, their dialogue makes it clear that the stakes of social prestige are every bit as serious as those of business or institutional power are in other Marx Brothers' films:

GRACE: Well, sis, it looks as if we deal the social honors of the season to Mrs. Rittenhouse.
MRS. WHITEHEAD: Isn't there something we can do?
GRACE: We might shoot ourselves.
MRS. WHITEHEAD: I'd rather shoot Mrs. Rittenhouse.

The allusion to shooting oneself as a response to losing social prestige seems particularly resonant in the context of the stock market crash, an oblique reference to the many investors who took their own lives.

The film is also permeated by the theme of fakes and falsity, in terms of both art works and social status. When the Beaugard painting is dis-played in Mrs. Rittenhouse's fashionable Long Island residence, it is replaced twice with fakes: one a meticulous copy made by Parker and the other a bad imitation painted by Mrs. Whitehead's sister. As Musser has noted, "the original and Parker's copy are virtually indistinguishable, making us ultimately question the authenticity of Chandler's canvas" (80). The film also introduces a series of social fakes: Groucho as Captain Jeffrey T. Spaulding the "African Explorer," and Zeppo as Horatio W. Jamison his "Field Secretary"; Chico as Signor Emanuel Ravelli, a musician hired for the party (who has a very limited repertoire consisting primarily of an unfinished and maddeningly repetitive version of "Sugar in the Morning"), and Harpo as his partner "The Professor," who has more talent for chasing women and wreaking general havoc than for musical performance. Finally, there is Louis Sorin as Roscoe W. Chandler, a "wealthy art patron" who is in fact a swindler and former fish peddler. Chandler, like Spaulding, has designs on marrying Mrs. Rittenhouse for her money; he also speaks with an apparently phony French accent, unexplained either by his WASP-sounding name or by his shady origins in Czechoslovakia. Finally, since Chandler cannot tell Parker's copy from the original Beaugard, we also wonder about his skills as a connoisseur.

The theme of false identities proliferates in a number of smaller ways as well. Spaulding takes on the persona of a Scotland Yard inspector in order to investigate the stolen painting; the Rittenhouse butler, Hives, is an ex-convict who is secretly in league with Mrs. Whitehead; and Mrs. Whitehead herself pretends friendship with Mrs. Rittenhouse while actually attempting to undermine her social position. There is even an inside joke about Chico's fake Italian identity: when Chico asks Chandler how he got to be "Roscoe W. Chandler," he asks Chico how he got to be Italian. The confusion of names – and thus of identities – becomes a kind of comic leit-motif in the film. One gag involves Chandler and Spaulding trying to sort out which name belongs to whom, and later in the film Groucho says that "Mrs. Beaugard lost a valuable painting by Rittenhouse." Artist and patron, commodity and consumer become interchangeable in a world that seemingly lacks any substance. Names are also mispronounced, in inadvertent (or intentional) slights: Arabella calls Ravelli "Ravioli," and Spaulding calls Mrs. Rittenhouse "Mrs. Rittenrotten."

The entire film works as a comic deflation of the art world, and more generally of the upper-class world of social and aesthetic pretension. The featured painting depicts a scene after a fox hunt, an allusion to English aristocratic life, and the entire film is made up of such parodies of elitist culture. Groucho parodies Eugene O'Neill's *Strange Interlude,* delivering a series of mock-dramatic soliloquies directly to the camera; Groucho (as Spaulding) also mocks the stories recounted by explorers and big-game hunters about their African adventures (including the famous gag of shooting an elephant in his pyjamas). A discussion of art by Chandler and Spaulding and an art lecture by Chandler are both interrupted, one by Spaulding's objection to Chandler taking the subject too seriously and the other by the lights going out; a musical performance in the salon turns into a football game and a fistfight; a bridge game ends with Harpo (The Professor) wearing Mrs. Whitehead's shoes; and a letter to Spaulding's attorneys, dictated to his secretary Jamison, is the occasion for an extended parody of lawyers and legalese.

The film begins with an article from the society pages of the newspaper. A photo of the Rittenhouse home ("one of the showplaces of Long Island") is accompanied by the headline, "Social Season Opens with Brilliant House Party at Home of Mrs. Rittenhouse." The first scene immediately establishes the scale of the Rittenhouse mansion and the nature of class relations within it. In a brief patter song, Hives instructs the rest of the male staff on how to treat the guest of honor, Captain Spaulding. The song's lyrics themselves parody the absurdly hyperbolic logic governing social relations within the world of the excessively wealthy and their celebrity guests:

> HIVES: You must do your best tonight, be on your toes, men.
> There's another guest tonight, it's one of those men who are
> being feted by the smart set.
> CHORUS: We'll see that he gets what he deserves.
> HIVES: Treat him as you do a king, in manner royal. Like a subject to a king, you must be loyal. On this subject you must
> have your heart set.

In the stage version of *Animal Crackers,* this opening scene was a more extended satire on the relations between the servants and those upon whom they wait, as "the butlers deride[d] the 'trash' spoken by society people, while the maids impl[ied] multiple infidelities among the guests."[36] The pretension and conspicuous consumption represented by the Rittenhouse household becomes even more apparent with the appearance of Mrs. Rittenhouse herself, who instructs Hives to put Mr. Chandler in the "Blue Suite" and Captain Spaulding in the "Green Duplex," with "two baths."

As in *Duck Soup* three years later, the Brothers make brilliant use of the device of Groucho's delayed arrival. By the time Spaulding actually arrives, carried in on a sedan chair supported by four Africans (with another two to carry his collection of guns), his entrance has been well prepared. The assembled guests have already sung a round of "Hooray for Captain Spaulding," and his secretary Jamison has announced in song the conditions under which the captain is prepared to "camp here." Spaulding's first gesture is vintage Groucho. He asks the head African porter what he owes, and when told it comes to $1.85 he refuses to pay and sends him off, asking to see his license plate. While the joke comparing the African porters to overcharging New York taxi drivers might be dismissed as a tasteless, and even racist gag, it reveals the unequal socioeconomic relations constituting Depression-era America. The porters literalize the gap between rich and poor that is suggested in various ways throughout the film. The fact that discussions of money appear continually, one might even say obsessively, throughout the film is no coincidence in this post-crash environment. The painting is said to have cost $100,000; John Parker tells Arabella he only made $150 off the sale of his paintings last year and that a cousin of his made $50,000 on Wall Street; Ravelli discusses the terms of his pay in some detail with Spaulding ($10 an hour for playing, $12 an hour for not playing, and $15 for rehearsing); Spaulding tries to sell Mrs. Rittenhouse a life insurance policy for $1500; Ravelli and the Professor blackmail Chandler into offering them a check for $5,000 in hush money; Ravelli and The Professor also try to get Mrs. Rittenhouse and Mrs. Whitehead to play cards with them for money; and at one point Spaulding asks Mrs. Rittenhouse how much she pays Hives, a man who, despite his admonitions to his staff about "loyalty," has already left the Whitehead residence after receiving a higher offer from Mrs. Rittenhouse.

In the most direct allusion to the economic context in which the film was made, one of Groucho's O'Neillesque soliloquies segues brilliantly into a series of stock market quotations: "And in those corridors I see figures . . . strange figures . . . weird figures . . . Steel 106, Anaconda 74, American Can 138."[37] In another scene, Spaulding and Chandler engage in a lengthy discussion of the value of a nickel:

CHANDLER: Well, you see my dear captain, in the last analysis it is a question of money. A nickel today is not what it used to be ten years ago.

SPAULDING: Well, I'll go further than that: I'll get off at the depot. A nickel today's not what is was worth *fifteen* years ago. Do you know what this country needs today? A 7-cent nickel. Yessirree, we've been using the 5-cent nickel in this country since 1492. That's pretty near a hundred years, daylight savings! Now why not give the 7-cent nickel a chance? If that works out, next year we could have an 8-cent nickel. Think what that would mean. You could go to the newsstand and buy a 3-cent newspaper and get the same nickel back again. Why, one nickel carefully used could last a family a lifetime.

Spaulding's speech is a clear parody of the kind of economic remedies that were proposed in the period following the market crash, when President Hoover and other political and business leaders continued to make upbeat pronouncements about "prosperity" and a speedy economic recovery.[38] It can also be read as a statement of class inequality. While the people assembled at Mrs. Rittenhouse's party live in excessive luxury, the average family is struggling to make a nickel go further. Despite all the talk of money and finances, the wealthy are protected from having to deal with money directly: Arabella has "a charge account in every shop on Fifth Avenue," which she naively suggests she and John can live on after they get married.[39]

Arabella's offer to support John brings up another important aspect of the film's social relationships. Issues of class, and of the power and privilege that accompany socioeconomic status, are mapped onto gender relationships in significant ways, perhaps anticipating anxieties about gender order that would become more prevalent during the Depression years. With the exception of the dubious Chandler—whose mysterious origins cloud the legitimacy of his claim to social status—all the male characters in the film occupy a lower place on the social ladder than the women. There is no Mr. Rittenhouse or Mr. Whitehead to balance their socially powerful wives, or even a suitably upper-class suitor for Arabella. Parker, a somewhat feminized man, faces the prospect of being shunned by Arabella's social set and supported by her money (or else giving up his career as an artist to get a "real" job). The characters portrayed by the Marx Brothers are con-men who seek to make a quick buck off wealthy women who appear desperate for masculine attention.

That the Brothers resent these upper-class women is clear from the beginning. Aside from the usual jokes Groucho/Spaulding makes at Dumont/Rittenhouse's expense, there are attempts to efface her presence quite literally from the screen.[40] When Mrs. Rittenhouse begins a speech in praise of Spaulding by proclaiming "You stand before me as one of the bravest men of all time," Groucho literalizes the statement by stepping between her and the camera, temporarily blocking her from view. Later, in a scene with both Mrs. Rittenhouse and Mrs. Whitehead, Groucho walks toward the camera and away from the two women (upstaging them, in the most literal sense) in order to deliver his soliloquy while the two women are frozen in space and out of camera focus.

The most unambiguous display of gender and class resentment in the film comes not from Groucho, but from Harpo (The Professor), who, in league with Ravelli, seems determined to disrupt the party in any way he can. The Professor chases and harasses women, shoots at the guests, kills the pet canary, wrestles Mrs. Rittenhouse, sits on Mrs. Whitehead's lap and steals her shoes, destroys the card table, steals the silver, takes both the original Beaugard and the Parker imitation, and, at the end of the party, puts the entire cast to sleep with chloroform gas. Harpo, with his highly ironic nickname, "The Professor," embodies all the contradictions of the Depression era. He represents the period's violence on the one hand (he carries a blackjack and is associated with criminality), and its innocence and sentimentality on the other (he is treated as a child throughout the film and his harp number is a wistful version of "Why Am I So Romantic?"). He represents an affront both to social respectability – appearing at the party wearing only a bathing suit under his coat – and to economic security. A figure for incipient fears of poverty and homelessness, he sleeps on a bench in the garden, using the Beaugard painting as a blanket.

The film's final scene is also its most effective imagetext, as the police inspector decides not to arrest The Professor after he returns the paintings, but tries instead to give him a paternalistic lecture:

INSPECTOR HENNESSEY: You're running around with the wrong
kind of people. Do you want to be a crook?
*(Harpo nods his head. Hennessey looks surprised.)*
HENNESSEY: Oh, why don't you go home?
RAVELLI: He's got no home.
HENNESSEY *(ignoring him):* Go home for a few nights. Stay home.
Don't you know your poor old mother sits there . . . *(a piece of
silverware falls out of Harpo's pants pocket, then another)* . . . sits
there night after night waiting to hear your steps on the stairs.
RAVELLI: Got no stairs.
HENNESSEY: And I can see a little light burning . . . *(more silver-
ware falls)* . . . burning in the window.
SPAULDING: No you can't. The gas company turned it off.
HENNESSEY: Now what I'm telling you is for your own good,
and if you listen to me you can't go wrong.
*(Cut to shot of a huge pile of silverware falling out of Harpo's pocket
and lying on the floor at his feet.)*

Here the physical embodiment of conspicuous upper-class consumption
– the silverware – continually interrupts the paternalistic officer's
attempts to appeal to an outdated vision of domestic sentimentality. The
falsity of Hennessey's narrative is displayed both by the running commentary of Ravelli and Spaulding – which he chooses to ignore – and by
the fact of the stolen silver itself – which he cannot.

The "happy ending" proposed by Hennessey is rejected in favor of a
more ambiguous closure. When the inspector decides he will have to
arrest The Professor after all for the theft of the silver, Harpo pulls out a
spray canister filled with chloroform gas and puts the policeman and all
the guests – including the other Marx Brothers – to sleep. Seeing a beautiful blonde lying on the floor, Harpo tries to lift her up, but realizing that
she is out cold and cannot be awakened, he lies down beside her, putting
himself to sleep to end the film. Harpo's desire for the luxury represented
by the Rittenhouse mansion – a desire intensified by the sight of the
fetishized upper-class female body – participates in the utopian desires of
American society for romance and material satisfaction. Yet Harpo's
utopian solution is at best a temporary one. His desire to stay with the
party guests at the end of the film rather than use the opportunity to

make an escape signifies the powerful appeal such a world and its commodities (silver, paintings, and attractive women) still holds for him.

As in several of the Marx Brothers' films of the early 1930s, the social transgressiveness of the ending – one in which the representatives of both the law and the dominant social class are put to sleep by a member of the unemployed and homeless underclass – are placed in a strange and finally unresolved tension with the film's utopian energies. What makes the ending of particular interest is the fact that its form of social transgression – or, as we might say from another standpoint, its form of utopia – involves the silencing of the film's verbal dimension. High society and its phony, pretentious, and manipulative language are finally silenced by Harpo. Even Groucho and Chico, whose verbal gymnastics have shared the screen with Harpo's visual gags throughout the film, are rendered silent by the oxymoronically nonspeaking "Professor." Finally, the film itself can be seen as reverting generically to the era of the silent film, with Harpo as its silent clown. In this apparent reversal of film history – one that replaces the imagetext with the silent image – we can perhaps read a desire to turn back the clock to an earlier and happier time, a time before the market crash and the onset of greater class antagonisms created troubles in paradise.

# 2

# WORKING LADIES AND FORGOTTEN MEN

## Class Divisions in Romantic Comedy, 1934–1937

I

If films like the Marx Brothers' *Animal Crackers* made clear the object of their social satire, many of the comedies made later in the decade – including the romantic "screwball comedies" by directors such as Gregory La Cava, Mitchell Leisen, and Leo McCarey – were far more equivocal in their treatment of class and other social issues. La Cava's *My Man Godfrey* (1936), for example, begins with a satire on upper-class society that seems equal in its subversive potential to the most anarchic comedies of the Marx Brothers, yet it ends with an unexpected and rather sudden reversal of its underlying social critique.

The film begins when two wealthy young women – Irene Bullock (Carole Lombard) and her sister Cornelia (Gail Patrick) – discover the apparently destitute Godfrey Parke (William Powell) among the homeless men living on the city dump, bring him as their "forgotten man" to a scavenger hunt party at the "Waldorf Ritz," and subsequently hire him as the family butler. Throughout most of the film, La Cava's satirical lens is directed toward the screwball antics of the conspicuously pampered upper classes, as we witness the total lack of sensitivity displayed by upper-class characters toward the situation of their less privileged counterparts. When Irene first encounters Godfrey at the dump, she fatuously asks him why he lives in such a place when there are so many nicer homes. Irene appears not even to have registered the fact of the Depression, and the Bullock family as a whole retains a pre-crash mentality in the midst of the Depression era.

The scenes at the beginning of the film – especially the juxtaposed scenes that take place at the dump and the Waldorf-Ritz ballroom – suggest the potential for strong social comment. At the ballroom, for example, we see elegantly dressed men and women carrying and dragging various discarded objects for the scavenger hunt. With the appearance of Godfrey as one of these unwanted objects, the scene captures better than any other in Depression-era comedy both the insane gap between rich and poor and the utter lack of social consciousness displayed by the wealthy few. By the end of *My Man Godfrey,* however, the film's apparent sociopolitical message appears to have undergone a radical reversal. The film concludes not with the kind of class satire with which it began, but with a utopian celebration of private enterprise during the Depression. Godfrey – as it turns out – is no real bum at all, but a wealthy member of the "Boston Parkes," an upper-class New England family actually higher on the social scale than the family for which he is working. At the end of the film, Godfrey builds a nightclub ("The Dump") on the site of the old dump, thus providing jobs for his hobo friends as cooks and waiters and restoring a sense of social harmony. What is most remarkable in this scenario is that Godfrey accomplishes his project without resorting to New Deal methods of social engineering. As Rita Barnard suggests, La Cava's vision of a utopian entrepreneurial solution to economic hardship appears to anticipate "the wishful thinking of the Reagan years" more than it reflects the stereotypical vision of the "lean and angry" 1930s.[1] Nevertheless, the film's use of juxtaposed wealth and poverty to create an entertaining spectacle for the film audience is quite typical of filmic representation during the Depression years, and it is a formula repeated in a number of films, including La Cava's *Fifth Avenue Girl* (1939) and Mitchell Leisen's *Easy Living* (1937). The tension between utopian desires and transgressive social energies more often than not gets resolved in favor of utopian solutions conforming to the myths promoted by the American culture industry: those of social harmony and an idealized classless society.

Yet while the romantic comedies of the mid-1930s to early 1940s were less openly subversive of social norms than earlier comedies such as those of Charlie Chaplin and the Marx Brothers, they were nonetheless highly ambivalent in their exploration of social class, social conformism, and the establishment of social order. As Mike Cormack argues, screwball films such as Leo McCarey's *The Awful Truth* (1937) can be read as "ideologically subversive" productions that contain "some of the strongest social criticism to be found in Hollywood films of the middle and later thirties."[2] It was in part in order to defuse the screwball comedy's "potentially subversive form," according to Cormack, that the films adopted a relatively conservative cinematographic style. Given their static visual style, and the fact that many of them were adapted from theatrical plays, screwball comedies are most strongly defined by their use of language. The same "uneasy social vision" that Ed Sikov has located in the love and marriage plots of these films – the "cultural distress" the characters manifest in their words as well as in their awkwardly manic physical actions – can be related to a larger social distress, a "dis-ease" located in the ideological contradictions caused by various forms of socioeconomic and class upheaval.[3]

Critics have been reluctant to examine in depth the social, ideological, and cultural dynamics of 1930s comedies. Stanley Cavell, for example, in the most frequently cited study of romantic comedies of the 1930s and 1940s, pays scant attention to the question of class or to the broader issue of social relations within the films he discusses.[4] While the questions he treats – principally those surrounding love, sex, and marriage – were important to Depression-era comedies, these films were crucially concerned with class and social relations as well. In fact, the intersection of issues of class with those of gender and sexuality is central to any understanding of the comedies of the period.

Given the generally hostile sentiment toward the wealthy few expressed by both the working class and the increasingly proletarianized middle-class populations that constituted the bulk of theater audiences, any naively positive view of the upper classes would have proved unacceptable to many, if not most, contemporary viewers. Although it is difficult to assess the response of working-class audiences to particular pictures, class antagonisms were strong enough by the mid-1930s that at least a portion of the film-going audience would have rejected overly flattering depictions of the rich. As Brian Neve suggests, these less affluent film audiences of the 1930s "were unable to check their anxieties at the door [and] substantial numbers of viewers may have been aware of the ambiguities of the films that they were viewing, despite or because of their optimistic conclusions."[5] Hollywood films of the 1930s, Giuliana Muscio remarks, "did not so much project a seamless band of dominant ideology as explore [its] contradictions."[6] Muscio provides the example of the gangster film, in which the gangster is punished only after his violent gestures have been glorified and his sexually transgressive behavior has been presented "in the most minute and seductive detail." A similar contradiction can be seen in screwball comedies, which present the wealthy in an ultimately forgiving light, but only after exploring the inherent conflicts and potential fissures within the class system.

These ideological contradictions in 1930s films are symptomatic of larger contradictions within American society of the Depression era. As Rita Barnard observes, the 1930s represented as much the emergence of a "culture of abundance" and a growth in the consumer society as they did a time of poverty and deprivation. Motion pictures, along with other consumer products and institutions such as the radio, the automobile, the photonewsmagazine, installment buying, and the self-service supermarket, became central features of American life, changing both patterns of consumption and the social relations affected by such patterns. These changes helped to create a society that was more dependent on the "commodity spectacle" than ever before. While class discrepancies – measured in strictly economic terms – may have been greater during the 1930s than in preceding decades, the fact of an increasingly consumerist ethos paradoxically produced interests that brought the various classes closer together.

It is within this context of growing disparities in wealth and social status and a simultaneous development in the national consumer economy that cross-class interactions – and especially cross-class interactions of a sexual nature – become of central importance to film comedy. The two most common versions of the screwball plot of the 1930s and early 1940s involve either an upper-class heiress involved with a middle-class man or a wealthy man involved with a woman of working- or middle-class background. These two basic narrative structures constitute the bread-and-butter plots of screwball comedy films, and a number of the best-known films of the genre conform to one formula or the other.[7] Garson Kanin's *Tom, Dick, and Harry* (1940) is a unique hybrid of the two kinds of plots, in which a middle-class woman has to choose between a working-class auto mechanic, an upwardly mobile (middle-class) car salesman, and a wealthy playboy. Other variations on the class theme include the confrontation of "respectable" middle-class status with more questionable or marginal social status (*Ball of Fire* and *Vivacious Lady*), and a sudden change in class status caused either by inheritance *(Mr. Deeds Goes to Town)*, mistaken identity *(Nothing Sacred)*, or deliberate subterfuge *(Midnight, The Princess Comes Across)*. Although few comedies of the period depict actual poverty or working-class conditions in any meaningful terms, such films as *My Man Godfrey*, Capra's *Mr. Deeds Goes to Town* (1936), and Sturges' *Sullivan's Travels* (1941) involve significant interactions between the more privileged classes and the world of Depression-era poverty.

Even if the Hollywood system as a whole had little interest in producing comedies that challenged the status quo of American social life, individual writers and directors were committed to using their films as a means of explicit social comment. Norman Krasna, for example, who worked his way up from the position of copy boy at *The New York World* to become one of the most successful Hollywood screenwriters of the 1930s and 1940s, intended his screenplays for such films as *Bachelor Mother* and *The Devil and Miss Jones* to be "as much as a protest as I [could] make against the existing system" within "the framework of a comedy."[8] In emphasizing the position of the "underdog" in society and in providing as realistic a vision as possible in a Hollywood comedy of "how tough life is," Krasna's treatment of the class theme in *The Devil and Miss Jones* offended some viewers, including one reviewer at the *Los Angeles Times* who wrote an editorial condemning the film. In an interview from the mid-1980s, Krasna characterized the film as a form of "propaganda" and a "dangerous picture" (233). Similarly, in the case of George Cukor's *Holiday* (1938), Donald Ogden Stewart rewrote Philip Barry's original play in order to strengthen its critique of patriarchal capitalism.

Given the explicit sociopolitical commentary offered in Depression-era comedies like Cukor's *Holiday*, Capra's *It Happened One Night, Mr. Deeds Goes to Town,* and *You Can't Take It with You,* La Cava's *My Man Godfrey* and *Fifth Avenue Girl,* Leisen's *Easy Living,* and Garson Kanin's *Bachelor Mother* and *The Devil and Miss Jones,* it seems clear that Hollywood comedy contained a significant potential for social and political critique. This critique is not to be found primarily on the level of plot, since these films, like most comedies, tend toward the resolution brought about by ultimate class harmony and social reparation. Instead, their social subversiveness must be located primarily on the level of nonnarrative elements such as characterization, visual imagery, and especially language.

The screwball comedies were intensely involved with the issue of language and with the class-inflected nature of all speech acts. As Giuliana Muscio suggests, the "verbal hyperactivity" of films of the 1930s – including the pace and energy of screwball comedy dialogue – was part of a "sensory revolution" that "can be interpreted as an expression of the restlessness and social confusion of the moment" (72). If it is in their narratives that 1930s comedies comment most overtly on the class system of the Depression era, it is through their *language* that they engage in a more subtle analysis of class relations. One indication of the singularly important role language plays in these films is the preponderant representation of professions concerned with language and spoken discourse. Depression-era comedies are filled with writers (Richard Boleslawski's *Theodora Goes Wild,* William Keighley's *No Time for Comedy,* William Seiter's *The Moon's Our Home,* Hawks's *Ball of Fire,* George Stevens' *Vivacious Lady*), and even more commonly, with newspaper reporters (Capra's *Platinum Blonde, It Happened One Night* and *Mr. Deeds Goes to Town,* Hawks's *His Girl Friday,* Cukor's *The Philadelphia Story,* Wellman's *Nothing Sacred,* Tad Garnett's *Love Is News,* Van Dyke's *Love on the Run,* Edward Griffith's *Cafe Society,* Hal Roach's *There Goes My Heart,* Leigh Jason's *The Mad Miss Manton,* and Jack Conway's *Libeled Lady*).

The linguistic production of these reporters and writers creates a carnivalesque environment for the screwball film, one in which socially inflected forms of speech are constantly thrust into dialogic encounters with those from other registers of discourse. Writers and reporters also represent a mediating class function within many of these films, allowing an acceptable crossing or blurring of class boundaries during the Depression years. Belonging neither to a traditional working class nor to an established bourgeoisie, writers in these films are often capable of greater class mobility than other characters.

Significantly, the proliferation of cinematic speech in screwball comedies was occurring at exactly the moment when the censors were beginning to crack down on the free flow of screened language. While the Production Code administered by the Hays Office had first been introduced in 1930, it was not until 1933 that a combination of forces led to increased pressure for more rigid enforcement of the codes.[9] Discussions between the Hays Office and representatives of both the church and the government began in the summer of 1933, and by the spring of 1934 William Hays and the head of his censorship office, Joseph Breen, had written a new and more strongly worded document urging the necessity for "moral compensating values" in the movies. According to this document, which would determine the restrictions on Hollywood film for the next two decades, films were required to contain "sufficient good to compensate for any evil that might be depicted," and to balance any morally questionable behavior with at least one "virtuous" character who spoke "as a voice 'for moral behavior.'"[10] This revised code, formally implemented in July 1934, not only restricted films far more in their use of sexually explicit language, theme, and behavior, but also encouraged them to serve as vehicles for moral improvement and to avoid sensitive issues in both moral and political arenas. Divorce, adultery, sexual passion, and "modern living" now had to be handled with much greater finesse, and political and social controversy were increasingly avoided in the fear of ultimate rejection by the censors.

Most of the films that came into direct conflict with the censorship codes in the 1930s were not comedies, although one of the primary battlegrounds for the first attempts at censorship – the early films of Mae West – illustrates the direction film comedy might have taken within a less restrictive atmosphere. Although the censors did not succeed in destroying West's screen career entirely, they managed to minimize her ability to exploit her sexual persona on screen, thereby helping to divert popular attention away from her distinctive brand of sexually suggestive comedy and toward less sexually explicit genres like screwball comedy.

Ironically, the enforcement of the notorious Production Code inadvertently made screwball comedy one of the most successful genres of its day. The screwball comedy did not abandon sex as a topic. Instead, it managed to replace the direct representation of sexuality with a brilliant use of language composed largely of cleverly disguised sexual innuendo and a verbal foreplay between the sexes. The change from pre-code liberation to post-code restriction did as much as the Depression itself to change the genres of motion pictures. One of these changes was to put a greater burden on language to fill in the gaps left by the imposition of greater restrictions on explicit content.

## II

In order to examine more closely the representation of class relationships in 1930s comedies, I shall begin by looking not at a canonical example of the screwball genre, but at a comedy that can be seen as a transitional film between earlier forms of romantic comedy and screwball comedy. *The Girl from Missouri,* directed by Jack Conway, written by Anita Loos, and starring box-office sensation Jean Harlow, was made at a pivotal moment in the development of Hollywood comedy: between April and June of 1934. This was only a few months before the Hays Office applied the more stringent morality code, and it was in the same year that the screwball comedy was to emerge as a popular new genre. Although *The Girl from Missouri* has never been hailed as a classic 1930s comedy on the level of Hawks's *Twentieth Century* or Capra's *It Happened One Night* – both made in the same year – it deserves more attention than it has previously received because of the unique way in which it articulates a number of the factors that more generally inform 1930s comedies: the impact of the new censorship codes; the use of a strongly inflected class-based narrative; and the thematizing of language as a crucial aspect of class relationships.[11]

The story concerns a young woman from small-town Missouri who leaves an unwholesome home situation (where her mother and stepfather – proprietors of a dance hall – require her to entertain the male customers) in order to pursue a better life in New York City. Eadie (Harlow) travels with her female companion Kitty to the big city, where she plans to work as a chorus girl until she can meet a man – preferably one with a lot of money – and get married. After quickly garnering what she assumes to be a genuine proposal from a banker, Frank Cousins, who gives her his ruby cufflinks as an engagement present, she finds herself in a difficult situation when Cousins, who is actually bankrupt and heavily in debt, commits suicide in the next room. Undaunted in her search for a rich husband, however, Eadie goes on to pursue a real millionaire, T. R. Paige (Lionel Barrymore), and ultimately falls for his son Tom, whom she finally convinces to marry her. Despite the obstacles on her road to marital and financial success (the death of Cousins, a compromising situation involving the rubies Cousins gave her before his death, Tom's unwillingness to propose, and, most importantly, his father's resistance to the match), the plot seems more linear than that of the typical screwball feature, lacking the comic twists and turns of screwball narrative. Eadie's singlemindedly earnest pursuit of a rich husband leaves little room for screwball silliness. The film also differs from screwball in its more blatant presentation of the sexual theme. Eadie is clearly a golddigger with few scruples other than her insistence on marriage as the final outcome of her flirtations; given her background as a dance-hall hostess and showgirl, her sexual purity is always somewhat in question. In an early scene of the film, after telling her friend Kitty that she intends to go "straight" (in other words, remain a virgin) until she can find a man to marry her, she declares: "Nobody ever believes I have ideals, but I do have, and I'll show 'em I have." Later, after sneaking into Cousins' room and engaging him in conversation, she replies to his insinuation ("so you have no 'minor vices'?") by defending the questioned virtue of chorus girls. Yet when she receives the rubies from Cousins, she hides them provocatively in her stocking; and when the police are about to search her, she shows little embarrassment in asking Paige to remove them. Throughout the film, Eadie engages in active flirtation and sexually suggestive repartee. Finally, at the end of the film, she gets drunk and almost commits a sexual indiscretion with another admirer before she is "rescued" by Kitty and Tom.

The various proposed titles of the film reflect the sexual ambiguity epitomized by the film itself. Beginning with the suggestive "Eadie Was a Lady," the film progressed through the diametrically opposed titles "Born to Be Kissed" and "100% Pure" before settling on the innocuous "The Girl from Missouri." The film also contains scenes of partial undress which might easily, as the reviewer for *The New York Times* put it, have "disarm[ed] the more squeamish of its auditors by declining to be too serious about the controversial subject of amour." It is hard to imagine, despite Eadie's frequent assertion of her "100% pure" morals, that *The Girl from Missouri* could have been made in the post-code era. In fact, while it did manage to slip by the censors, the film initially encountered considerable trouble from the Hays Office. Following the lead of the Legion of Decency, which had already attacked Harlow, along with Mae West, as an actress responsible for the decay of American sexual morals, Breen and the Hays Office initially decided to ban "Born to Be

Kissed," calling it "one of the most torrid efforts to emanate from any studio at any time." Even the proposed change of the title to "100% Pure" failed to sway Breen, and it took considerable pressure from MGM, along with a further change of title to the final "The Girl from Missouri," to persuade the office to approve the movie for its August release.[12] The film was quite successful at the box office, grossing $1.1 million, and it received positive reviews in both *Variety* and the *New York Times,* but it was overshadowed by films like *It Happened One Night* and Van Dyke's *The Thin Man.*[13]

*The Girl from Missouri* explores the class theme in provocative ways. Class relationships in the movie are fairly complex and clearly related to gendered and sexual relationships. Eadie herself, despite her pretensions of being a "lady," is from a working-class background, and she is constantly reminded of this fact by the presence of her companion Kitty. Whereas Eadie holds out for a wealthy husband, Kitty provides a comic foil for Eadie's aspirations by going after every man she meets (including, in the course of the film, a butler, a doorman, a lifeguard, a policeman, and a sailor). When Eadie begins dating Tom, he refuses to take her desire for marriage seriously, and in one scene he humiliates her in front of his friends, who treat her as a cheap floozy. What makes the film's class relationships more complex than a simple "poor girl meets rich boy" plot, however, is the fact that Tom's father, T. R. Paige, is himself a thinly disguised product of the working classes (a "roughneck," as he puts it). We learn this first in the scene in which Cousins asks Paige for leniency on a loan he has made; the humiliation of Paige's blunt refusal leads to Cousins' suicide.

Within the class structure of the film, Paige represents an intermediate link between the working-class Eadie and Kitty on the one hand and upper-class characters like Cousins, Lord Douglas, and Senator Titcombe on the other. Paige understands Eadie better than the upper-class sycophants who surround him, and he is more resistant to her charms. His reluctance to accept the marriage of Eadie and Tom is in large part based on his own desire to consolidate the social position he has worked so hard to achieve. Despite his wealth and influence in business, and, increasingly, in social and political circles, T. R. is insecure about his own class status, realizing that the deference shown him by lords and senators is only circumstantial. In the course of the film, he is appointed the

American representative to important disarmament talks in Europe, and a dinner is given in his honor at an exclusive men's club to which in earlier days he would never have been admitted as a member, much less be an honored guest.

In one revealing scene early in the film, Eadie mistakes T. R., who is holding a tray of drinks, for the butler, and asks him, in an affected upper-class accent, about his "mah-ster." T. R., amused by Eadie's crude attempt at "passing" socially, mocks her by repeating the word with the same phony pronunciation. When she realizes she is being ridiculed, Eadie slaps T. R. for not "keeping his place," only later discovering that the man she slapped is actually a millionaire. The relationship between Eadie and T. R. is the most interesting one in the film in terms of its class dynamics. T. R. immediately recognizes Eadie for what she is: a golddigger. He shows a kind of grudging respect for her efforts to pull herself up in society, and he is willing to be her "friend," helping her to hide the rubies and giving her money. On the other hand, he draws the line at anything more than casual flirtation. He is firmly set against the idea of Eadie as a wife either for him or for his son. When it appears that Tom is serious about marrying Eadie, T. R. reverts to the kind of tactics he has learned from his experience as a hard-nosed entrepreneur. He frames Eadie for stealing the jewels, and he hires another man to pose as her lover in order to discourage Tom's affections. Eadie, however, is no pushover. She frames him in return, at the moment of his triumphant trip to Europe, by posing next to him in her negligée for the press photographers. The movie ends when T. R. decides to accept Eadie as a daughter-in-law, though it remains unclear whether the motive is really his respect for her fighting spirit, as he says, or only the fact that by claiming her as daughter-in-law he can provide an explanation for the compromising photos and avoid damage to his social and political career.

Language plays an important role throughout the film in delineating class relationships. Eadie and her companion, Kitty, attempt to change their lower-class accents in order to be accepted by high society, but they never quite manage to do so successfully. Eadie even offers to take elocution lessons in order to conform to Tom's social world: "I know my English is lousy . . . I mean bad . . . but I'll take lessons, you know, for enunciation." In another humorous exchange with Kitty, Eadie corrects her friend's pronunciation of "vase":

KITTY: We have every vase in the place.

EADIE: Vahze.

KITTY: Very well: we have every vahze in the plahze.

Kitty's failed attempt to effect a "correct" upper-class pronunciation is a satiric comment on the fundamental affectation of the people Eadie wants so badly to emulate. At the same time, however, T. R.'s use of a phony and pretentious mode of speech designed to impress his upper-class friends is only a more sophisticated version of Eadie's more naive attempts to act the part of a "lady." Barrymore gives an impressive linguistic performance as the self-made millionaire roughneck: in the course of the film, he shifts his accent up and down the class scale, depending on the occasion. In the scene toward the end of the film when Eadie gains her revenge on T. R. by framing him, T. R. had just been giving an impromptu speech for the press in which his puffed-up rhetoric and upper-class accent duplicate the posture of the cultural ambassador he hopes to become: "I'm going to give this job all I've got, of dignity, sincerity, and reverence for the fine traditions of our great country." By this point the film's audience is well aware of T. R.'s hypocrisy and is all too happy to witness the ironic reversal of his linguistic and social pretensions when Eadie, dressed only in a negligée, appears from the door behind him and embraces him just as the cameras shoot his picture for the newspapers. At this point, T. R. reverts to the language of the street with which he is more comfortable ("Why you little rat . . ."), thus revealing his class origins to be identical to Eadie's. It is *language,* then, and not money, that serves as the common currency by which Eadie and T. R. are brought to the same level at the end of the film.

*The Girl from Missouri* is unusual for comedies of the 1930s in its unapologetically negative portrayal of the wealthy. If it is true, as Andrew Bergman suggests, that in most mid-1930s comedies "class conflicts . . . were really personality conflicts, and hence easily resolved by a good chat," that is certainly not the case in this film.[14] Rather than the lovably harmless upper-class patriarch who occupies the position of the father in many screwball comedies, T. R. Paige is a real antagonist for Eadie, a man who has had to rise to the ranks of the wealthy by his own less than salutory efforts. While the rich in most screwball comedies appear to have always been that way – a kind of pseudo-aristocracy who inhabit their Fifth Avenue residences, Palm Beach mansions, and Connecticut summer houses like English country manors – Paige is a character who still displays the seams of class ideology. That he is unapologetically *nouveau riche* is apparent in the scene where he gives Eadie the "tour" of his Palm Beach mansion, announcing the historical importance of each piece of furniture they pass.

Although Eadie finally gets her rich husband, this is no fairy-tale environment such as we find in typical screwball comedies. With the exception of Paige – who remains a morally ambiguous figure – the rich are portrayed as either upper-class sycophants like Lord Douglas and Senator Titcombe, alcoholic playboys like Charlie, or weak aesthetes like Cousins. The only characters in the film who display any real vitality are Eadie and T. R., both of whom have had to rise from working-class backgrounds rather than inheriting wealth.

To understand the difference between the treatment of class issues in *The Girl from Missouri* and that of the screwball film as it was to evolve throughout the decade, we need only compare the portrayal of T. R. Paige with that of the wealthy fathers played by actors from Walter Connolly to Edward Arnold to Eugene Pallette in comedies by Capra, Leisen, La Cava, and Sturges. In the same year as *The Girl from Missouri*, Capra's *It Happened One Night* presented the character of Alexander Andrews (Connolly), a patriarch who would serve as a model of the "grumpy plutocrat [with] a heart of gold," as one reviewer for the journal *New Theatre* remarked. While he is presented in a less positive light in the early scenes, Andrews becomes completely sympathetic at the end of the film when he buys off the fortune-hunting playboy fiance and connives Ellie's elopement with the working-class hero Peter Warne (Clark Gable) whom he has liked from the start. Unlike Paige, Andrews has nothing to gain from a more socially prestigious marriage for his child. He greatly prefers the down-to-earth honesty and humble background of Peter to the social pretensions of the playboy aviator King Westley. Even with the father in Capra's 1939 comedy *You Can't Take It with You* – the tycoon Anthony P. Kirby (Edward Arnold) – we do not find the hypocrisy or moral ambiguity of a T. R. Paige. Kirby appears for most of the film as a tough nut for the Vanderhof family to crack, and he does symbolize in some sense the evils of conspicuous and rapacious wealth (he attempts to gain a monopoly of munitions plants). Yet at the end of the film he abandons his merger, rushes off to join the Vanderhofs, and sits down to play harmonica with Grandpa Vanderhof in a scene of ultimate social reconciliation. That no such scene exists in *The Girl from Missouri* indicates that—despite its nominal "happy ending"—the film enacts only an uneasy truce between rich and poor, not a utopian vision of cross-class harmony.

## III

As *The Girl from Missouri* makes clear, class relationships are often sexualized or eroticized in Depression-era comedy. Eadie, as played by Harlow, is an eroticized version of the working-class female. She is associated with sexuality through her family background, her manipulation and sexual control of men throughout the film, and her sexual indiscretion with Charlie. Although Eadie may indeed remain "100% Pure" throughout the film, Harlow's performance creates just enough ambiguity that the audience – along with the various male characters in the film – can have some doubts about her sexual mores. When we link Eadie with the only other working-class female represented in the film – the blatantly promiscuous Kitty – we see an even clearer pattern of associating class and sexuality.

This tendency to identify working-class women as sexual objects in Depression comedy can also be seen, though in more farcical terms, in Mitchell Leisen's *Easy Living*. Here the story concerns an honest working girl named Mary Smith (Jean Arthur) – an underpaid employee of the magazine *Boys' Constant Companion* – who is mistakenly identified as the mistress of the fabulously wealthy New York banker J. B. Ball, "The Bull of Broad Street." Though Arthur's performance is much less overtly sexualized than that of Harlow in *The Girl from Missouri*, and the treatment of class and sexuality in this post-code film is more implied than explicitly stated, we see the same tendency to enact parallels between class relations and sexual relations. The film could in fact be seen as a screwball rewriting of *The Girl from Missouri*. Rather than a golddigger in search of a rich husband, Mary is an innocent young woman who has both fortune and sexual innuendo literally fall on top of her in the form of an expensive sable coat thrown from a rich man's apartment. Although both films involve triangles in which the woman uses a relationship with the wealthy father to gain access to the son, Preston Sturges' screenplay for *Easy Living* adopts a fairy-tale mode rather than the more realistic social narrative of *The Girl from Missouri*.

Mary, a writer of boy's stories, represents the kind of downwardly mobile salaried employee whose situation was seen as an emerging social problem of the Depression years. One day, as she rides the top deck of a New York bus, a fur coat miraculously falls on her. Through a series of unlikely coincidences, she manages to meet and befriend not only the Wall Street banker who threw the coat from his penthouse but also his son, whose recent falling-out with his father has resulted in his working as a busboy in an automat (apparently the only job he could get without relying on his father's support). In this film – as in other screwball comedies like *My Man Godfrey* – the world of wealth is parodied as ridiculously extravagant, especially in the context of the mid-1930s. Ball, the "third biggest banker" in the city, has so many servants that he is constantly bumping into them. Far from earning the respect of his household, Ball is a figure of ridicule and contempt. His servants laugh at him when he trips and falls down the stairs, his cook calls him a "dirty capitalist," and his wife and son Johnny spend his money as if it quite literally grew on trees. Ball finally reaches the limits of his tolerance when he discovers that his wife has spent the outrageous sum of $58,000 on a new fur coat, and his son has bought an expensive Italian sports car.

In a fit of anger, Ball refuses to continue supporting the son and throws his wife's coat off the balcony. These two acts set off a series of narrative twists that appear at times to be little more than excuses to display in ironic fashion the gulf between rich and poor. The contradictions are spelled out quite specifically: Johnny's sports car cost $11,000, while Mary asks J. B. for a 10 cents bus fare; J. B. Ball owns actual banks, while Mary has to use the heel of her shoe to break open a nearly empty piggy bank; the Balls live in a luxurious Fifth Avenue mansion with a staff of servants, while Mary can barely afford to keep up with the $7 a week rent on her small apartment on West 112th Street; Mrs. Ball, who already has a closet full of furs, spends $58,000 on a superfluous sable, while Mary informs J. B. that a perfectly decent fur coat can be bought for $2 down plus payments; the stingy J. B. Ball complains about the cook's extravagant use of butter at breakfast, while Mary cannot afford to buy herself a decent meal at the automat.

Whatever else it may say about economic inequalities and class politics, *Easy Living* is a playfully satirical commentary on the relations between capitalism, consumer culture, and commodity fetishism. The film appears to comment on the ever-present dream of consumerist abundance. When Mary is mistaken for Ball's mistress after he gives her the coat and buys her an expensive hat to go with it, she is given the Imperial Suite at the luxurious but practically empty Hotel Louis, run by the French chef and failing hotelier Louis Louis. An icon of conspicuous consumption in the midst of the meagre 1930s, the Imperial Suite includes five reception rooms, a salon with white grand piano, an exercise room, two bedrooms, and a kitschy bathtub as big as a swimming pool. The real-life model for the Hotel Louis was the Waldorf Towers; like the Louis, it was an expensive hotel finished "just in time for the Depression to keep it empty" (Sikov, 124).

The practical Mary is more excited by the prospect of free food than by a desire for the luxurious accommodations of the Hotel Louis. Finding the refrigerator empty – another symbol of the hollow center within the masquerade of abundance – Mary heads for a nearby automat, the working-class alternative to the Louis' dining room. Lacking the money for even a decent automat meal, she hungrily eyes the food on other diners' plates. The busboy (who is none other than Johnny Ball) sneaks her a slice of beef pie, but he is caught by a guard who tries to arrest him. In the ensuing struggle, Johnny accidentally hits a lever that simultaneously opens the doors to all the automat entrees. The anarchic rush of the hungry patrons as well as a crowding mob from outside the restaurant to put as much food on their plates as possible precipitates a food riot, representing perhaps more directly than any other scene in 1930s comedy the desperation and material deprivation of the average American.

The following morning, Mary is awakened from her slumbers at the hotel by a string of calls from merchants, offering her everything from expensive chauffeur-driven cars to diamond jewelry from Cartier. In a parody of the rags-to-riches story, Mary enters a utopian dream of instant commodity gratification merely by being wrongly identified as J. B. Ball's mistress. In its use of consumerism as a utopian dream, the film recalls Charlie Chaplin's *Modern Times,* a film made two years earlier, in which the drudgery of modern life is temporarily forgotten amidst utopian visions of the department store. When Chaplin and his female companion enter the store after hours, we see what Rita Barnard describes as "a land of wishes, where the delights of the deli counter are free, where the tramp sleeps on the finest bed linen, and where the tattered gamine can don a fur and (for a frame or two) be transformed into a glamour girl" (22–23). While Leisen's screwball farce adopts a very different tone from Chaplin's silent morality tale, the resemblance of certain Depression-era motifs – the lure of free food, the fur coat, the promise of endless commodities – cannot be overlooked. Like Chaplin's glamorized gamine, *Easy Living's* Mary Smith takes on the elegant trappings of the wealthy without ever shedding her working-class innocence.

Yet despite the persuasiveness of the film's sociopolitical commentary, it ultimately backs away from Chaplinesque satire and ends, like *My Man Godfrey,* on a note that seems more utopian than subversive. Johnny, having decided he can swallow his pride and take his place in the family business—thereby also supporting the woman he loves—offers Mary the "job" of "cooking his breakfast." In both socioeconomic and gender terms, harmony is restored through an abrupt return to a masculine order and a corporate ethos. Mary, whose unruly female presence had caused problems for J. B. Ball on both a personal and a financial level, will give up her position as a working woman in order to marry a rich husband. The "easy living" she acquired through mistaken identity will now be hers through a legally sanctioned cross-class relationship.

Although Mary's marriage to Johnny would appear to clarify both her social and her sexual role, the film as a whole makes her sexual identity more complex in ways that are associated with her questionable class status. If two of the main themes of the film are money and food, the film's third preoccupation is sex, and sex, like money and food, is closely related to class. When Louis invites her to take up residency in the Hotel Louis, he suggests her need of a social "background" befitting her role as Ball's mistress: "A beautiful young girl like you has got to have a background. . . . This [hotel] is what you call a background!" Although sexuality is never made explicit here in the way it is in *The Girl from Missouri,* it is constantly invoked through both language and narrative situation. When Ball innocently insists on buying Mary a new hat to replace the one that was damaged by the falling coat, he immediately arouses the suspicions of Van Buren, the nosy proprietor of the hat-shop. Later that day, when Mary arrives at work wearing the fur coat, she again becomes the object of sexual innuendo. Though she continues to protest her innocence, she is obliged to invent a story about buying the coat in order to cover up the still more unbelievable story of it falling on her head. Neither of her stories convinces her boss and co-workers, and when she is fired from her job for violating the "ethical requirements of the *Boys' Constant Companion,*" she is driven to break a framed picture of the "typical American boy" over her boss's head in retaliation for his insinuating remarks.[15] Suspicion of Mary's illicit relationship with Ball causes a number of side-effects: it revives the business of the Hotel Louis; it threatens to break up Ball's marriage; and it throws the stock market into a tailspin when her prognostications – believed to be informed by her unique insider status as Ball's mistress – turn out to be the opposite of Ball's own market positions. Even Mary's "innocent" relationship with Johnny has a sexual undertone: Johnny stays overnight at her room in the Hotel Louis, and at one point they end up together (fully clothed, of course) in the suite's enormous bathtub.

The film can also be read in terms of 1930s consumer culture, especially in relation to its production of gender ideology. When Mary changes from female worker to female consumer in the second half of the film, she also comes to embody the increasingly dominant cultural image of women as shoppers rather than as productive workers. At a time when manufacturers, stores, and advertisers looked to women as the primary purchasers of consumer goods, the female shopper embodied, in the words of Elizabeth Melosh, "[a] widespread conflation of erotic and consumer desire."[16] As Mary Smith – whose ambivalent image in the film simultaneously denotes both an extreme sexual naivete and a locus of sexual desire – Jean Arthur represents the gender contradictions within a 1930s American culture that saw women as both erotic and pure, as both the agents of excessive consumption and the household regulators of consumer desire. From the moment she has a fur coat unexpectedly land on her at the beginning of the film – signaling her move from the world of economic deprivation to that of material and sensual abundance – Mary is associated with gestures and images of excess, most of which can be linked to money, food, or sex. She is the unwitting recipient of a fur coat, an eroticized object whose absurdly inflated value represents more than a lifetime's discretionary income for most Americans; she moves into the outlandishly luxurious Imperial Suite; and she is the cause of a literal eruption of food (a kind of culinary ejaculation) when Johnny attempts to get her a free meal. The gossip resulting from her presence at the Louis drives up the prices and desirability of the previously abandoned hotel, and her predictions cause wild gyrations in the stock market that nearly wipe out Ball's fortune. In the very process of turning capitalism upside down, Mary herself becomes a visual icon of excessive consumption. Wrapped in a fur coat, driving in an enormous V-16 automobile, and accompanied by two large English sheepdogs, she begins to resemble the parody of a wealthy woman out on a very expensive shopping spree.

Even the film's language tends toward excess, reflecting the excesses of a capitalist ideology run amok. Ball's hyperbolic rhetoric when pleading poverty to his wife and servants ("we're so close to being broke I can feel the wolf snapping at my pants") is matched by Mrs. Ball's equally hyperbolic language in refusing to return the coat to the fur store ("I'd rather *die* than humiliate myself in front of Mr. Zickle"). The film's carnivalesque use of language can be seen in the many different speech genres it displays or evokes: the family squabble; the language of money, business, and finance; the gossip of Louis Louis and Van Buren; the language of food, cooking, and menus; the language of advertising, shopping, and consumerism; the newspaper "help wanted" ads; the stock market "tip." Mary herself is a writer of stories who uses language for her own ends, making up a story in order to cover up yet another story. Louis is a foreigner (presumably French) whose heavy accent and colorful malapropisms lend an additional dash of flavor to the linguistic goulash of the film.

Finally, however, *Easy Living* does not choose to examine in any profound way the implications of consumeristic excess at a time of continuing poverty and joblessness. Even if it signals the contradictions that lay at the heart of Depression-era America, the film stays closer to the level of verbal and visual gag than to that of meaningful social critique. It was only in the 1930s films of Frank Capra – the subject of the next chapter – that the semiotic possibilities of sound comedy as a medium of social commentary would reach their full potential.

# 3

# "THE SPLIT-PEA SOUP AND THE SUCCOTASH"

## Frank Capra's 1930s Comedies and the Subject of Class

### I

Among the Hollywood directors who made comedies in the Depression era, Frank Capra was the most consistently concerned with themes of class and social distinction. As Leland Poague has suggested, the unifying thread of Capra's films is an examination of "moral questions having to do with class, economic status [and] life style as defined by class and economic status."[1] Like the Marx Brothers, Capra emerged from a working-class immigrant background that informed his views of class relations and made him highly critical of the upper-class WASP establishment.[2] At the same time, as an auteurist director within the Hollywood studio system, Capra repeatedly presented the story of a social outsider who is forced to work within the structure of a restrictive, manipulative, or corrupt social order. In Capra's films of the 1930s, we see the juxtaposition of two dominant narratives of class in America. On the one hand, Capra's comedies enact a celebration of the American success ethic (or "American Dream") in which Capra had himself participated. On the other hand, the films reflect an acute awareness of the reality of the class conflict to which Depression-era Americans were subject.

In many of Capra's films, the upwardly mobile trajectory of the success story is brought into tension with some form of class conflict; the ultimate resolution of this tension determines whether the film offers an ultimately utopian social vision or a more subversive view of American society. Although comedies like *It Happened One Night* (1934) and *You Can't Take It with You* (1938) suggest a more affirmative vision of a leveling of class differences and of both social reconciliation and upward mobility for ordinary Americans, a film like *Platinum Blonde* (1931) is far more cynical about such possibilities, depicting, in the words of Vito Zagarrio, "the decadence of a world riven by class distinctions" and presenting the potential for social "catastrophe."[3] Social conflicts exist in Capra's comedies both on the level of the bourgeois family—for example, in *Platinum Blonde, Broadway Bill,* and *You Can't Take It with You*— and on the larger social level of the crowd, which acts in potentially hysterical or dangerous ways in *American Madness, Broadway Bill,* and *Meet John Doe.* Even in *Mr. Deeds Goes to Town,* where the crowd of angry farmers is given a generally more positive role, there is the potential for a dangerous breakdown of social order. Finally, I would argue, there is a third category of Capra comedies—including the films *Lady for a Day* (1933), *Broadway Bill* (1934), and *Mr. Deeds Goes to Town* (1936) – which are more ambivalent in their social attitudes, hovering uneasily between utopian solutions and a critical reexamination of such solutions.

On the most obvious level, many of the plots of Capra's films depend on an unequal class position between the romantic leads. In *Platinum Blonde* (1931), *It Happened One Night* (1934), and *Broadway Bill* (1934), an upper-class woman becomes involved with a working-class or middle-class man. The reverse plot structure – involving a rich hero and a poor or middle-class heroine – can be found in several of Capra's other films, starting with the silent *That Certain Thing* (1928) and continuing in the sound era with *Ladies of Leisure* (1930), *Lady for a Day* (1933), and *You Can't Take It with You* (1938). All of these films, with the exception of *Platinum Blonde,* end with successful resolutions of the cross-class conflict. Thus, although Capra may have felt a distrust of wealth and the wealthy, he seems by and large to be less interested in denouncing or satirizing the upper class than in finding common ground between the classes, or at least in suggesting that the rich are capable of learning humility and humanity from their working-class and middle-class counterparts.

*That Certain Thing* is a paradigmatic example of what Steven Ross calls the "cross-class fantasy," the Cinderella story that ends with a reconciling vision of interclass harmony. It is a narrative structure that will provide the basic material for Capra's comedies in the decade to follow. The film involves a romance between the wealthy WASP Andy Charles – son of restaurant magnate A. B. Charles, Sr. – and a working-class Irish girl, Molly Kelly. Disinherited by his father when he marries Molly, Andy must work his way back from the bottom of the social ladder to attain socioeconomic respectability and regain his father's respect. The box lunch company founded by Andy and Molly proves so successful that A. B. ends up buying them out for $100,000 and accepting Molly as a daughter-in-law. The film's utopian vision of social relations involves a reconciliation between working-class determination and upper-class capital. As Lee Lourdeaux suggests, the story is "an immigrant's dream-come-true."[4] As the story of an Irish-American woman marrying into a wealthy WASP family, the film presents not only a class-based fantasy but also a narrative of ethnic assimilation and upward mobility.

It is with *Platinum Blonde* that Capra departs from the cross-class fantasy model of his earlier films, rejecting the utopian narrative to which the film ironically alludes. The film's hero, news reporter Stew Smith (Robert Williams), marries the wealthy Anne Schuyler (Jean Harlow) but soon rejects Anne's upper-class existence for his own more plebeian social *milieu* and proceeds to leave Anne and marry the faithful but unglamorous Gallagher (Loretta Young), a fellow reporter. When Smith marries Anne, he is teased by his colleagues at the newspaper about his marriage to a "society dame," and the bureau chief predicts that he will end up as "Mr. Schuyler," a bird in a gilded cage. When the prediction proves accurate – as Smith becomes a "kept man" in the Schuyler mansion and even begins wearing garters on his stockings to satisfy Anne's upper-class tastes – he finds the situation increasingly intolerable. Anne's attempts to transform him into her vision of social acceptability come into conflict with his own dreams of making his living as a playwright and supporting them both. Things come to a head when a reporter from a rival newspaper offers Smith a job writing a column but says it must be signed "by Anne Schuyler's husband." When Smith punches him in the jaw, the papers run the headline "Cinderella Man Grows Hair on Chest," causing embarrassment both to Smith and to the Schuyler family. Smith proceeds to throw a raucous party at the Schuyler mansion for his "gang" from the newspaper, and when Anne insists he cannot behave this way in her home, he takes the opportunity to leave her and marry the suitably working-class Gallagher.

Once again the story has important overtones of ethnicity as well as class. Smith rejects the WASP wealth and social privilege of the Schuylers – and its physical embodiment in the form of their "platinum blonde" daughter Anne – in order to marry the Irish-American Gallagher. As Lourdeaux puts it, the film critiques the opulent lifestyle of the Schuyler household, an example of "the success ethic gone bad," while bringing together "the feisty Anglo-American working stiff [Smith] with the Irish-American woman" (145). Of all the upper-class families in Capra's films, the Schuylers are the most repellent in their class snobbery. In one conversation with the family lawyer, Grayson, Anne wonders aloud whether there is a "finishing school" to which they can send Stew: "Yes—Sing Sing," replies Grayson. When Anne suggests that it will be "a very interesting experiment" to try to change Smith, Grayson reminds her of how much it cost to get rid of a baseball player with whom she had previously been involved. The Schuylers display obvious and undisguised contempt for Smith's lowly socioeconomic status. As Mrs. Schuyler says to Anne, "A reporter! Of all things, a reporter! A barbarian who lets his socks come down!"

The class tensions informing *Platinum Blonde* receive more nuanced treatment in three of Capra's comedies from the mid-1930s: *It Happened One Night* and *Broadway Bill,* both from 1934, and the 1936 *Mr. Deeds Goes to Town.* It is on these three comedies that I will focus the remainder of this chapter. Capra's comic triad of the mid-1930s demonstrates the director's range of comic styles: the romantic screwball comedy of *It Happened One Night,* the broader social comedy of *Broadway Bill,* and the dramatic sociopolitical comedy of *Mr. Deeds Goes to Town.* These films also demonstrate Capra's growing awareness of social issues and his developing ability to translate class relationships into effective images and imagetexts.[5]

**II**

*It Happened One Night,* like *Platinum Blonde,* is a film involving a middle-class reporter and a spoiled heiress. Although the plot of *It Happened One Night* superficially resembles that of *Platinum Blonde,* both the film's less cynical tone and its more utopian outcome differ significantly from that of the earlier film. Capra's biographer Joseph McBride has argued that the appeal of *It Happened One Night* to American audiences of the mid-1930s was largely a result of its presentation of class themes. The spectacle of the more proletarian hero "humbling, educating, and finally winning over the 'spoiled brat' heiress ... not only provided a fantasy of upward mobility, both sexual and economic, but, more important, represented the levelling of class barriers in the Depression."[6] The interclass dynamic of the film was largely absent from the original story by Samuel Hopkins Adams, which represented Peter Warne as an out-of-work gadabout, college-educated but recently fallen on hard times. The explicit class theme was also missing in the first version of Robert Riskin's screenplay, in which Warne was depicted as a bohemian Greenwich Village painter.[7]

In Riskin's final script, however, Warne appears as the famous character so memorably portrayed by Clark Gable, a hard-drinking and streetwise reporter. Critics have had a somewhat difficult time determining Warne's class. While his education and aspirations appear to be higher than those of a typical working-class protagonist, his evident class anxieties and his antagonism toward Ellie's class privilege, combined with his degree of comfort with the rougher aspects of the bus trip, would seem to indicate something below a typical middle-class affiliation. Although Warne functions structurally as the "lower-class hero" who "demonstrates his worth by overcoming class obstacles to the romance," his values are more those of "middle-class male normality": a strongly defined work ethic, a refusal to accept charity or to take something for nothing, and a need to live within one's means.[8]

The change in Warne's character for the filmed script provided the opportunity not only for another cross-class romance (and the first of a series of Depression-era reporter-meets-heiress comedies), but also for a more extended commentary on the structure of social class in Depression-era America. The primary choice Ellen Andrews (Claudette Colbert) must make in the film is itself fraught with class implications: she must decide between her playboy aviator fiance King Westley – his name already signifying the pretensions of his class status – and Peter Warne, the unglamorous but honest "man of the people."[9]

As Rita Barnard and Barbara Ching suggest, every event in the story of Ellen Andrews' journey – from her millionaire father's yacht to her honeymoon in an auto camp – "foregrounds the question of class":

Although Capra's depiction of workaday life is sentimental and unsubversive, it still provides an education for his heiress. Ellie, though sophisticated in appearance, doesn't know about bus schedules or standing in line; she hasn't been allowed to be alone with a man, and she hasn't even been given a decent piggyback ride, since, as Peter cantankerously maintains, no rich person could ever be a decent piggybacker. ... In short, the basic premise and source of laughter in *It Happened One Night* is that all experience is mediated or filtered by class.[10]

The plot of *It Happened One Night* is perhaps more familiar than that of any other Depression-era comedy, but I will summarize it briefly in order to suggest the many class-based elements it contains. At the beginning of the film, Ellen has married King Westley against the wishes of her overprotective father, the millionaire Alexander Andrews (Walter Connolly). Representing both wealth and power, Andrews has been holding Ellie prisoner on board his yacht off the Florida coast until she agrees to give up Westley, but she has started a hunger strike in protest (the movie's first reference to the Depression-era hunger and poverty that will be a constant motif). After an argument with her father, Ellie jumps off the boat, evades capture by Andrews' servants, and swims to Miami, where she boards a bus for New York and finds herself sitting next to Peter Warne, a reporter who has just been fired by his New York office.

The bus is Ellie's rude awakening to the realities of life away from her protected upper-class existence. Crowded and filled with unsavory characters, the bus is a place of potential danger. At the first rest stop, her suitcase is stolen, and she leaves her ticket on her seat, almost losing it as well. The bus teaches Ellie an important social lesson: the real world does not revolve around her upper-class needs and desires. The uncomfortable conditions of bus travel level the social classes, creating an entire community – and by extension an entire nation – of economy-class citizens. When Ellie asks the bus driver to wait for her in Jacksonville while she goes to freshen up at a fancy hotel – another assertion of her assumed class privilege – he ignores her request and leaves without her. Peter, who has discovered Ellie's true identity through a picture in the newspaper, stays behind with her, but when she tries to buy his silence, he labels her the "spoiled brat of a rich father" who thinks she can buy her way out of any jam.

From this point on, the Depression-era bus trip reverses the roles of the two protagonists. As Elizabeth Kendall suggests, Ellie quickly loses the social privilege she has always enjoyed as her father's daughter and becomes "just a solitary, vulnerable woman."[11] As her class ascendancy wanes, Peter's gender ascendancy becomes increasingly apparent, and for the middle third of the film it is the working-class Peter who is placed in the role of Ellie's guide, protector, and instructor in the ways of ordinary life. When Ellie finds herself seated next to a traveling salesman, Shapely, who makes an obnoxious pass at her, Peter intervenes, exploiting the advantage of his gender by pretending to be her husband. The bus is forced to stop for the night because of a washed-out bridge, and the passengers spend the night at an auto camp. In the interests of saving their dwindling funds, Peter gets Ellie and himself a cabin together, registering them as husband and wife. The mock marriage is another step in the breakdown of the social difference between them, but barriers to real connection still remain. The blanket Peter hangs between their beds to ensure their separation has a social significance as well as a sexual one, since Peter is intimidated by the seemingly impenetrable class barrier between him and Ellen Andrews. The famous "Walls of Jericho" that are raised between their beds represent not only a sexual barrier, but also an uncrossable social divide.

Peter, an embodiment of the ineffectuality of the American male during the Depression, becomes increasingly nurturing and domestic during the course of the film, even cooking breakfast for Ellie while she sleeps. Ellie, on the other hand, a stereotypical "spoiled brat" heiress at the beginning of the film, becomes more fully humanized by her relationship with Peter and by her experience of working-class America. As she encounters for the first time the America of ordinary working people – with its uncomfortable and crowded buses, its dreary auto camps, its hunger and deprivation, and its many hardships and dangers – she gains a form of experience that allows her to overcome her own class prejudices. While she is completely incapable of taking care of herself in the first part of the film – relying on Peter to budget her cash, tell her what and when to eat, protect her from aggressive men, and have her clothes ironed – she soon learns how to survive away from the protections of her pampered upper-class life.

Much of the comedy of the film results from the juxtaposition between Ellen's expectations and the reality she encounters. As Joseph

McBride suggests, "the humor in *It Happened One Night* comes from watching the heiress being reduced to living on a subsistence allowance, strictly regulated by Peter, whose ability to stretch a dollar struck a chord with the Depression audience" (306). Both Riskin's screenplay and Capra's direction make the most of their opportunities to exploit the class-based differences between Ellen and Peter, and more generally between Ellen and the Depression-era world she confronts on her cross-country journey. But the cross-class fable has a happy ending. Ellen's ability to adjust to a version of working-class life on the road – sleeping on a haystack, eating raw carrots, piggybacking across streams, hitchhiking on a rural highway, waiting in line with working-class women for an auto-camp shower, and even transforming herself into a rumpled, lower-middle-class housewife in order to evade her father's detectives—ensures that she can no longer marry a man like King Westley, the embodiment of social privilege and pretension. She is saved from the marriage at the last minute by Peter Warne and her father, whose collusion with Warne itself represents an important interclass alliance. Although the alliance of the two men may appear reactionary in its reassertion of male dominance over the "confused" Ellie, it presents a more progressive social message as well. The marriage of Peter and Ellie signifies, as Kendall puts it, "the end of the extravagant, wasteful, snobbish life of the upper classes of the twenties," the "unclassing" of the heiress to create "a new kind of unit held together by something besides class" (49). In his next comedy, *Broadway Bill*, Capra and Riskin ask the followup question: What happens when a cross-class marriage doesn't work, when the utopian solution necessitated by the cross-class romance plot proves an untenable one?

## III

*Broadway Bill* is a lively and entertaining film in its own right, yet it is something of an anomoly among Depression comedies, conforming neither to the screwball format Capra had so successfully invented with *It Happened One Night* and would revisit with *You Can't Take It with You*, nor to the form of more explicitly social comedy exemplified by *Mr. Deeds Goes to Town*. As Charles Wolfe points out, *Broadway Bill* was reasonably successful at the box office and enjoyed favorable reviews, but it has been largely ignored in surveys of Capra's career, "which typically move directly from the grass-roots success of *It Happened One Night* to Capra's excursion into social and political commentary with *Mr. Deeds Goes to Town*."[12] The film's lack of critical attention can be attributed to several factors: it was overshadowed by two very successful and popular Capra comedies made directly before and after it; it was not promoted by Capra himself as one of his important films (it does not even rate a mention in Capra's autobiography *The Name Above the Title*); and it became unavailable for a time after the remake, *Riding High,* in 1950. Nevertheless, it is a film that bears some scrutiny, particularly in terms of how it functions as a transition between the cross-class romantic comedy of *It Happened One Night* and Capra's more socially conscious films beginning with *Mr. Deeds.* The film depicts the working-class class hero Dan Brooks (Warner Baxter), a man of uncertain origins who has married into the wealthy Higgins clan but who ultimately rejects the family's materialist values for the more fulfilling if financially risky life of the racetrack. Brooks's antagonist throughout most of the film is J. L. Higgins (Walter Connolly), the president-owner of the Higgins National Bank. Higgins' bank is the center of a conglomerate that holds a virtual monopoly on the subsidiary industries in the town of Higginsville, each of which is run by one of Higgins' three sons-in-law.

The leading role of Dan Brooks was written with Clark Gable in mind, and there are clearly resemblances between his character and that of Peter Warne. Although it has taken Dan somewhat longer than Peter to come to a full realization of his scorn for the upper classes, he is ultimately just as adamant about his preference for a life made on his own terms and by the sweat of his own brow. Like Peter, Dan is a man of apparently humble beginnings, a man who, as J. L. reminds him, "came to this town three years ago penniless [and] with a questionable background." If anything, Dan's association with the racetrack business – a connection J. L. claims to have been "broadminded enough to overlook" in allowing him to marry his daughter Margaret – is even more problematic than Peter's job as a newspaper reporter. J. L.'s obvious condescension toward Dan at the beginning of the film makes him a less sympathetic version of the wealthy patriarch than Andrews, and his rapaciousness in expanding his business enterprise with no thought for the human cost anticipates the character of Wall Street banker Anthony

Kirby in *You Can't Take It with You*. Kirby is a far more extreme and dangerous example of the tendency than the small-town Higgins. Kirby's goal of forming the world's largest munitions firm, however, and his tactics of buying up the residential property around his rival's factory in order to prevent him from expanding, reenact on the national or multinational level Higgins' more local monopolization of the town's businesses by "gobbling up the little fellas," as Dan puts it. Nonetheless, the theme of "the little fella" as a victim of big business establishes a link between *Broadway Bill* and the Capra films of the late 1930s and early 1940s, including the social comedies *Mr. Deeds Goes to Town* and *You Can't Take It with You,* with their more explicitly ideological reading of class issues. Whereas in *It Happened One Night* the sociopolitical difference between Ellen and Peter functions primarily as part of the more central romance plot, *Broadway Bill* begins to introduce a distinctly Capraesque politics in the characters of Dan Brooks and Alice Higgins, J. L.'s youngest daughter. The class rhetoric adopted by Dan, who accuses J. L. of "snatch[ing] the Acme Lumber Company away from some poor people who spent their lives building it up," is the first sign of an emerging politics in Capra's films, a politics that will be more obviously foregrounded in *Mr. Deeds Goes to Town.*

Dan is married to Margaret, the oldest of the Higgins daughters, but he is temperamentally and ideologically much closer to Alice (Myrna Loy), the youngest daughter, who is secretly in love with him. When Margaret will not leave Higginsville to join him when he offers his resignation from her father's company in order to pursue a career racing horses, Alice goes instead. Like Ann Schuyler in *Platinum Blonde,* Margaret is the figure of the upper-class woman unwilling to move beyond the rigid confines of a bourgeois life in order to enable her husband to fulfill his dream of success and financial independence. Alice, on the other hand, resembles Ellen Andrews in her rebellion against the patriarchal domination of her father and the excesses of upper-class life, and she is attracted to Dan's lack of social pretense in much the same way Ellen is drawn to Peter and the life he offers. For both Dan and Alice, the stables and the racetrack represent a pastoral retreat in opposition to the stuffy Higgins mansion and to the capitalist ethos as embodied in the various companies operated by the family, including his own paper-box division. The racetrack functions as an egalitarian space where anyone can participate and where everyone – at least in theory – has a chance of winning and building a stake on which to build a life. It is when Alice first accuses Dan of becoming "another Higgins slave" that he decides to renounce the comforts of an affluent but sterile existence in Higginsville and try his luck at the races. Dan's goal, as he confesses to Alice in one of his more self-revealing moments, is not to run someone else's paper-box business but to become the kind of enterpreneurial small businessman he accuses J. L. of "gobbling up": "I've got to get the money to do things: buy more horses, train them right. I don't know, I may even go in for breeding. ... Take my word for it, Princess, I'm going to have the finest collection of thoroughbreds in the country."

In contrast to the democratic possibilities represented by the stables and the racetrack, the Higgins family represents a rigid patriarchal system with strongly aristocratic, even monarchic overtones. The motif of J. L. Higgins as a king within his court of sycophantic followers is foregrounded throughout the film. Not only is the youngest daughter called "Princess," but the eldest daughter Margaret expects a higher position for her husband based on her primogeniture. In the first scene in which we see J. L., he is sitting with his back to the camera, enthroned in the "mausoleum" of his study, as Dan at one point calls it, while his daughters and sons-in-law enter one by one to pay their respects and systematically take their places to either side of him. At dinner, J. L. is equally imperial, sitting at the head of the table with the daughters arranged in order of age on one side and the sons-in-law opposite them on the other. An extra place setting is even made up for Alice's future husband, a symbolic reminder of the sense of absolute monarchic order J. L. Higgins demands for his family, household, and business interests. When Dan decides to leave Higginsville, Alice teases her father about his failed attempt to exercise full control over his kingdom:

Daddy dear, your little monarchy is fast folding up. Your crown prince has flown. ... You're a strong and powerful ruler, o mighty king, but you're not going to crush *him* under your heels any longer.

Later in the film, another dialogue between Dan and Alice repeats the same motif. When Alice tells Dan she is going to stay with him until the race rather than return to Higginsville, Dan jokingly protests:

DAN: Well, what'll the emperor think?

ALICE: Oh, hang the emperor!

DAN: Well ... another revolutionary. First the crown prince con-
sul absconds, and then the little princess.

Like Ellen in *It Happened One Night*, Alice realizes that she can live
under physically demanding circumstances in order to be near the man
she loves. Renouncing her coddled existence as a Higgins daughter, she
engages in a series of proletarian gestures: she stays at the barn with Dan
and Broadway Bill rather than going to a hotel for the night; she abandons her fancy dress and fur coat for a pair of Dan's dungarees; she
befriends the black stable-hand ("Whitey") and sings songs with him;
she stocks the barn with canned goods and cooks a plebeian dinner of
canned split-pea soup and succotash (once again playing on Capra's concern with food as a marker of social relationships); and she stays up all
night helping to keep Broadway Bill dry in a leaky barn.

The static world of the affluent but repressive Higgins household
which both Alice and Dan seek to escape – a world full of material privilege but devoid of any pleasure in its consumption – is represented visually in the opening shots of the film. The opening montage moves with
the perspective of someone entering the town and moving toward its
center of power. Starting with a shot of the "Welcome to Higginsville"
sign, we see a statue of Jeremiah Higgins, "Founder of Higginsville," a
plaque of the Higgins National Bank ("J. L. Higgins, President"), and
finally the plaque on J. L.'s office door. The absolute hegemony of the
Higgins name and the Higgins family within the town – represented by
these images of permanence and stasis – creates a dystopic atmosphere
that has driven Dan to the town's limits at the stables and that will eventually drive him out of town entirely. "Everything seems lopsided to me,"
Dan tells J. L., "Higginsville, the Higgins family, the Higgins enterprises." As another disgruntled Higginsville citizen puts it even more
forcefully in the film's opening moments: "Higgins, Higgins ... that's not
a family, it's a disease."

The repression of both pleasure and dissent by a conservative upper-
class patriarchy is a common trope in Depression-era comedies. In
George Cukor's 1938 *Holiday*, for example, the palatial Seton house
functions as a symbolic landscape in which physical spaces reflect class

divisions. Cukor uses the elevator, the formal salon, and the children's playroom as distinct social spaces, within each of which the characters nogotiate their class relations. In *Holiday,* the playroom functions as a space where individuals can create an alternative community based on a sense of play, where the protagonists can take a "holiday" from the pressures of bourgeois conformity.[13] In *Broadway Bill,* no equivalent "playroom" exists, and Dan is forced to create his own spaces in which to escape the tomblike Higgins house. Before the directors' meeting, Dan tries to get Margaret to skip the meeting, sit with him under the moonlight, and throw rocks at the house; on his return at the end of the film to claim Alice—to "release the princess from the dark tower," as he puts it—Dan does throw rocks through the dining room windows, another shattering of the "Walls of Jericho" which combines screwball irreverence with an undertone of social and political transgression.

The most important alternative spaces in *Broadway Bill* are those associated with horse racing. In the world of the racetrack, we find everything in opposition to the Higgins house: speed, change, movement, fun, and risk. The first appearance of Dan and Alice in the film is in a fast-moving car, driving alongside Broadway Bill as Dan clocks his run. Similarly, when Dan arrives at the racetrack after leaving Higginsville, a montage composed of crowd scenes, betting windows, a marching band, and an exciting horse race functions as an inversion of the earlier montage depicting the signs, statues, and plaques of Higginsville. The economy of the racetrack also differs markedly from that of the Higgins enterprises. Whereas the Higgins fortune is based on sure and steady profits from banking and solid manufacturing businesses, the economy of the racing world is based on risk, luck, and the ability to raise money through any possible means. In order to raise a stake to put Broadway Bill in the Derby, Dan and his friends work together: Alice hocks her jewelry and fur coat, Dan sells his old Ford truck, Whitey tries to win money in a craps game, and Dan's friend Colonel Pettrigrew attempts to sell phony racing tips to unwary fans. As opposed to the centralized control of the Higgins companies – and of the gambling syndicate led by Eddie Morgan which tries to rig the race Broadway Bill ultimately wins – Dan organizes a kind of grass-roots community who rally around him and Broadway Bill.

The difference between the Higgins conglomerate and the racetrack economy can also be read as an allegory for the finances of filmmaking itself and for Capra's own career in filmmaking and production. Capra's rebellion against what he considered the "class-structured" studio system in his attempt to produce his own pictures later in the decade is analogous to Dan's "revolutionary" gesture of abandoning the Higgins enterprises in order to pursue his own entrepreneurial goals. Throughout the 1930s, Capra promoted a vision of himself as a Hollywood outsider, "a Poverty Row scrapper at a second-class studio like Columbia rather than at a 'palatial' major, a 'class-structured' studio like MGM."[14] By the time of *Broadway Bill,* Capra had already accumulated an unusual amount of power within the studio system, exercising control over the writing, casting, and editing of his own films. In 1937, he sued Columbia for breach of contract and requested release from the studio, attempting to organize an independent production company with directors Wesley Ruggles, Gregory La Cava, and William Wellman. It was not until 1939 that Capra was finally able to leave Columbia and form Frank Capra Productions with his screenwriter Robert Riskin. The story of Dan Brooks arriving penniless in Higginsville, making a success in the business world, and then leaving to pursue his career goals with greater creative freedom must have appealed greatly to Capra, whether or not he intended the film as explicitly autobiographical.[15]

As in many of Capra's films, the use of language and speech has important social implications. J. L. and Dan are polar opposites in their use of speech. As Dan says in explaining their differences, "It's just that we don't speak the same language, that's all." J. L. uses both speech and the withholding or forbidding of speech as a means of gaining and holding power. The ritualistic "directors' meeting," held at the Higgins dining table on the first of every month, is really no more than an opportunity for J. L. to give executive orders and keep both fiscal and symbolic control over the family enterprise. From the start, language, and in particular any form of extemporaneous utterance that might be seen as a threat to the rigid social code, is strenuously forbidden. When Dan arrives at the house with Margaret, J. L. says simply "you're late," thus effectively ending any attempt at communication and going into the dining room without listening to Dan's explanation. At dinner, no small talk is allowed. After announcing the acquisition of a new subsidiary – the Acme Lumber Company – J. L. decrees that no more business will be discussed until after they have eaten, and it appears that no other form of speech will be tolerated either. One of the most effective visual scenes in the film involves the Higgins family eating their dinner in complete silence, picking up their spoons in unison and eating their soup with machinelike uniformity.

For Dan, on the other hand, life without talk is unthinkable. Unlike J. L. and the other sons-in-law, he is a man who has had to live by his wits and charm, and he enjoys the simple pleasures of talking, joking, and singing. He teases and flirts with Alice throughout the film, and while his sweet-talking no longer appears to have much effect on Margaret, we have the sense that it was his verbal ability, as much as anything, that helped him win over both Margaret and J. L. on his arrival in Higginsville. The racetrack is the place where Dan can relax, have fun, talk freely, make jokes, sing songs, and role-play. If the Higgins household represents the monologic discourse of big business, the racetrack is a heteroglossic space in which financial reward is only part of the equation. As in *It Happened One Night*, where the rendition on the bus of "The Man on the Flying Trapeze" functions as a form of egalitarian communal experience, singing in *Broadway Bill* is an important indicator of a society defined not by class hierarchy but by a sense of familiarity and solidarity.[16] Dan sings with Whitey as they leave Higginsville; Alice sings spirituals in the barn with Whitey, thus cutting through both racial and class barriers; and Dan, inspired by Alice's gesture of cooking him dinner, makes up a nonsense song about the split-pea soup and the succotash that becomes a kind of musical motif tracing the progress of Dan's prospects in the race and his relationship with Alice.

The class relations in the film are duplicated on the level of the horses in the Derby. Gallant Lady, a famous thoroughbred owned by a wealthy stable and the heavy favorite to win the race, arrives by train to much fanfare and gets an entire stable to herself while Broadway Bill has to sleep in a nearby farmer's barn. Broadway Bill is the classic underdog, who triumphs over adversity in order to win the race. In a rainstorm a few days before the race, while Gallant Lady stays dry in her stable with the thermostat kept to within two degrees, Broadway Bill is under a leaking roof in the barn and becomes sick as a result. A 100–1 shot, Broadway Bill symbolizes the aspirations of ordinary people during the Depression, hoping for some miraculous change in their fortunes. By the time of the race, helped by a rumor about a bet by a famous millionaire, his odds have dropped to 6–1, and in the race itself Broadway Bill again overcomes adverse circumstances by winning despite a jockey who has been bribed to hold him back.

As originally written by Robert Riskin, based on an unpublished story by Mark Hellinger, the script of *Broadway Bill* was an unambiguous allegory for the American success story, a triumphantly utopian vision of the regular working man (or horse) beating out the more pampered thoroughbreds who were favored by every circumstance to win. While the original story had the film ending happily with Broadway Bill beating Gallant Lady by a nose, Capra asked Sidney Buchman to rewrite the script with a more ambivalent ending in which the horse dies after winning the race. Although the film does end happily, with Dan returning two years later to reclaim Alice and take her on the road with him and his two new racehorses, the sudden death of Broadway Bill suggests Capra's discomfort with overly formulaic solutions to complex social issues. It is questionable, however, whether Broadway Bill's death really works either symbolically or narratively in the picture. Its sudden rupture of the comic tone of the film puts into question the farcical twist of the ending, in which J. L. announces his intention to sell off the last of the Higgins companies, including the bank itself, and decides to join Dan and Alice on their horse-racing adventure rather than stay within the static household he himself created. Although the transformation of Higgins had been suggested in earlier scenes, it seems a rather abrupt and somewhat unbelievable narrative turn to a form of radical social populism. Perhaps Capra and his screenwriters wanted to salvage the rich from what seemed to be an overly total indictment, or perhaps they simply wished to infuse the film's ending with a more "screwball" sensibility in order to capitalize on the success of *It Happened One Night.*

## IV

With *Mr. Deeds Goes to Town,* Capra was already moving decisively away from the screwball mode he had invented in *It Happened One Night* and used with somewhat less conviction in *Broadway Bill.*[17] *Mr. Deeds* centers on two important changes for its protagonist, both of which involve a renegotiation of class status and class allegiances. The first of these changes is the sudden inheritance of a great deal of wealth. A seemingly typical representative of the American middle class, Longfellow Deeds (Gary Cooper) is instantly transformed by the sudden death of his uncle Semple, and a bequest of $20 million into "one of the richest men in the country," as his uncle's attorney Cedar puts it. The second change is the move from the small town of Mandrake Falls, Vermont, to the big city of New York. Deeds, who has never left Mandrake Falls in his life, begins the film as the proverbial country bumpkin, a man innocent of big-city ways and of the kinds of social relationships that exist in the urban environment, and is forced to gain the experience necessary to survive the cynical mores of high society.

*Mr. Deeds* differs from Capra's other cross-class films of the 1930s in one significant respect: the change in class status experienced by Longfellow Deeds is brought about not by a marriage or romantic attachment but by inheritance. This is not an insignificant fact in understanding the film's class dynamics. Deeds personifies the American myth of upward mobility more fully than characters like Stew Smith, Peter Warne, or Dan Brooks. His upward trajectory, unlike that of Smith, Warne, or Brooks, is no longer contingent on his ability to conform to the desires and expectations of a wife and her upper-class family, or on his acceptance by them as a social equal. Like Smith, Deeds may still be a "Cinderella Man," as the newspapers mockingly call him, but he is one who by virtue of his direct inheritance of wealth controls his own destiny to a far greater extent than those who have risen to their current social status through marriage.[18] Whereas *It Happened One Night* ends with Peter's marriage to Ellen – never showing us the details of how they will work out their social differences – and whereas Stew's marriage to Ann and Dan's marriage to Margaret are depicted as total failures, Deeds has the chance to remake himself as a millionaire without changing his fundamental values and without looking to a wife or father-in-law for employment, income, or social respectability.

Whether we see Deeds as another "Cinderella Man" of the 1930s or as the icon of a more generic myth of upward mobility, what is most striking in the film is his *reaction* to the wealth he inherits and the change in social status that goes along with it. The sudden and unexpected inheritance of $20 million in the midst of the Depression would appear to be the fantasy of every American, a jackpot beyond our wildest dreams. Yet when Deeds first hears of the bequest from Cedar, he treats the event as an abstraction that has little significance for him personally. "$20,000,000. That's quite a lot, isn't it?" he asks, feigning a greater naivete than even a citizen of Mandrake Falls could honestly claim. When the press agent Cobb ironically answers that "it'll do in a pinch," Deeds continues, "Yes, indeed. I wonder why he left me all that money? I don't need it."

What makes possible Deeds's lukewarm reaction to the news of his sudden inheritance – aside from his somewhat eccentric or "pixilated" character – is his comfortably, we might even say ideally, middle-class status. Deeds is not a representative of the new middle class. Rather, he is an exemplar of what at that time constituted the "old" middle class. He represents the nineteenth-century ideal (still alive but rapidly disappearing from the American social landscape of the 1930s) of independent farmers, business owners, and self-employed professionals rather than the emerging middle class of urban professional and clerical workers. As we learn in the course of the film, Deeds's father was a doctor who delivered many of the town's babies, and Deeds himself (with his literary, patrician, and somewhat quaint first name of "Longfellow") is the part-owner of a tallow factory as well as the landlord of other real estate in town.[19] He is comfortable enough to afford a housekeeper, and although he derives some income from his greeting-card poetry, he does not need to hold a regular job, leaving him plenty of leisure time to engage in his favorite activities: playing the tuba, working for the town's volunteer fire department, and making up humorous poems based on people's names.

All this changes when Deeds comes to the city, where he is immediately marked as easy prey for every kind of self-serving vulture. In addition to Cedar and the other lawyers in his firm – who seek power of attorney over Deeds's fortune – there is the Opera Board which wants him to make up its annual deficit of $180,000; there is a woman claiming to be his uncle's common-law wife and demanding, through her attorney, a third of Semple's fortune; and there is another Semple cousin and his wife who charge Deeds with insanity when he threatens to give away the inheritance. Finally, and most destructively, there are the newspapers, who want a piece of Deeds for a front-page story. The chief representative of the newspapers in the film is Babe Bennett (Jean Arthur), a tough-talking, Pulitzer prize-winning reporter who impersonates an unemployed stenographer in order to meet Deeds and exploit his confidences.

Babe is herself an interesting foil for Deeds. Unlike Deeds, who shows little interest in money, she is presented in her opening scene as entirely mercenary, demanding a month's paid vacation before she will agree to write the story. Babe is a highly successful reporter, standing at the top of her profession just as Cedar stands at the top of his. It is Babe who embodies, more than Deeds himself, what Charles Maland identifies as the major tension in the films of Capra: the tension in American middle-class life "between capitalism and democracy, self-interest and the common good."[20] Like Cedar and the other New Yorkers with whom Deeds comes into contact, she begins the film lacking the human warmth and decency necessary to be a fully rounded person. She must be humanized by Longfellow just as Ellen Andrews is reformed and softened by Peter Warne in *It Happened One Night*. Babe also enacts an inversion of Deeds's own form of social mobility: whereas Longfellow has moved up the class scale from middle-class "hick" to urban millionaire, she descends the class scale from ace reporter to starving stenographer in order to meet him. Taking advantage of Deeds's "democratic" symphathies and small-town naivete, she dresses herself in the shapeless tweed coat and battered hat of a hungry job-hunter (an early reference to Depression-era conditions which anticipates the hungry man who breaks into Deeds's mansion later in the film). Babe transforms herself into the seemingly plebeian "Mary Dawson," fainting into Longfellow's arms, accepting his invitation to dinner, and effecting the meek self-deprecation of a working-class woman: "Oh, I'm really just a nobody."

Yet as the film progresses, the personas of Babe Bennett and Mary Dawson begin to merge: Babe takes on some of Mary's humility and changes from wordly skeptic to empathetic nurturer. Babe originally introduces Mary as having family in "a small town near Hartford" – a story the audience assumes to be a cover for Babe's own more urban background. As the film progresses, however, it turns out that Babe, too, has small-town origins. In the scene with Longfellow in Central Park – still in the guise of Mary Dawson – Babe begins to reveal the truth about certain aspects of her own background:

BABE: I'm from a small town too, you know.
LONGFELLOW: Really?
BABE: Probably as small as Mandrake Falls.

LONGFELLOW:  Gosh! What do you know about that!

BABE:  It's a beautiful little town, too. A row of poplar tress right along Main Street. Always smelled as if it just had a bath ... I've often thought about going back.

In Babe's depiction of her idyllic small-town childhood, we see the convergence of her social origins with those of Longfellow: her father, like Longfellow, used to play in the town band. Babe, as it turns out, has forgotten her solidly middle-class roots in her quest for fame and success. As she tells her friend Mabel, she has become too caught up in "a crazy competition for nothing." As in all Capra's films, the notion of competition is fraught with ambivalence. Like Capra himself, who possessed a burning desire to succeed yet who also entertained lingering doubts about the status of his own success, his characters have to negotiate between the values of success, ambition, and the urge to compete, and the often opposed virtues of contentment, generosity, and democratic community. Unlike the chosen career of Dan Brooks, whose more democratic desire to train and race horses represents a healthy form of competition, the tactics employed by an overambitious reporter like Babe signify a destructive and morally questionable form of competition.

The word "competition" seems to hold particular significance in *Mr. Deeds Goes to Town*. Although Deeds himself seems almost peculiarly to lack a sense of competition, the rest of the film's world is marked by various forms of competitive behavior, whether the form of that competition is literary, journalistic, legal, or social. As Longfellow suggests in his metaphor at the trial, the success ethic of getting one's own car over the hill in high gear must be tempered with the altruistic imperative to "stop once in a while and help those who can't."

The film is structured by a series of oppositions, beginning with the obvious contrast between Mandrake Falls and New York City. This contrast is further exemplified by the difference between Deeds and his uncle, Martin W. Semple, a hedonistic playboy who made a habit of inviting up to twenty women to the house for his own pleasure and who spent most of his time traveling and "enjoy[ing] himself." Unlike Deeds, who in the spirit of American self-sufficiency is determined to oversee his own financial affairs, Semple left everything up to the crooked law firm of Cedar, Cedar, Cedar, and Budington, who doctored the books in order to cheat him out of a good part of his fortune. Other oppositions in the film reinforce these same categories. Deeds's tuba and the Mandrake Falls town band represent an unpretentious and egalitarian approach to music as opposed to the elitist, greedy, and hypocritical world of the opera. Deeds's simple poems represent a folk charm and wisdom in opposition to the verbally sophisticated but morally hollow works of the New York literati who attempt to make fun of the homespun postcard poet. Finally, Deeds's sincere and moving courtroom speech represents a common-sense decency in opposition to the dishonesty, manipulation, and double-talk of the newspapers, the courtroom attorneys, and the court-appointed psychologists.

These various instances of language use within the film function to establish a connection between the forms of language people use and the forms of social discourse they represent. Spoken language in the film contains a number of different kinds of rhetoric: from Morrow's exaggeratedly "poetic" usages to the legal rhetoric of Cedar and the other lawyers; from the use of newspaper "hype" to the psychiatric jargon adopted at Deeds's trial. In all of these instances, speech is shown to be either superfluous or corrupted by manipulative or distorting use.[21] In the world of Cedar and his associates, language is a cynical game rather than an honest representation of the self. As Raymond Carney suggests, Cedar's world is one of "social overdetermination," just as Deeds's is one of social openness and possibility. Through both language and cinematography, Capra expresses the "narrowing of performative possibilities" represented by Cedar and his allies (275). Like J. L. Higgins in *Broadway Bill,* Cedar wants to control human and social movement, and this control or containment is reflected in the more mechanical blocking and camera movements used in the scenes in which he appears. Deeds, on the other hand, is never restricted by the movements of the camera or followed in such a mechanical way.

Similarly, the response to *language* by Cedar and his circle is highly circumscribed. Near the beginning of the film, when Cedar, his assistant Anderson, and the press agent Corny Cobb arrive at Mandrake Falls, Cobb reads aloud the poem on the railway station's welcome sign and comments sarcastically, "That's pretty." Cobb and Cedar are similarly unresponsive when Deeds's housekeeper, Mrs. Meredith, reads them one of Deeds's poems. A few scenes later, at Deeds's house, Longfellow is playing his favorite game of attempting to find rhymes for people's names. When he is unable to find a rhyme for "Budington" (a fact itself suggestive of the lack of linguistic playfulness allowed within the social universe of the law firm and its clients), he makes one up for Cobb instead. Cobb takes the last line of the limerick, "And now poor Cobb's out of a job," literally, suspecting that it is Deeds's clever way of firing him: "I've gotten the sackaroo in many ways, but never in rhyme." Cobb's inability to "read" Longfellow's lighthearted poetic joke as it is intended again suggests his inability to enter into the spirit of poetic language, to adjust himself to its difference from ordinary discourse. It is only when he is able to dismiss the line as "just poetry" that he feels secure.

The character of Cobb is important as a symbol of the hardened and cynical approach to language and society associated with Cedar and New York who comes increasingly to act as an ally of the democratic Deeds rather than the elitist Cedar. An ex-newspaperman, Cobb had been employed as a press agent, or "buffer," by Deeds's uncle, primarily for the purpose of protecting him from the media. Cedar explains to Deeds the necessity of such a "buffer":

> You see, rich people need someone to keep the crowds away. The world's full of pests. Then there's the newspapers to handle. One must know when to seek publicity and when to avoid it.

Cedar's rationale indicates social attitudes that are so inimical to Deeds's own philosophy that Deeds fails even to respond. The world-view that sees the rich as a pampered class needing to be protected from "crowds" and "pests," as well as shielded from all social accountability, will increasingly come into direct conflict with Deeds's egalitarian approach. This tension culminates in the trial scene, where Deeds expresses most eloquently his support of the poor farmers in opposition to rich lawyers and selfish millionaires.

The other scene in which Capra makes brilliant use of both language and imagetext to critique particular forms of social or class relations is the "echo scene" that takes place in the huge marble foyer of Deeds's mansion. The scene itself "echoes" a similar scene in *Platinum Blonde* in which Stew Smith plays hopscotch on the marble floor of the Schuyler house. In *Mr. Deeds,* the scene is more elaborate: Deeds breaks down the upper-class decorum represented by his New York mansion by engaging in a round of shouting with the hired help. After playfully chasing his valet Walter out of his room and down the stairs, he stops him at the bottom of the staircase and orders him to try making an echo with his voice. Soon the butler and another servant join in, and the four men make a harmonious chorus of hoots, shrieks, and yells, with Longfellow conducting them like a symphony orchestra.

On one level, the male chorus and its resonant echoes is a mockery of the opera, a cultural form that represents the opposite end of the musical and social spectrum from this spontaneous and democratic performance. In an earlier scene, Deeds had refused to subsidize the opera's annual losses, which amounted to $180,000 a year. With his suggestion that the opera might be losing money because it is a fundamentally undemocratic institution ("maybe you charge too much"), he declares his suspicion of elitist cultural productions organized with only the wealthy in mind. In the echo scene, the enormous hall becomes a parody of the opera house where he and the servants can make music for free. The scene reintroduces the motif of music as a form of democratic communion, reminding us both of the Mandrake Falls band and of the scene in which Deeds and Babe play an impromptu duet of "Humoresque" and "Swanee River" in the park. As Lee Lourdeaux has suggested, the "harmonious chord" made by the men "introduces innocence and communal celebration to the cold surfaces of Anglo-American wealth" (150). The use of the echo also suggests the hollowness of language as it is used to reinforce established social relations in the city. By forming an imaginative community within the overwhelming private space of the mansion, Deeds overcomes both the social burden and the sense of spatial alienation produced by his new status.

Leland Poague has located in the echo the "dominant narrational trope" of *Mr. Deeds Goes to Town.* The "echo trope" functions as an element of filmic self-consciousness (the scene itself echoes *Platinum Blonde* and the entire film is an echo of Capra's *American Madness*), and it also operates as a linguistic device throughout the film.[22] Echoes or repetitions can be found in Longfellow's own name, an echo of another and more famous popular poet; in conversations (like the one early in the film in which Cedar and Cobb have to ask the stationmaster several times for directions to Deeds's house); in Deeds's penchant for rhymes and rhyming games; in the repetitive title of "Cedar, Cedar, Cedar, and Budington"; and most conspicuously in the courtroom scene, where a series of doublings takes place. In the courtroom (a scene in which Deeds himself alternates between silence and speech, a kind of large-scale echo effect), we have the two Faulkner sisters, whose tendency to repeat each other causes the judge to ask, "must we have the echo?" The scene also contains *two* appearances by Babe Bennett (herself a double for "Mary Dawson"): one when Cedar calls her as a witness against Deeds, and the second when she voluntarily takes the stand in his defense. Dr. Von Holler's charts, with their lines signifying the wavelike patterns of manic depression, is a visual representation of the alternating or echo rhythm. And finally, Longfellow's explanation of various forms of repetitive behavior (including his own tuba playing as well as "doodling" and other habits) can be seen as a formal thematization of the echo motif.

The precise significance of all of these echoes, doublings, and repetitions within the film is not altogether clear. My own reading, given my interest in the film as a social critique and in particular one concerned with the question of social class in America, would emphasize the doubling or fracturing of Deeds himself as a social being, the disjunction of the coherent social self he had maintained throughout his life in Mandrake Falls. In *Mr. Deeds,* we no longer find the doubling of the protagonist by another character from a different social class – as in the case of Peter Warne and King Westley. Nor do we find a character who can move spatially from one social persona to another, like Stew Smith or Dan Brooks. For Longfellow Deeds, the pressure of being both small-town hick and urban millionaire almost leads to a psychic fracture reproducing the social fracturing that has already taken place.

It is in the final courtroom scene that we find the most complex instance of language use in *Mr. Deeds Goes to Town,* and perhaps the most sustained and sophisticated treatment of spoken language in any of Capra's films. As Carney has observed, it is the courtroom scene that finally gives the lie to the vision of Deeds – held by the film's other characters and to some extent by the audience as well – as a country bumpkin unable to understand the complexities of life in the urban fast lane, and lacking the verbal sophistication to counter the attacks of articulate lawyers like Cedar. In this scene, Deeds demonstrates "his ability to play … with linguistic tones, styles, and metaphors as creatively and wittily as he showed himself capable of playing for and to himself on the tuba all along" (291). Unlike Capra's earlier comedies, this film does not allow its protagonist simply to rebel against society and its arbitrary codes of class, privilege, and status, or to run away in pursuit of some pastoral or imaginative world: "Codes are everywhere, and everything is encoded. There is no nature, or reality, to run away to. Any momentary leverage over social discourse can and must be achieved from within the system." It is only through the medium of language, then, and not through any decisive action such as those actions taken by Stew Smith, Peter Warne, and Dan Brooks, that Longfellow Deeds can restore an affirmative social order in place of the corrupt status quo.

As the audience knows, the fact that Deeds is willing to give away his entire fortune to buy land for needy farmers does not make him insane – despite Cedar's characterization of "an insane desire to become a public benefactor." But the audience also knows that in order to convince the judge and his team of psychiatric "experts" of this fact he will have to play by the rules, rules set up by a legal system run by the likes of Cedar for the benefit of those like himself and their wealthy clients. The scene begins with Deeds's persistent silence while a series of witnesses testifies against him, each with his or her own agenda, and each conforming to a particular sociolinguistic style. Each character speaks in an exaggerated, even caricaturized version of social type: the policeman speaks in a Irish brogue; the waiter from Tullio's uses street slang; Madame Pomponi, the famous opera singer, makes operatic expostulations; the bodyguard talks in the tough-guy language of a gangster film; the Cockney cabman tells a sentimental story about his horse; and Dr. Von Holler speaks like a Freudian psychiatrist, complete with Viennese accent. Finally, the judge himself addresses Deeds in a stiff legalese. Each of these speakers embodies a different form of linguistic habitus, representing markedly different positions within the social order.

At this point, the film has moved far away from what we might think of as the comic mode toward something like melodrama. It is through Deeds's own linguistic performance that he will not only save himself, but also set the film back on the comic trajectory from which it has strayed. When Babe takes the stand in Longfellow's defense, her language takes the melodramatic form of a woman trying desperately to confess her own sins while exonerating the man she loves:

He's been hurt! He's been hurt by everybody he met since he came here, principally by me. He's been the victim of every conniving crook in town. The newspapers pounced on him – made him a target for their feeble humor. I was smarter than the rest of them. I got closer to him so I could laugh louder. Why shouldn't he keep quiet? Every time he said anything it was twisted around to sound imbecilic.

Babe's testimony is more heartfelt than that of the other witnesses, yet it still remains the sensationalist language of the newspaper reporter, a language defined by her professional training. It will require several others to speak before Deeds can begin his own testimony. Nevertheless, it is Babe's language, and her admission that she is in love with Deeds, that prove to be cathartic in the scene: Babe's speech turns the tide in the hearing and begins the flow of language away from the cynical manipulation of discourse by Cedar and back toward a discourse of sincerity, creativity, and comedy. Cedar, a crafty rhetorician, attempts to undermine Babe's testimony by calling it "a tribute to American womanhood – the instinct to protect the weak." But this underhandedly sexist approach fails when two other characters – Babe's editor MacWade and Corny Cobb – take up the banner for Longfellow. It is significant that both of these men are journalists – "Mac" the editor of the "Morning Mail," and Cobb a former newspaperman – and that both of them represent class positions subordinate to those of Cedar and the other lawyers and psychiatrists. The journalist, as in all of Capra's films, represents the self-made man, the working-class man (or woman) who lives for the pursuit of at least some version of the truth, as opposed to the lawyer who lives by the wholesale manipulation of others for his own financial gain.

Mac begins by deflating Cedar's puffed-up rhetoric in his own colloquial style, getting his "two cents in" by calling Cedar a "windbag" and declaring what a "swell fellow" Babe has reported Longfellow to be. Cobb tries to get in his own "couple of cents" but is interrupted by the judge, who refuses to hear more testimony. By now, however, the floodgates have been opened: a farmer in the audience stands up and demands to be heard, at which point the entire crowd of farmers begins to admonish Deeds for allowing himself to be framed and leaving them "out in the cold." It is at this point that Deeds himself first speaks in the scene, and it is not without significance that he adopts the language of Mac and Cobb, immediately establishing a social and linguistic solidarity with them by echoing their words: "I'd like to get in *my* two cents' worth."

What we have seen in the shift from the testimony of Dr. Von Holler to that of Longfellow's defenders is not only a change from a purely functional and rhetorical use of language to a more personal and colloquial use, but also a progression from one end of the social order to the other: from the position of upper-class authority represented by Von Holler (whose name implies an aristocratic association) and the judge to the descending social scale of Babe, Mac, Cobb, and finally the poor farmers. In Capra's populist vision, it is the members of the urban working class and even the destitute rural class who save Deeds from himself and from his own inability to speak on their behalf. Deeds, who has moved from his position as "one of the people" to that of pampered millionaire, must be embraced by the people before he can become one of them once again, reverse his own upward mobility by giving away most of his money, and rejoin the middle class by moving back to Mandrake Falls and marrying Babe. At the same time, Capra's film, which had shifted modes from screwball comedy to a combination of political drama and personal melodrama, must revert once more to a form of comedy before it can be successfully integrated into Capra's fundamentally optimistic social vision. This is achieved through Longfellow's speeches: first when he points out the compulsive habits of people considered to be quite sane (such as doodling, "O-filling," and nose-twitching), and then when he turns the tables on the arguments of the various witnesses concerning his own antisocial or "pixilated" behavior.

It is remarkable, in a film made less than a decade after the advent of sound, to find spoken language so masterfully brought to bear on the representation of social relationships. If some critics complained about the film's mixture of comedy and serious social commentary, others, like Graham Greene, immediately grasped its importance. Calling *Mr. Deeds* "Capra's finest film" and "a comedy quite unmatched on the screen," Greene located in Capra's film "a complete mastery of his medium, and that medium the sound-film, not the film with sound attached to it."[23] *Mr. Deeds* was not only Capra's most important comedy, but it was also the most powerful synthesis of screwball comedy and social critique among all the Depression-era films made in Hollywood. Although Capra was to make the more obviously comic *You Can't Take It with You* two years later, *Mr. Deeds* was as far as he could extend the comic mode while still moving in the direction of greater social commitment. When Capra turned away from comedy in the 1940s, the mantle of Hollywood's preeminent comic filmmaker would fall on the shoulders of two other directors – Preston Sturges and Howard Hawks – who would continue to explore new directions for comedy in the waning moments of screwball comedy's success.

# 4

## IS CLASS NECESSARY?

### Preston Sturges and Howard Hawks
### in the Early 1940s

### I

In the opening scene of Garson Kanin's screwball comedy *Tom, Dick, and Harry* (1940), Janie (Ginger Rogers) and her boyfriend Tom (George Murphy) are sitting in the movie theater watching a typical Hollywood tearjerker of the period. As Janie and Tom listen attentively, the following on-screen dialogue is heard:

MAN: But you don't understand. I want you to marry me.
WOMAN: Marry you?
MAN: Yes, I want you to become my wife.
WOMAN: Your . . . wife?
MAN: Yes, of course, you silly little goose. What did you think?
WOMAN: Oh, but John, we live in two different worlds. You have money, position, power . . . everything. There's too great a gulf between us.
MAN: Our love will build a bridge across that gulf.
WOMAN: Oh darling, darling . . . *(she begins to cry)*
MAN: Why are you crying?
WOMAN: Because . . . I'm so happy.

Kanin's film is a comic send-up of exactly the kind of hackneyed cross-class love plot the scene represents, one so familiar by the end of the 1930s that it could be already parodied as a cliché of the Depression era. In *Tom, Dick, and Harry,* middle-class Janie is no longer satisfied with her fiancé. Tom, a rising car salesman whose obsession with his progress in the automobile business overshadows their relationship. Instead, she dreams of marrying a millionaire like the wealthy playboy Richard Hamilton (the "Dick" of the title), a man who drives fancy European cars and flies to Chicago in his private plane. After receiving marriage proposals from both men – along with another proposal from the poor but contented auto mechanic Harry – Janie throws over both wealth and status for true love and poverty in a life with Harry, the embodiment of the working class. This decision comes as no big surprise to the audience, which has already dismissed her relationship with Dick as a trivial affair. The film, with a brilliant screenplay by Paul Jarrico, is a play on the Depression-era fairy tale (Janie meets her rich man by wishing on a star but hears bells when she kisses her true love), and it is ultimately a cynical farce in which the dream of every girl to marry a rich husband is shown to be a hollow one after all.

By the early 1940s, romantic comedies had become more self-conscious about their own social conventions, more willing to parody their own conventions while challenging prevailing values of materialism, greed, and the desire for easy money. If romantic comedies of the 1930s like those of Frank Capra, Gregory La Cava, and Mitchell Leisen had established the screwball comedy as one of the most successful Hollywood genres, it was comedies of the early 1940s by Preston Sturges and Howard Hawks that brought a new level of satirical wit to the comic treatment of class issues. In Sturges's *The Lady Eve* and Hawks's *Ball of Fire,* both released in 1941, and Sturges' *The Palm Beach Story* (1942), we see the conventions of screwball comedy – including the treatment of class issues – taken to their parodic extreme. While they lack the overt social agenda of Capra's 1930s comedies, these films challenge constructions of social class by undermining or parodying conventions of the cross-class romantic comedy, including those of Capra, George Cukor, and other Hollywood filmmakers.

## II

Although class is clearly one of the central issues underlying *The Lady Eve,* the class theme is not presented as explicitly as in films like *The Girl from Missouri, It Happened One Night,* or *Easy Living.* Jean Harrington (Barbara Stanwyck), the female protagonist of *The Lady Eve,* is a woman without a past, and only her profession and vocabulary identify a class background. As a professional card shark and con-artist, Jean, along with her father and their companion Gerald, makes a livelihood of disguising her actual social origins and mixing successfully with the wealthy upper class. Jean is not only able to "pass" socially, but in the second half of the film she is able to move *beyond* the American upper class by successfully acting the part of Lady Eve Sidwich, a member of an aristocracy rich New Yorkers can only imitate.

The film is almost symmetrically divided into two parts, which we can designate as Act I and Act II. The first act begins in South America, where Charles Pike (Henry Fonda) has just completed his part in a scientific expedition (the "Pike Expedition") having something to do with snakes and clearly subsidized by his father. Charles and his valet-bodyguard, Muggsy (William Demarest), board a luxury liner, the S.S. *Southern Queen,* headed for New York. We soon learn that Charles's father owns a very profitable brewery whose most profitable product is "Pike's Pale Ale." After Jean Harrington and her father, "Colonel Harrington" (Charles Coburn), decide to play Charles for a sucker, Jean trips Charles up in the ship's dining room and then entices him to her room. There she takes advantage of his lack of familiarity with women (as he mentions several times, he has been "up the Amazon" studying snakes for the past year) and uses her charms to get him to fall in love with her. The next day Jean and her father play a game of bridge with Charles, letting him win in the hopes of winning back more in the next game. But Jean, who is by now becoming quite fond of Charles, forbids her father to win back more than he lost, and finally she prevents the undissuadable "Harry" from doing so by outcheating him. When Jean leaves the table, however, Harry promptly finds a way to cheat Charles out of $32,000. On discovering that her father has been cheating Charles again, she forces him to tear up the check Charles has written, but Harry secretly pockets the torn check. Charles takes Jean out on deck and proposes to her, but before Jean can tell him the truth about herself, Muggsy secures a police photo identifying Jean and her companions as professional con-artists. Charles refuses to hear her explanation and breaks off the relationship.

Act II begins at the racetrack, where Jean and her father meet a fellow con-man, Pearlie, who, in his assumed identity of Sir Alfred McGlennan Kieth, is currently conducting a card game in the wealthy Connecticut suburb where the Pikes have their mansion. Jean concocts a plan to pay "Sir Alfred" a visit as his niece Eve Sidwich. At a party at the Pike's, Charles is introduced to "Eve" and falls for the deception, especially after hearing from Sir Alfred that Jean is really Eve's sister, the dark sheep of the family who was secretly fathered by Lord Sidwich's coachman, "Handsome Harry." Charles falls for Eve just as he had for Jean, and once again he proposes. This time the wedding does take place, but on the train to their honeymoon, Jean/Eve gets her revenge for Charles' treatment by confessing to a series of previous love affairs. Completely disillusioned, Charles gets off the train at the first available opportunity. Pike and his lawyers are willing to make a settlement to have the marriage annulled, but Eve, claiming not to want his money, asks only to see Charles one last time. Charles, it turns out, is bound for the Amazon once again on the same ship. Eve, now transformed into Jean once again, rushes to the ship where she finds Charles, who now realizes it was really Jean he loved all along.

This synopsis of the film already suggests a far more complex comedic plot than that of the typical Depression-era comedy. Critics seldom mention the class elements of the film, however, although these elements are obviously integral to the film's story and its language. Class is not discussed partly because the film works on so many other levels. *The Lady Eve* is certainly not direct social commentary on the level of Capra's films, for example; in fact, the class relations are somewhat disguised by the film itself. But if the film has been read both as an allegory of female deception and male innocence and as a quintessential comic love story, it can also be read as a highly inventive twist on the class confrontation theme of the 1930s romantic comedy. Charles ("Hopsie") Pike is not only innocent – the "Adam" in this Adam and Eve story – but also extremely wealthy. It is his wealth, and Jean and her father's desire to prey upon it, that functions as the initial motivating factor in the plot.

At the same time that the film plays with the convention of the cross-class love plot, it also works in certain ways to disguise the significance of class relationships. Although Jean and the other con-artists are part of a different social class from the Pikes and their wealthy friends, they do such a convincing job of pretending to belong to that class that they manage to fool everyone with the exception of Muggsy, whose own class background and more skeptical tendencies allow him a more accurate reading of the con-game they are playing. Jean dresses well (she carries a whole trunk full of shoes for different occasions), and she is well-spoken, at least in public. As her father indicates early in the film, the success of a con-artist lies in never showing his true "cards," his actual class background: "Don't be vulgar, Jean. . . . Let us be crooked but never common." The idea that "crookedness" (criminal behavior) need not entail commonness or vulgarity is central to the premise of the film. Not only must Charles accept Jean, and later Eve, for what she appears to be rather than for what she truly is, but on some level the audience must accept this deception as well, at least to the point of accepting as entirely plausible the romance between them.

The only scene in which Jean refers to her own socioeconomic situation directly occurs near the beginning of the film, when she tells Charles about her "ideal" husband:

> JEAN: You have a right to have an ideal. I guess we all have an ideal.
> CHARLES: What does yours look like?
> JEAN: He's a little short guy with lots of money.
> CHARLES: Why short?
> JEAN: What does it matter if he's rich enough . . . it's so he'll look up to me . . . so I'll be *his* ideal.

Like Eadie in *The Girl from Missouri*, Jean wants a rich husband; but Jean's ideal man, as she goes on to reveal, is defined more by what he isn't than by what he is: "when he takes me out to dinner he won't ever add up the check or smoke greasy cigars . . . and he won't use grease in his hair either . . . and he won't do card tricks." Jean, it would appear, is speaking from personal experience, perhaps commenting on the kind of men she has dated in the past. Jean's composite portrait of a greasy, somewhat low-class hustler is at the opposite end of the social scale from her current surroundings aboard the S.S. *Southern Queen,* and yet her goals are not as lofty as the kind of upper-class life Charles could provide. Jean wants a "practical ideal," a man she could meet anywhere and who would provide a sense of middle-class stability: "What's the use of having an ideal you can't find anyplace? Mine is a practical ideal you can always find two or three of in every barber shop getting the works." Jean is tired of the continually deceitful and unpleasant life of the con-artist. As she complains to Harry when they first set their sights on Charles, her role usually consists in "danc[ing] in the moonlight" with their dupes, and "a sucker always steps on your feet."

One of the scenes from the screenplay that was shot but never used in the final film was the bank scene in which Charles, knowing he has been duped by Jean and her father, still helps her to cash the check for $32,000 that he had written to cover his gambling losses on the ship. Had this scene been included in the film, the relationship of Charles and Jean as a pecuniary transaction as well as a purely amatory one would have been clearer, as would Charles's superior class position. The scene as written ("Sequence E" of the screenplay) is brief, but it occupies a pivotal point in the screenplay, connecting the entire first half of the film to the second half in which Jean, as Eve, gets her revenge. In the scene, Charles happens to see Jean in a New York bank as she is attempting to cash the check; the bank manager is explaining to her that he cannot cash a check for such a large amount. Charles steps forward to the window, examines the check, and directs the manager to pay it: "I believe we have ample funds to cover this." Charles's sarcastic understatement of his own wealth (in an earlier scene he had declared to Harrington the statistic that "every time the clock ticks fourteen people swig a bottle of Pike's"), along with his rejoinder to Jean about the check – "You'd never know it had been crumpled, would you? A good trick" – indicates his feelings of both moral contempt and socioeconomic condescension toward Jean and her father. It is the one scene in the screenplay in which Charles's class identification outweighs his generally more sympathetic personality. It was perhaps for that reason that the scene was ultimately cut, even though its inclusion might have provided greater motivation for Jean/Eve's seemingly unwarranted revenge on Charles in the second half of the film.[1]

Even without the bank scene, however, the film indicates that Sturges was well aware of class differences and that he was interested in puncturing class pretensions. Sturges' penchant for parodying high society had clear biographical origins. He was raised in Europe by a mother, Mary Desti, whose social and artistic pretensions were almost obsessive, and his second wife Eleanor was an heiress from the very wealthy Hutton family. Eleanor's parents, founders of the General Foods Corporation, had estates in both

Long Island and Palm Beach and a 350-foot yacht with gold and marble interior. Eleanor's yacht and Palm Beach mansion, Mar-A-Lago, were the models for the Hackensacker yacht and mansion in *The Palm Beach Story.* By the time his marriage was annulled, Sturges had had considerable exposure to what he considered the ridiculous excesses of upper-class culture. Although he remained fascinated by the wealthy, he saw their world as "more/absurd than anything conceived by the Brother Florenz Ziegfeld."[2]

In *The Lady Eve,* the satire of the upper class is most evident in the scenes at the Pike mansion, where we find an even more exaggerated version of the typically eccentric wealthy household of screwball comedy (one that bears a distinct resemblance to the Bullock family in *My Man Godfrey*). The slapstick elements in the depiction of the Pikes, along with their total lack of sophistication in dealing with the likes of Eve and "Sir Alfred," indicate that they are not to be taken very seriously. Sir Alfred makes this clear in his speech to Jean at the racetrack, when he indicates how easily the rich can be taken in by the trappings of English aristocratic life: "I have my horses, I have my dogs, I have my little house, I have my antiques." The Pike family here presents no obstacle to the marriage of Charles and Jean/Eve; they are thrilled to see their son marry into what they believe to be the English aristocracy, and they are too busy trying to impress Sir Alfred and Eve to ask any impertinent questions. In one of the more humorous interchanges in the film, Mrs. Pike asks Sir Alfred about Eve's arrival in America. When told that Eve has only recently arrived, she queries him further:

> MRS. PIKE: How did she come over? I didn't know the boats were running.
> SIR ALFRED *(confidentially)*: Battleship.
> MRS. PIKE: They sent a . . . *(mouths the word "battleship")*
> SIR ALFRED: Oh yes . . . actually a . . . cruiser.
> MRS. PIKE: But then she must be very . . . very . . .
> SIR ALFRED: Very.

Use of the single word "very" conveys brilliantly the fact, never directly alluded to, of Eve's social position, a position so elevated it can only be suggested. The Pikes and their other guests accept this position on faith, despite the somewhat suspicious details of her arrival. (In a later scene, the story has been exaggerated still further, and she has come over on a submarine.)³ At the racetrack, Jean had declared that she could "be" English just as easily as she could "be" anything else. Just like her father, who can take on any number of fictitious identities and aliases, Jean lacks any real social identity: "I've been English before . . . I'll be as English as necessary." At the Pikes' party, Jean plays her part to the hilt, telling humorous stories to show her ignorance of American customs and geography, tossing about British words like "dray" and "tube," and outclassing Charles with references to Deauville, Biarritz, and Le Touquet. Only Muggsy sees through Eve's thin disguise, and while he is unable to convince Charles, his own brand of no-nonsense language cuts through the pretense: "That's the same dame. . . . She looks the same, she walks the same and she's tossing you just like she did the last time." Significantly, Charles points to the linguistic difference as the one remaining barrier to identifying Eve as Jean: "She doesn't *talk* the same." Muggsy, however, is not fooled: "Anybody can put on an act," he says as he illustrates his point, somewhat inappropriately, by performing an impression of Hitler.

This exchange is significant because it is through language that Jean/Eve demonstrates her most profound difference from Charles and, as we might put it, her fundamental superiority to him. Where Jean always uses language effectively, whether narrating stories, telling jokes (which Charles never gets), or role-playing, Charles is most often tongue-tied and in important moments either stumbles over his words or resorts to set speeches. The film's critique of the pretensions of language as used by Charles and those surrounding him is introduced in the very first scene, when Charles leaves the Pike Expedition to board the S.S. *Southern Queen* and reenter society. Brian Henderson describes the dialogue here between the professor leading the expedition and Charles as "cartoonish," and there is no doubt that there is a staged and phony aspect to the "undue formality" with which the professor speaks and Charles responds.⁴ When Charles speaks here of "spend[ing] time . . . in the company of men like yourselves . . . in the pursuit of knowledge," his language anticipates the awkward formality of his proposals to both Jean and Eve.

The difference between Charles's and Eve's ability to use and manipulate language is apparent in several key scenes. The first is the famous scene on board ship when Jean first observes Charles in the dining room and narrates what she sees through a hand-held mirror. Charles is reading a book (with the ridiculous-sounding title *Are Snakes Necessary?*), and he is completely silent throughout the scene, while Jean both supplies the play-by-play commentary and invents the dialogue as a series of women walk by his table trying to attract his attention. Jean performs a symbolic castration of Charles in the scene, as Kathleen Rowe suggests, but she does it as much through language as through the gaze.[5] It is primarily through her verbal narration of the scene, and not through the visual image she frames in her mirror, that the humor and satire are created. It is also significant that it is the attempts of the women to be noticed by Charles, as well as his oblivi-ousness to them, that is being satirized: Jean immediately identifies the class-based phoniness of the women, from the "nice store teeth" of one to the dropped-handkerchief ploy of another.

The second key scene is that in which Charles proposes to Eve, using exactly the same language he had used to propose to Jean earlier. Both pro-posals take place in prototypically romantic settings (the first on the bow of the ship in the moonlight, the second at sunset on a ride in the country), but whereas the first is presented without apparent irony, the second is made thoroughly ironic by its context – (it is seen through the imagination of Eve, who has already predicted all the details of Charles's falling in love with her) – by the repetition of the same trite phrases ("you seem to go way back . . . I see you here but at the same time, further away and still further away, way, way back"), by Eve's interruptions of his speech to show that she knows exactly what is coming (a fact that Charles attributes to "telepathy" rather than to the fact that Eve is actually Jean and has heard it all before), and to the additional sight gag of a horse's head that keeps whinnying and nuzzling Charles from behind as he attempts to propose. In one of the most obvious shot changes in the film, the end of the scene moves from a front-facing shot of the two characters to a reverse shot, showing the romantic clouds in the sunset in the background. As the music swells and Charles delivers his most passionate lines – "I hardly have to tell you of the doubts I've had before I brought myself to speak like this. . . . You see, darling, you're so beautiful, you're so fine, you're so . . ." – the horse nuzzles his head and he looks back, almost as if he is speaking to the horse rather than to Eve. This brilliant comic imagetext culminates in a shot of Charles kissing Eve while the horse licks Charles's head.

The third key scene establishing the difference between Charles and Jean/Eve is the climactic moment on the train when Eve finally achieves her revenge. Here again, it is through language rather than through any overt action on her part that Eve emotionally destroys Charles and puts to rest any ideas of a workable marriage between them. Here Jean/Eve's verbal domination of Charles is more apparent than ever. After having told him a story about an affair with a stableboy named Angus when she was sixteen, she proceeds to torment him with accounts of a series of other lovers. The gradual buildup of Charles's shock and outrage throughout the scene (represented both by the thunder and lightning and the smoking, howling train roaring through tunnels) functions as an ironic substitution for the sexual excitement and climax that never occur. The train, like the horse's head in the previous scene, provides the visual image that completes the comic imagetext, but it is the timing of Eve's increasingly outlandish declarations, and her determination to undermine Charles's attempts at understanding and reconciliation, that ultimately make this one of the most brilliant scenes in all of American film comedy.

Once again, Charles resorts to one of his set speeches, as he speaks nobly of "the qualities of mercy, understanding, and sweet forgiveness," but this time he has the added problem of being drowned out by the sounds of the train and the thunder. Not hearing his last words (or at least pretending not to hear them), Eve asks, "Sweet what?" and an exasperated Charles replies "Sweet forgiveness!"[6] When he has regained his composure, Charles finishes his speech, forgiving her for her youthful indiscretion and agreeing to "smile and be as we were." Eve, however, continues to play verbal games with him, like a cat toying with a mouse:

> EVE: I knew you'd be both husband and father to me. I knew I could trust you and confide in you . . . I suppose that's why I fell in love with you.
> CHARLES: Thank you.
> EVE: I wonder if now would be the time to tell you about Herman.
> CHARLES: Herman?! Who was Herman?

At that moment, the train passes into a tunnel, and we miss a section of the dialogue. As the train exits the tunnel, we hear only the name of the next lover:

> CHARLES: Vernon?! I thought you said Herman!
> EVE: Vernon was Herman's friend.

By the time Eve corrects Charles's pronunciation of "Cecil" (after passing through another tunnel), the scene has become so absurd that only the virtuosity of Sturges's verbal wit is able to keep it going. When Charles steps off the train and slides promptly into the mud, we know this screwball romance and its male participant have fallen as low as they can go. With nowhere left for the film to take its central characters except toward reconciliation, the ending of the film is rather perfunctory, depending on the highly unlikely coincidence of Charles leaving on the same boat for South America just as Jean/Eve asks to see him one last time. It is significant, however, that the last line of the film is given to Muggsy, who declares as Jean and Charles enter Jean's cabin, "Positively the same dame!"

It is only fitting that Muggsy should have the last word, bringing the film's language back from the falsity of "Eve" and from the world of social pretension represented both by her and by the upper-class society that produced "Hopsie." It is Muggsy, after all, who is at once the greatest abuser of language (he at one point commits the malapropism of proposing a "hypothermical" situation to the ship's purser) and one of the most inventive users of the colloquial American idiom. Muggsy has little use for double-talk or for deception of any kind: he is a version of the wise fool character who exposes the hypocrisy and falseness around him. When he fails to elicit a straight answer from the double-talking purser about the presence of card sharks on the ship ("what do you mean by 'cheating'"? the purser sophistically asks), he accuses him of "talk[ing] like a law school."

Muggsy's vigilance, though it fails to save Charles from his own gullibility, would seem to be an important trait in a world in which communication is rarely direct and most often the source of misunderstandings or deceptions. Nothing in the world of this film is quite what it seems, a fact that makes for a good deal of the comedy. In the scene where we first meet Horace Pike, for example, he marches down the stairs and passes a table with several telephones, one of which is ringing. He first picks up the wrong telephone, and when he picks up the right one he misunderstands a question about the proper attire to be worn at the party to take place that evening: "Black tie or white tie? You can wear a green tie for all that I care." The wealth and class position of the Pikes is itself largely dependent on a catchy advertising slogan used to sell their beer: "Pike's Pale: The Ale That Won for Yale." Even the difference between "beer" and "ale" (a distinction on which the Pike fortune depends) is a matter of confusion to Charles, who is unable to explain it to Jean: "There's a big difference. Ale is sort of fermented on the top or something and beer is fermented on the bottom . . . or maybe it's vice versa. There's no similarity at all."

The distinction between beer and ale – one that Charles can only assert without being able to define – is parallel to the more important distinction between Jean and Eve, which he also cannot define with any certainty, making only the illogical argument that they must be different because they look too much alike to be the same person. In both cases, the difference is rhetorical rather than real. Muggsy's assertion that Jean and Eve are "positively the same dame" debunks the Eve myth, returning things from the world of rhetoric to the world of reality and allowing the comedy to reach its necessary resolution.

It is in large part Muggsy's class position that allows him the final word. Muggsy is not only a member of the working class, but he is literally hired to be a protector of the upper-class Pike progeny, as Charles relates to Jean: "My father took him off a truck to watch over me when I was a kid . . . you know, kidnappers and stuff like that . . . and he's been sort of bodyguard, governess and a very bad valet ever since." Muggsy's voice, delivery, and pronunciation all accentuate his working-class roots. William Demarest – whose gruff delivery and gravelly voice helped make him a successful character actor and one of Sturges's favorites (he appears in most of his films) – was himself an actor with populist roots: a veteran of the vaudeville stage, he was also a former boxer. In *The Lady Eve,* his casting opposite Fonda is particularly effective. This was a rare comic role for the usually serious and dignified Fonda, and his only role in a Sturges picture. Sturges exploits the smooth, modulated, somewhat boyish quality of Fonda's voice in creating the portrayal of the rich, innocent Charles Pike.

The very different acting styles of Demarest and Fonda and the different traditions they represent (classical Hollywood leading man vs. vaudevillian comic) also contribute to the film's irony. As an adult, Charles may no longer be vulnerable to kidnappers, but he is still extremely naive, and he is subject to more subtle dangers including card sharks and scheming women.[7] Charles's trip "up the Amazon," with all its hidden dangers, was merely an allegorical prelude to his entry into the real world as a wealthy and pampered adult male. In order to take his place in the symbolic order of things, to marry and perhaps even take over his father's brewing business (the two are explicitly linked by

Charles in an early speech to Jean), he must leave behind the protection of Muggsy, along with his juvenile passion for snakes, and engage in a mature adult relationship with a woman. As Charles and Jean enter Jean's cabin (both already "married" but only now ready to consummate that marriage), Muggsy slips out, leaving Charles to survive without his protection. Yet even now it is unclear whether Charles has the wherewithal to survive in a relationship with a woman like Jean, who has already twice demonstrated her ability to play him for a fool. Charles in fact relinquishes his right (or his capacity) to judge the situation at the end of the film. When Jean asks him if he will forgive her, he is still unaware of what she has done to him: "I don't want to understand. I don't want to know. Whatever it is, keep it to yourself."

If read from a class perspective, the film's ending represents a triumph of the more proletarian Eve over the wealthy, overprotected, and usually befuddled "Hopsie," whose nickname itself denotes a certain lightness in the head.[8] Diane Jacobs has noted the number of images of descent in the film, and while she does not explicitly connect these images to class relationships, such a connection is clearly warranted (238). In order to meet Charles, Jean must literally bring him down to her level by tripping him. In her cabin, she brings Charles down another level by having him kneel at her feet to put on a new pair of slippers, while she provocatively crosses her legs from above his vantage point. Later, at the Pike's party for Eve, Charles descends the staircase three times – each time after having spilled something on his suit – and he is so distracted by Jean/Eve that he takes a number of dramatic falls in the course of the evening. Finally, Charles and Jean run down flights of stairs to her cabin (which is on a lower deck than his) both at the beginning and at the end of the film. Each of these instances can be read as representing the process of Charles "falling for" Jean/Eve in the colloquial sense (making a fool of himself in his relationship with her), but they also establish a pattern of his descent from the upper-class position of privilege (a position symbolized by his trips up the Amazon and by his Connecticut mansion) to the "real world" represented by Jean. At the film's conclusion, Jean stands for all those from the less privileged classes who have had to lie or cheat, or simply to use their charm and brains – as Sturges himself had to do – to find their way to a more economically secure position. If we read Sturges's comedies at least in part as parodies of Frank Capra's films, the triumph of Jean also represents a more cynical version of the Capraesque plot, in which the "common man" triumphs over the corruption of the upper classes.

## III

While Hawks's *Ball of Fire* has received less critical and popular acclaim than the director's most famous comedies, it achieves in its own quieter way a comic eloquence equal to that of *Twentieth Century, Bringing Up Baby,* or *His Girl Friday.*[9] The film may be in part a response to *Bringing Up Baby,* as critics have suggested, in its more positive treatment of academic learning and its retreat from the celebration of excess and irresponsibility represented in Hawks's earlier comedy. With its witty screenplay by Billy Wilder and Charles Brackett, and its softer performance by Barbara Stanwyck, it also forms an interesting contrast with *The Lady Eve.* Sugarpuss O'Shea, like Jean Harrington, is a character who operates outside the mainstream of society and to the side of the law. But whereas in Sturges's film the final capitulation is by the wealthy and respectable Charles Pike to the charms of the con-artist Jean, in this film it is the showgirl and gangster's moll Sugarpuss who ultimately capitulates to the stuffy, brainy, and respectable professor Bertram Potts (Gary Cooper). Potts heads a group of eccentric college professors who have been housed in a townhouse off Central Park for the past nine years while they prepare a new encyclopedia for a private foundation. They are – in the film's fairy-tale plot – the seven dwarves to Sugarpuss's Snow White. When he goes out in search of the "living language" for his article on slang, Potts discovers the sexy Sugarpuss singing in a nightclub and invites her to become a subject for his research. Little does Potts know that Sugarpuss is also wanted for questioning in connection with crimes committed by her boyfriend, the gangster Joe Lilac (Dana Andrews). In order to avoid the police, she decides to hide out at the professor's house, on the pretext of taking part in the research.

Even in this introductory segment of the film, the structuring of class relations is clear. The opening shots of a statue and well-maintained walking paths of Central Park establish the highly respectable region in which eight professors take their morning "constitutional," walking two by two in orderly fashion and timing their outing to the minute. The professors are a caricature of ivory tower academics: extremely knowledgeable in their respective fields, but pedantic, desexualized, hopelessly out of touch with the world outside, and infantilized in various ways, as when the house-keeper Miss Bragg accuses one of them of stealing the blackberry jam. Bertram Potts is the youngest and handsomest of the professors, and it is he who is responsible for convincing Miss Totten, the daughter of the wealthy endower of the foundation, to continue funding the encyclopedia, even though it has run over its allotted schedule and budget. Potts is not a member of the upper class in economic terms, but his links to the Totten Foundation and his Ivy League background (he later gives as references the Rockefeller Foundation and the president of Princeton University) give him the credentials of a cultural aristocrat. What Potts lacks in economic capital, he more than makes up for in cultural and intellectual capital, making him the direct opposite of his chief antagonist in the film, the wealthy but uncouth and uneducated gangster Joe Lilac.

The film is narratively and even visually constructed by such opposi-tions. Just as Sugarpuss is torn between two men – Potts and Lilac – who represent opposite ends of the class spectrum, Potts is himself framed by two women – Miss Totten (Mary Field) and Sugarpuss – who represent social opposites. Miss Totten, whose patronym with no first name attached already signifies her elevated class position, is portrayed as gen-tle and soft-spoken, but also as rather stiff, unattractive, and spinsterish. In short, she is an embodiment of upper-class decorum and respectabil-ity. Miss Totten is socially awkward and relaxes from her formal demeanor only when she receives Potts's attention. She is also strongly associated with visual signs of authority: the plaque next to the door of the house, the portrait of her father Daniel S. Totten on the wall, and the foundation lawyer Larsen, who always accompanies her on her visits to the professors. Sugarpuss, on the other hand, displays a physical freedom and social self-confidence, as we see in her nightclub act and later in her interactions with the professors. If Sugarpuss is the link to popular cul-ture and entertainment Potts is looking for, she is also a link to the world of gangsters: a world of violence, danger, and sexuality that is antithetical to the world of the professors and the Totten Foundation.

On stage and in her interactions with the nightclub crowd, Sugarpuss displays a bodily hexis that disrupts the overly stable and uneventful world of the Totten Foundation, and marks a clear contrast with Miss Totten. Where Miss Totten wears a conservative tailored suit and black hat for her visits to the professors, seeming almost physically imprisoned in her attire, Sugarpuss is first seen in the quintessentially "vulgar" outfit of the nightclub singer: a dress with glittery sequins, bare midriff, and spaghetti skirt. Where Miss Totten's language and physical movements are contained and forbidding, Sugarpuss uses both speech and body language to invite physical intimacy. In the nightclub, she breaks the traditional separation of performer and audience by coming down from the stage and gathering the crowd close around her for a participatory rendition of "Drum Boogie."[10] Later, at the Totten Foundation, she has the same effect on the professors, who quickly relax from their stiff and orderly routine and enter her personal space in a way never permitted by Miss Totten or the housekeeper Miss Bragg. Even the film's cinematography emphasizes the difference between the two women: Miss Totten's stiffness and lack of physical form is emphasized by shots from above and in front, while Sugarpuss is shot from the back and side with low camera angles in order to display the curves and movement of her body. In fact, the scene in which Sugarpuss first enters the Totten Foundation mimics the structure of a strip-tease act: she enters wearing a fur coat and veil over her dance outfit, and proceeds to take both of them off. Potts is literally knocked several steps back when he sees her revealed in her full splendor (another fairy-tale element), and he asks if she wouldn't rather keep her coat on. She replies provocatively that she is fine except for a run in her stocking, after which she walks sensually over to a chair, sits, and stretches her legs out toward Potts, revealing their full length. As the scene goes on, Sugarpuss continues the "act" by removing her shoe and then her stocking. Over the embarrassed objections of Potts, who tells her that all the professors are bachelors (with the exception of one widower), she insists on staying the night, holding up her wet and cold foot and showing her raw throat as evidence that she is in no condition to travel.

Like Stanwyck's Jean Harrington in *The Lady Eve,* Sugarpuss uses her body language to seduce and confuse the helpless male.[11] Even more than the freedom and sensuality of her body, however, it is the unfettered libidinal energy of her language that gives her power over Potts, a man who, as a professional student of language, fetishizes linguistic difference. When he first tells the other professors about his meeting with Sugarpuss at the club, Potts cannot remember the color of her hair, but he immediately recognizes the seductiveness of her language: she spoke in "words so bizarre they made my mouth water." Unlike the pedantic language used by Potts, Sugarpuss uses a a colorful and active idiom, turning even grammatical errors into eloquent speeches.[12] In one scene, when Potts attempts to correct her use of the construction "on account of because," she repeats it for dramatic effect:

> SUGARPUSS: I came on account of because I wanted to see you again.
>
> POTTS: Miss O'Shea, the construction "on account of because" outrages every grammatical law.
>
> SUGARPUSS: So what? I came on account of because I couldn't stop thinking about you after you left my dressing room. On account of because I thought you were big and cute and . . . pretty.
>
> POTTS: Pretty?!
>
> SUGARPUSS: Yeah, I mean you. Maybe I'm crazy, but to me you're a regular yum-yum type.
>
> POTTS: Yum-yum?
>
> SUGARPUSS: Don't you know what that means?
>
> POTTS: No, we never got to that.
>
> SUGARPUSS: Well, we got to it now.

Sugarpuss proceeds to stand on Professor Gurgikoff's reference books, facing Potts.

> SUGARPUSS: I'm going to show you what "yum-yum" is. *(Putting her arms around his neck.)* Here's yum . . . *(kisses him)* Here's the other yum and . . . *(kisses him again)* here's yum-yum *(another kiss, during which both fall back onto a chair).*

This brilliant piece of dialogue illustrates the playful tone of the film at its best. If the pedantic Potts insists on interrupting Sugarpuss's display of affection by correcting her grammar, she is perfectly capable of throwing the offending construction back in his face. If he is dense enough not to know what an expression like "yum-yum" means, she will demonstrate it to him through concrete action. Sugarpuss mocks the conventions governing Potts's academic study of language, but she is able to appropriate the tools of academic research, standing on a stack of reference books in order to kiss Potts on the lips. Sugarpuss's superior "reason" (that of the flesh over the intellect) prevails, and a flustered Potts runs up the stairs to cool himself off with a cold washcloth.

Unlike Miss Totten, Sugarpuss uses language for seduction and manipulation. In her first scene at the Totten Foundation, Sugarpuss's language is already laden with double entendres: "This is the first time anybody moved in on my brain," she says, suggesting that Potts might want to "start working on [her] right away." When he replies stiffly that he "wouldn't think of imposing" on her "at this hour," Sugarpuss turns on her most mischievous charm in order to heighten the sexual innu-endo: "Listen, I figured on working all night."

Potts and his seven dwarfs are knocked out of their socially protected existence by the entrance of Sugarpuss, the kind of woman, according to the highly proper Miss Bragg, who "makes whole civilizations topple." The casting of Stanwyck in the role of Sugarpuss was a significant part of the film's success. Born in Brooklyn and having begun her own career as a cho-rus girl, Stanwyck was to play "tough" women or women from lower socioeconomic positions in such films as *Remember the Night* and *The Lady Eve,* as well as in *Ball of Fire* and later Wilder's *Double Indemnity.* Although she was not the first choice for the role, Stanwyck's performance brings exactly the right combination of brains and looks, of a no-nonsense practicality with a capacity for warmth and sentimentality.[13] In this film, we first see her as Potts does, on stage, singing and moving. Her vulgarity, her charismatic ability to entertain an audience, and the seemingly non-sensical repetition of lyrics in her song ("drum boogie, drum boogie, drum boogie-woogie"), all fascinate Potts and send him on a collision course with a new kind of language, with new experiences (love and sex), and, finally, with the more suspect elements of society.

The thematization of language in the film begins even before the entrance of Sugarpuss. Potts's search for a "living language" to replace the "dead" language of his bookish encyclopedia entry on slang begins with the unexpected appearance of the garbage man, who sneaks in through the kitchen door to ask the professors for help with questions for a radio quiz contest. The lower-class identification of the garbage man is clear, especially when the overly fastidious Miss Bragg orders him out, telling the professors "you can't tell me he isn't infested with germs." Later in the film, Bragg will have much the same reaction to Sugarpuss, telling her she will have to have the room "fumigated" after she leaves. In social terms, Bragg represents the cultural snobbism and overcompensation of the lower-middle class. She feels an urgent need to distance herself from those class fractions represented by the garbage man and the gangster's moll, and she is obviously proud of her identification with the professors and the Totten Foundation, even though she seems unable to appreciate the more creative or intellectual side of their endeavor. Her habitual verbal tick of using the split infinitive (always corrected by Potts), indicates a somewhat affected mode of speech, perhaps resulting from an attempt to sound more educated than she really is. Bragg serves as another foil to Sugarpuss, whose "natural" language of the street is clearly in opposition to Bragg's exaggeratedly "proper" language.

Potts and the other professors are fascinated by their encounter with the garbage man, a piece of "real life" who seems to be a kind of walking slang machine. It is this meeting that inspires Potts to go out in search of "the streets, the slums, the theatrical and the live professions," where he hopes to find speakers of authentic American slang. Potts never gets as far down the social order as the slums, but he does investigate a streetcar, a pool hall, a baseball game, and a college campus, as well as Sugarpuss's nightclub.

Use of the streetwise Sugarpuss to satirize the narrow, pedantic, and childlike world of academics in the first half of the film is more typical of Hawks's comedies (consistent with the portrayal of the ineffectual pale-ontologist David Huxley in *Bringing Up Baby* and the absent-minded scientist Barnady Fulton in *Monkey Business*). The second half of the film, however, enacts a subtle but important change in tone, distancing it from the screwball conventions of both Hawks's other comedies and Sturges's *The Lady Eve* (which also contains a professor type in the amateur ophiologist Charles Pike). Here, as Todd McCarthy remarks, it is the "world of civilized values" represented by the professors that is "respected and reaffirmed," while the gangsters appear increasingly laughable in their tough-guy roles. The change begins when the professors drive Sugarpuss out to New Jersey for what they believe is to be her wedding with Potts, but which is actually meant to be her marriage to Joe Lilac. In the ensuing scenes, the film allows an increasing sense of respect for the sensitivity, integrity, and even bravery of the professors, who outwit and overpower the gangsters to restore law and order and ensure the marriage of Potts and Sugarpuss (the Handsome Prince and Snow White) at the end.

It is the scene at the New Jersey inn where the professors give Potts his prenuptial dinner that the audience is drawn beneath the eccentric carica- tures of the professors. The scene culminates in Professor Oddly's some- what pathetic but moving speech about his honeymoon with his now-deceased wife Genevieve. Comparing his bride to a highly sensitive flower (the "anemone nemorosa"), Oddly suggests that he did nothing more than kiss his wife's forehead during the two weeks of the honeymoon. Potts, who feels he needs permission to express his own passionate feelings for Sugarpuss more directly, goes to look for Oddly in his hotel room, but he enters Sugarpuss's room by mistake. In the dark, with Sugarpuss listen- ing from the bed, Potts gives his most emotional speech of the film:

> POTTS: I'm a man in love. It's the first time in my life. I want to take her in my arms. I thought because I was young I had self- control, but that's not true. I think of her every waking moment. Why, if this marriage had been delayed, I mean should have been delayed, I mean should be. . . . Listen to that! I don't know my tenses anymore. I've gone goofy, com- pletely goofy, bim-buggy, slap-happy. Can a man like that keep his mind on the anemone nemorosa?

When Potts speaks from the heart about his feelings for Sugarpuss, he not only loses control of his speech – forgetting the correct verb tense – but he even begins speaking in the slang-inflected language of the street. Here language defies the imposed cultural boundaries of class and educa- tion, allowing Potts for the first time to let down his guard and speak in a more relaxed idiom.

The action of the last section of the film is entirely predicated on speech acts. After Potts and the other professors return to New York, Sugarpuss is held in Fulham, New Jersey, where Lilac attempts to force her to go through with the wedding ceremony – in effect, to say the words "I do." At the same time, Lilac's flunkies Pastrami and Anderson are holding the professors (as well as Miss Totten, Larsen, Miss Bragg, and the garbage man) at gunpoint in order to ensure Sugarpuss's cooperation. On both sides, however, the cap- tives use their superior linguistic abilities as a weapon that ultimately proves more powerful than machine guns: Potts uses a long diatribe in pseudo-aca- demic gibberish to distract the gangsters long enough so that the professors can use a reflected light to burn through the cord holding up Totten's portrait over the seated Pastrami. When the painting falls – in a reenactment of the "Sword of Damocles" – it knocks out Pastrami, and the professors overpower and arrest the two hoods and head for New Jersey in the garbage man's truck. At the same time, Sugarpuss uses *her* linguistic skills to undercut the wedding ceremony which Lilac insists on going through with, despite her objection that she loves Potts. Sugarpuss delivers wisecracks after every line of the service, which the nearly deaf justice fortunately cannot hear, but which are a reminder both to Lilac and to the audience of her resistance to the wedding:

LILAC: I, Joseph Lilac . . .
SUGARPUSS: Head of Murder Incorporated . . .
JUSTICE: Take thee, Katherine O'Shea . . .
LILAC: Take thee, Katherine O'Shea . . .
SUGARPUSS: Who hates and despises him . . .
JUSTICE: To be my lawful wedded wife . . .
LILAC: To be my lawful wedded wife . . .
JUSTICE: For better or for worse . . .
LILAC: For better or for worse . . .
SUGARPUSS: For worse.
JUSTICE: For richer or poorer, in sickness and in health . . .
LILAC: For richer or poorer, in sickness and in health . . .
SUGARPUSS: I'm sick right now.

Here the contrast between Sugarpuss and Lilac is made clear by the contrast between the monotonous repetition of the wedding vows and the sarcastic rejoinders of Sugarpuss, left with only her wit and her tongue as defenses against the gangster. Sugarpuss may be a showgirl and a gangster's moll, but she shares with Potts an ability to enlist language as a weapon, and she will ultimately fit better into his ivory tower than into Lilac's dead-end criminal underworld. At the moment when Sugarpuss is to give her vows, the strains of the academic anthem "Gaudeamus Igitur" are heard, and the professors appear at the door, toting machine-guns and ready to take Sugarpuss back by force. Order is restored only after Potts, having read a boxing manual in order to avenge his earlier humiliation by Lilac, now knocks his adversary down with a flurry of punches, throwing the rules of the manual aside. Potts can become a Hawksian hero – and the Handsome Prince to Sugarpuss's Snow White – only when he learns the lesson that "words cease to be of use," as he says in the final scene, that erudition and fancy language can only take him so far. Language and action must come into a balance, as must the class structures represented in the film. When Potts embraces Sugarpuss at the end of the film he establishes a new household with himself as patriarch. It is the household as a model of the classless society, one that can include both the patrician Miss Totten and the more plebeian Sugarpuss, both professors and garbage men. This is as close as we come at the end of any screwball comedy to a truly utopian vision, one more in keeping with Hawks's comedy than that of Sturges, but moving even further in that direction than Hawks did in a film like *Bringing Up Baby*, where the tottering dinosaur skeleton still signaled an uncertain future for the film's protagonists.

## IV

After *The Lady Eve*, Preston Sturges went on to make seven more comedies in the 1940s, several of which can be categorized as screwball.[14] Parts of *The Palm Beach Story*, Sturges's 1942 release, can in fact be seen as reworkings of *The Lady Eve*. Like Jean Harrington, Gerry Jeffers (Claudette Colbert) is an ambitious, attractive woman, adept at using her feminine charms to get ahead in life. Like Jean, too, she meets an extremely wealthy man (this time by stepping on his head and breaking his glasses in a train's sleeping compartment) and secures a proposal from him. And finally, as with Jean/Eve, Gerry's success depends on pretending to be from a more elevated class position than she really is: in order to explain the sudden appearance of her husband Tom (Joel McCrea) in Palm Beach, she introduces him as her brother, a "Captain McGlue."

Here, however, the class elements are more exaggerated than in *The Lady Eve*. Where the wealthy in the earlier film were portrayed as dupes, in *The Palm Beach Story* they are reduced to caricatures. John D. Hackensacker III is no beer baron, but one of the richest men in the world, and his sister Maude ("The Princess Centimillia") is a real member (by marriage, anyway) of the European aristocracy. Hackensacker is a multimillionaire who painstakingly writes down every penny he spends and who claims that "tipping is un-American," yet who never adds up his expenditures and who seems to think nothing of buying an expensive ruby bracelet and an entire new wardrobe for Gerry. The Princess is an equally exaggerated portrait of an empty-headed high-society woman who has little to occupy her other than what man she will marry next ("I'll marry anybody," she at one point admits to Tom). She has already been through five divorces and two annulments, and she keeps as her current "pet" a babbling foreigner of indeterminate nationality named Toto.

The plot of the film is somewhere between a cartoon – as suggested by the names of the two protagonists, Tom and Gerry – and a fairy tale.[15] It contains not one millionaire benefactor but two, and it ends with not one marriage but two simultaneous weddings, along with a "remarriage," in Stanley Cavell's terms, between the two principals. If the Hackensackers are modeled directly on the Rockefellers, America's most famous upper-class icons, the film's other millionaire is a pure Sturges invention: "The Wienie King."[16] The Wienie King is an eccentric Texas sausage manufacturer, a true *deus ex machina* character who appears at two different points in the film to rescue the protagonists from poverty. And between "The Wienie King" and Hackensacker we find the members of the "Ale and Quail Club," a group of revelling millionaires who buy Gerry a train ticket to Palm Beach and adopt her as their mascot.

There is some truth to Diane Jacobs's claim that *The Palm Beach Story* is less a true screwball comedy than "a sort of mannerist recreation" of one, "with atmosphere and narrative ploys intact, but no real suffering or affirmation" (271). If there is no authentic love story in the film, there is also no real class tension. Any class difference appears to have little to do with fundamental social distinctions, and only to do with money.

In the depiction of class relations in Sturges's screwball comedies from *Christmas in July* (1940) to *The Lady Eve* (1941) to *The Palm Beach Story* (1942), there would appear to be a trajectory from a structure based on a form of social realism to one based on almost total fantasy. Of the three films, only *Christmas in July* takes place within a work environment, and its depiction of class dynamics is by far the most direct.[17] Jimmy McDonald and his girlfriend Betty are anonymous office workers at the Baxter Coffee Company, a firm at which there is obviously little chance of advancement. When Jimmy and his boss believe he has won first prize in a $25,000 contest to choose an advertising slogan for a rival coffee company, he is promoted to a position in management, with a big raise and his own office. As it turns out, however, Jimmy has not won the contest – his apparent victory was only a cruel practical joke played by his co-workers – and he is promptly demoted to his old job. In this film, class lines are fixed and hierarchical; there is no rich benefactor to make a miraculous appearance, and Jimmy's advancement beyond his lower-middle-class status is only a temporary one.

To see the change in Sturges's approach, we need only compare this relatively straightforward narrative with the outrageously improbable plot of *The Palm Beach Story*. Tom and Gerry are a middle-class couple down on their luck after five years of marriage. Tom, a struggling architect-inventor, has not been able to support Gerry in the style to which she aspires, or even to pay their mounting bills, and he needs the absurdly exact amount of $99,000 to fulfill his dream of building an airport in the center of a city. As the film begins, the management of the building where Tom and Gerry live has put their apartment up for rent. The first prospective tenant, however, is none other than "The Wienie King," who gives Gerry enough money to pay her bills and buy herself a new dress. Freed from the burden of debt, Gerry decides to go to Palm Beach and seek her fortune. As Sturges's early notes for the film indicate, Gerry is at least in part a golddigger or adventuress: "A young woman works her way to Palm Beach to see what life holds for her: a husband or adventure. . . . She chose Palm Beach because it contains more wealth in the shape of rich men per square mile than any other locale."[18]

The idea that marriage could be viewed as an essentially financial arrangement – only hinted at by Jean in *The Lady Eve* – is made quite explicit here, especially in the scene on Hackensacker's yacht when Gerry first discovers his real identity. Gerry levels with Hackensacker about her own designs: "I'm not really suited to being a poor man's wife . . . I tried it and it just didn't work out." She goes on to explain that her husband, from whom she is now seeking a divorce, needs $99,000. Hackensacker, though appalled at the implication that her husband would offer to "sell" her ("you read things like that in the Sunday magazine section but you don't run up against them in real life"), is forced to admit that Gerry is "probably worth twice that . . . three times." Gerry plays along with her own commodification, suggesting that her husband would want the money "in cash."[19]

Of course, if we are to accept the central premise of the film, Gerry's market value, under the right circumstances, is far higher than that. Yet the upper-class Hackensackers, despite all their millions, are not ultimately enough for Gerry and Tom, whose deep attraction for each other finally triumphs over the empty promise of the Hackensacker fortune. The film is a fairly devastating portrait of the idle and ineffectual rich, specimens who are not adequate potential mates for the film's protagonists even in the way that Hopsie Pike – with all his foibles – was an attractive match for Jean Harrington.[20] John D. is perhaps the most exaggerated version of the young millionaire of Sturges's comedies, a type that Manny Farber characterized as "heavily ornamented bugs . . . as moldy with leisure and tradition as an old cheese."[21] As Farber observed, John D., as played by Rudy Vallee, is "a pathetic creature in the last stages of futility." So ineffectual is John D. that he does not even manage a proposal to Gerry, but seems continually to get stuck at the stage of going down on one knee. Where Charles Pike at least had his passion for snakes to occupy him, John D. appears to have descended a couple of steps further down the ladder of futility. As Henderson points out, he is the one member of the family who has no real identity or vitality. (Even his sister is occupied with her flirting and compulsive marrying.) Like Hopsie, John D. needs a marriage with a solidly grounded middle-class woman to revitalize the family line; but unlike Hopsie, he lacks the charm to pull it off. Only the film's farcical fairy-tale ending (in which Sturges provides Gerry's identical twin for John D. to marry) prevents the extinction of the family line.

The deficiency of John D. Hackensacker – already suggested by his nickname, "Snoodles" – is demonstrated most tellingly in the scene toward the end of the film where he serenades Gerry from below her bedroom window while Tom seduces her. In a wonderful comic imagetext, Tom helps Gerry to undo her dress as we hear John D. singing outside. Gerry delivers the punch line from Tom's lap – "I hope you realize this is costing us millions" – and the scene ends as John D. hits the high note that finishes the song while Tom and Gerry embrace.[22]

If there is any tension in *The Palm Beach Story*, it has less to do with the film's plot than with its complex tone, which seems to hover between ebullient optimism and profound cynicism. Of all Sturges's comedies, this may be the hardest to read in terms of its implicit social commentary. On the one hand, the film presents a vision of a land of plenty where another millionaire can always be found just around the corner. On the other hand, the film's satirical portrayal of the upper class – who have even less in the way of redeeming qualities than the wealthy in the typical screwball comedy of a few years earlier – suggests that Sturges's real message may have been darker than its overtly optimistic narrative suggests.[23] Perhaps the ambivalent tone of the film also had something to do with the timing of its production. Although Sturges's screenplay was completed on November 21, 1941, the bombing of Pearl Harbor and the subsequent entry of the United States into World War II occurred during filming. Thus the making of *The Palm Beach Story* coincided with the official end of both the Depression era and the screwball era. Brian Henderson speculates that the event and aftermath of Pearl Harbor might have created enough of a distraction to allow the film to get past the censorship codes. They might also have contributed to the film's almost giddily irreverent treatment of the dominant themes of screwball comedy: love, sex, money, and class.

At the end, John D. marries Gerry's twin sister as the Princess marries Tom's twin brother. The film closes on an even more ironic (and even more improbable) note than *The Lady Eve*. Since there is no Muggsy equivalent to act as the voice of reason, the task of delivering the last line falls on Toto, who sourly pronounces his commentary on the proceedings: "Schnitz!" Toto's unpleasant-sounding utterance can be read in two different ways: it is the exclamation of disgruntled suitor left in the cold by Princess Maude's sudden marriage, but it is also a more general comment (by Toto as Greek chorus) on all that has gone before.[24] It is also significant that Sturges, who himself had important ties to Europe, puts the final word in the mouth of a foreigner.

The film can be read as an ironic comment on the American Dream of unlimited financial opportunity and the tendency toward nationalism and isolationism at the time of a global conflict in which the United States had decided not to become involved. Tom's airport project itself seems a symptom of the American tendency to do everything on a larger, more complicated, more visionary scale. Suspended on a grid of steel cables above the city ("like a tennis racket," as Gerry deflatingly describes it), the airport may be visionary, but it is also totally impractical, which explains why Tom has had trouble attracting investors. Finally, it is John D., a character as far removed from the all-American perspective as one could hope to find, who sees merit in the proposal, mostly because of his interest in Gerry and his lack of anything better to occupy his attention.

The characters of John D. and his sister also represent a commentary on America and Americanness. John D. engages in a jingoistic discourse, calling things he doesn't like (tipping, staterooms on trains) "un-American." Sturges's portrayal of John D.'s "Americanism" must be read as ironic, given the fact that he lives in a palatial Palm Beach mansion and has a yacht named "The Erl King."[25] Hackensacker sees tipping as un-American not only because he is cheap, but also because he believes in the myth of America as a classless society, a myth that the train porter who receives his dime tip debunks. John D.'s "democratic" beliefs miss the point as badly as Marie Antoinette's "let them eat cake": he and the Princess are a *de facto* American aristocracy, as real and as absolute in its own way as the British aristocracy to which Eve pretends to belong in *The Lady Eve*. The Princess has in fact been married to a series of Europeans, including "Stefan," "Serge," and "Baron Itsk," all of whom she has had to pay off with generous divorce settlements; John D. is so out of touch with normal American life that he wants to test Gerry's mothering abilities before marrying her by either renting or borrowing some children.[26]

What is apparent, however, in comparing this film with Sturges's previous comedies, from *Easy Living* (written by Sturges and directed by Mitchell Leisen) to *Christmas in July* to *The Lady Eve* to *Sullivan's Travels*, is the fact that Sturges's satire of the upper class – however caustic it may be – is no longer in the service of any real social critique. Nowhere in *The Palm Beach Story* does language become a vehicle for representing class difference, as it is in all the earlier comedies, and nowhere is a class background of any kind provided for either of the film's protagonists. As a result, the issue of social class is, within the economy of the film itself, a relatively superficial one. If the class theme is implicit in the almost continual discussion of money, it would appear to be removed from any real consideration by the procession of wealthy eccentrics, by the constant intervention of fairy-godmother benefactors, and by Gerry's complete confidence in the ability of "a long-legged girl" to find a "good provider."

As Kathleen Rowe has noted, many of the romantic comedies of the 1930s map the "slippery" issue of social class "onto the more readily managed ones of gender and generation" (125), thus "bridg[ing] the gap between social class" by "asserting that the differences between social classes are as illusory as those between the sexes" (126). But in *The Palm Beach Story,* Sturges appears to be parodying the "happy endings" of these earlier comedies. The differences between social classes may *appear* illusory, but by exaggerating wealth and privilege to the point of caricature, Sturges finally shows – paradoxically – that class is still very much with us, and that class divisions cannot be reconciled by love and marriage as they are in many Depression-era comedies.[27] Within the narrative structure of the film, class difference cannot be overcome by "true love," as it was in *The Girl from Missouri, It Happened One Night, Easy Living, The Lady Eve, Ball of Fire,* or many other Depression films. Gerry and Tom do *not* marry their respective partners from the upper class. Instead, Sturges manufactures – as if to ironize the too easy resolutions of previous screwball comedies – the totally artificial and emotionally unsatisfying ending involving the two sets of identical twins. There is no father figure, as in *It Happened One Night,* to restore class harmony by paying off the rich suitor and orchestrating the marriage of his child to a poor but honest mate. It is significant that no parental figure of any kind appears in the film. The class position so often represented by the parents, and usually by the father, in screwball comedies, is strikingly absent. Along with the maturing of the romantic comedy beyond its screwball phase comes a maturing of the protagonists of this comedy, who now act without parental consent or guidance. Although the patriarchal line is implied in the case of the Hackensackers, their money appears to be their own, with no strings attached. The characters, and especially the female characters, have become more jaded. Colbert is clearly older and wiser as Gerry Jeffers than she was as Ellie Andrews, and certainly no female character in screwball comedy has more worldly experience than the Princess. Finally, it is no longer the virtues of spunk, hard work, and principled independence that overcome class differences, as in the case of romantic comedies in the mode of *It Happened One Night.* Now class divisions are bridged by good looks, sex appeal, and the mercenary hunt for financial reward.[28] The metanarrative moment that follows the conclusion of the story makes Sturges's point very clear: the glass cover containing the printed title that is supposed to end the film – "And they lived happily ever after" – is shattered off-screen, thus also shattering the illusory promise offered by all the screwball comedies that had come before.

If my ironic reading of the film is correct, its title is significant in the way it tropes on the conventional titles of earlier films, and in particular on George Cukor's *The Philadelphia Story* of two years earlier.[29] *The Philadelphia Story*, which had garnered Oscars for best actor (James Stewart) and best screenplay (Donald Ogden Stewart), as well as nominations for best picture, best director, best actress (Katharine Hepburn), and best supporting actress (Ruth Hussey), would still have been very fresh in audiences' minds at the time *The Palm Beach Story* was being made. In the earlier film, which is only marginally a screwball comedy and which might better be seen as representing the romantic comedy tradition in its "straightest" manifestation, class issues are introduced, only to be deflected by a story that focuses on the growing emotional attachment and ultimate remarriage of Tracy Lord (Hepburn) and C. K. Dexter Haven (Cary Grant). As Stanley Cavell rightly argues, the film can be read as very much about class. It stages a debate – as did the original framers of the Constitution in Philadelphia – about "the nature and the relation of . . . classes" and about "whether the upper class, call it the aristocracy, is to survive and if so what role it may play in a constitution committed to liberty."[30] In the film, Tracy must choose between three men from very different social positions, and she ultimately chooses the one whose upper-class position – with all the trappings of yachting and horseback-riding that go along with it – most closely resembles her own. Although Cavell admits that the film treads on "dangerous moral territory," he is perhaps too generous in his interpretation of the film's apparently reactionary ideology. Cavell reads the defeat and expulsion of the *nouveau riche* George from the Lords' old-money family circle not as "a group of snobs ridding themselves of an upstart from a lower class," but as "a gesture to be rid of classes as such, and so to be ridded of George as one wedded to the thoughts of class division, to the crossing rather than the overcoming of class" (156). Yet it is clear that the remarriage of Tracy and Dexter, whatever other statements it hopes to make, reinforces established class divisions and reinstates the class-based ideology that both George and Mike are attempting in their own ways to challenge.

Sturges's film appears to rewrite aspects of Cukor's comedy as parody. Whereas the title of *The Philadelphia Story* contains a certain gravity – provided by associations with the city of Philadelphia and its part in our national history – *The Palm Beach Story* has none. Palm Beach, unlike Philadelphia, has no "story," no significant history. It is a playground created for the idle rich, with no regard to taste, good breeding, or family origins.[31] The Palm Beach aristocracy is not the old-money social establishment represented by the Lords, but a fabulously wealthy and completely tasteless society represented by the Hackensackers. Even the name "Hackensacker," while clearly an allusion to "Rockefeller," is a play on the lower-middle-class town of Hackensack, New Jersey, as well as a commentary on the way in which the family accumulated their wealth by ravaging and plundering the American people ("hack and sack"). The name is also in the tradition of ridiculous Sturges names, from "Trudy Kockenlocker" (the promiscuous pregnant heroine of *The Miracle of Morgan's Creek*) to names like Bildocker, Swandumper, and Diddlebock.

*The Palm Beach Story*, released in December 1942, appears to be Sturges's final treatment of the class theme that had fascinated so many filmmakers throughout the preceding decade. Sturges's next two comedies – *The Miracle of Morgan's Creek* and *Hail the Conquering Hero*, both released in 1944 – have little to do with issues of social class.[32] The change in Sturges's comedies coincides with the more general waning of the class theme within American film comedy. As America moved into the immediate postwar era, Hollywood comedies became far less concerned with the kinds of social issues explored by films of the 1930s and early 1940s. Film attendance and studio profits were at an all-time high, the Legion of Decency was consolidating its control over the content and style of American movies, and the incipient Cold War was dictating norms of social propriety to a greater extent than at any time during the previous two decades. As a result of these factors, Hollywood comedy settled into a cosy domesticity, venturing only a gentle satire of middle-class manners. The late 1940s and early 1950s was the age of films like *The Egg and I* (Chester Erskine, 1947), *The Bachelor and the Bobby Soxer* (Irving Reis, 1947), *Mr. Blandings Builds His Dream House* (H. C. Potter, 1948), and *Father of the Bride* (Vincente Minnelli, 1950), which established the genteel and mildly satirical mode that would become the dominant form of both film and television comedy. It was not until the mid-1950s, in a reaction against the complacent spirit that had overtaken Hollywood comedy, that filmmakers once again began to use comedies as a means of transgressing the boundaries of the social order as reflected and maintained by the American culture industry.

# 5

# DESPERATELY
# SEEKING STATUS

## Class, Gender, and Social Anxiety
## in Postwar Hollywood Comedy

A kiss on the hand may be quite continental,
But diamonds are a girl's best friend.
*Gentlemen Prefer Blondes* (Howard Hawks)

## I

In the screwball comedies of the 1930s and early 1940s, romantic attachments between members of different social classes functioned as allegorical representations of the more general class dynamics of Depression-era America. Through the screwball film, the problems and tensions inherent in an unequal and divided society could be safely explored. In many cases, the fantasy of social reconciliation could be embodied in a romantic union that overcame class barriers and thus demonstrated their fundamental artificiality. Hollywood films of the 1950s and early 1960s, on the other hand, treated the cross-class fantasy quite differently, reflecting fundamental changes in the prevailing social ideology of postwar America. Postwar comedies from Howard Hawks's *Gentlemen Prefer Blondes* (1953) and Jean Negulesco's *How to Marry a Millionaire* (1953) to Delbert Mann's *That Touch of Mink* (1962), for example, differ significantly from their Depression-era counterparts in their treatment of both class dynamics and gender relations. Unlike the 1930s screwball films, in which the man was as likely as the woman to occupy the socially subordinate role, postwar comedies tended to present only a one-dimensional vision: attractive women in search of rich husbands.

In *Gentlemen Prefer Blondes,* Marilyn Monroe plays Lorelei Lee, a blonde seductress on a mercenary quest for a millionaire. Monroe's performance as Lorelei makes the desire to marry wealth appear so naturalized as to require no concealment or apology. Lorelei and her friend Dorothy (Jane Russell) are, as they announce in one of their musical numbers, "Two Little Girls from Little Rock," who "come from the wrong side of the track." Their cynicism about meaningful relations between the sexes is made clear in the song's lyrics: "Find a gentleman who is shy or bold/ Or short or tall or young or old/ As long as the guy's a millionaire." As Ed Sikov suggests, these women "have joined together to parlay their looks and talents into economic gain": excluded from the male-controlled centers of socioeconomic power, they use the only power they have, the power to attract the male gaze. In his affirmative reading of the film, Sikov emphasizes the social mobility of Lorelei and Dorothy. The two women "are able to move between classes – from 'the wrong side of the tracks' to the first-class deck on the oceanliner – without ever belonging to either one."[1]

Although Sikov's analysis is persuasively argued, it reveals not so much a liberating or transgressive social mobility on the part of the characters as the film's lack of any attempt at social authenticity. Comedies of the 1950s, unlike their prewar counterparts, no longer attempt to articulate an authentic class experience or to depict realistic class relations. In a Depression-era film like Frank Capra's *It Happened One Night,* much of the narrative is taken up with establishing and defining the authenticity of working-class experience through the evocation of such class-coded activities as donut-dunking and piggyback riding, and, more seriously, the realities of working-class life: bus travel and auto camps, hitchhiking and raw carrots. It is only after such a painstaking definition of proletarian authenticity that Capra can juxtapose the social groundedness of working-class life with the inauthentic, affected, and socially insulated experience of the upper classes, as represented by King Westley and to a lesser extent by Ellie herself.

In *Gentlemen Prefer Blondes,* on the other hand, establishing a believable or authentic class identity for Lorelei is of little concern, since it is not so much class status that Lorelei is seeking as money, or, to be more precise, the materialized form of money as diamonds. When she learns that an unattractive older man on board ship is the owner of a diamond mine, she immediately takes an interest in him, envisioning his balding round head as an enormous gemstone. At the end of the film, there is no sense in which Lorelei and her fiancé will unite their disparate class experiences into the vision of a new social class, as Ellie and Peter do at the end of *It Happened One Night,* for example. In fact, Lorelei's commitment is at best a conditional one, motivated by the promise of wealth, and she is unabashedly honest about her socioeconomic motives. When the father of Lorelei's fiancé asks her to admit that she is marrying his son for his money, she politely demurs, "No, I'm marrying him for *your* money."[2]

In the lyrics of Lorelei's song "Diamonds Are a Girl's Best Friend," the appeal of "class" (i.e., the symbolic expression of sociocultural capital) is placed in direct opposition to the value of diamonds, the materialized and thus most permanent form of economic capital:

A kiss on the hand may be quite continental,
But diamonds are a girl's best friend.
A kiss may be grand but it won't pay the rental
On your humble flat, or help you at the automat.

In postwar Hollywood, the exterior signs of social class as cultural capital ("a kiss on the hand") are viewed as easily separable from economic wealth. If one has to choose between the cultural and economic capital, it is inevitably the latter that will prevail.

An even more blatant treatment of the same topic can be found in Negulesco's *How to Marry a Millionaire,* a film in which *three* young women devote their entire existences to the pursuit of a rich husband, using any possible means at their disposal, including dishonesty and theft, in order to achieve that goal. Unlike *Gentlemen Prefer Blondes* – where Lorelei's unrepentant desire for diamonds and cash is balanced by Dorothy's more wholesome wish for a marriage based on "true love" – *How to Marry a Millionaire* presents no viable alternative to the mercenary manhunt and never appears to question its underlying motive. The fact that only one of the three women actually hits the jackpot, and that unwittingly, does little to moderate the message that money in itself constitutes an acceptable, and perhaps even a laudable, objective for an attractive young woman of limited means.

In the postwar era, the more restrictive gender ideology governing the representation of both men and women in Hollywood comedy limited the range of social commentary that had been available to the prewar screwball genre. In the comedies of the 1950s, we see the prewar variations of the cross-class fantasy subsumed into a more rigid gender ideology. The blatant and crassly avaricious pursuit of money replaces the more complex search for a combination of social, sexual, and emotional fulfillment that characterized gender relations in the screwball genre.

The issue of social class – as an entire system of economic, social, and cultural relations rather than simply a bank account – seems to be of little concern in these films. With the rapid growth of the middle class that characterized the postwar U.S. economy, Americans wanted more than ever to believe in the myth of a socially homogeneous and virtually classless society, and Hollywood was happy to oblige them in this wish. Without the glaring social divisions of the Depression era staring them in the face, Americans could shift the fetishized object of their interest from class to money. Furthermore, where class relations were openly proclaimed and centrally important in prewar screwball comedy, they are more often hidden or cleverly disguised in postwar comedy. The overt barriers of class distinction – represented most memorably in the "Walls of Jericho" episode of *It Happened One Night* – are removed from the world of these films, allowing the impression of instant socioeconomic mobility. It may have been a struggle for Jean Harlow to marry the millionaire's son in a Depression-era comedy like *The Girl from Missouri,* but all Marilyn Monroe, Betty Grable, or Doris Day have to do is meet the right man and "biology" will take care of the rest.

This change toward a seemingly more egalitarian view of social class did come at a price, however, and especially for women. Whereas screwball comedies were often based on inversions of conventional gender roles, allowing female characters to be the intellectual and moral equals or even superiors of their male counterparts, women in 1950s comedies were more likely to be portrayed as sex objects with little to offer their potential partners beyond physical attributes. In the case of the characters portrayed by actresses like Marilyn Monroe and Jayne Mansfield, their iconic sexual identities obviate any need for a more realistic social history. Monroe's character in *How to Marry a Millionaire,* for example, has little in common with 1930s screwball heroines like those portrayed by Katharine Hepburn, Irene Dunne, Claudette Colbert, Jean Arthur, Ginger Rogers, or Barbara Stanwyck. So vain about her appearance that she refuses to wear her glasses in public, Monroe's character is constantly running into things and can hardly even see the men she is talking to. (In one scene, she is unaware that her date is wearing an eye-patch; in another, she pretends to be reading but has the book turned upside down).

In general, women in 1950s comedy were placed on display, a spectacle of the idealized female image. As sexual projections of the male spectator (both within the film and in the audience), they are either infantilized, domesticated, or sold to the highest bidder. In postwar comedies, visions of material and social success were literally mapped onto women's bodies as class relations were mapped onto gender relations. In *How to Marry a Millionaire,* the three female characters are models who in one scene literally put on a fashion show for a prospective suitor. Jayne Mansfield, a star in Frank Tashlin comedies such as *The Girl Can't Help It* (1956) and *Will Success Spoil Rock Hunter* (1957), was an even more exaggerated (and more obviously parodic) version of Monroe's sexy "dumb-blonde" persona. In *The Girl Can't Help It,* the talent agent Tom Miller (Tom Ewell) declines an offer to make the girlfriend of a gangster famous. At that point, a door opens behind him to reveal Jerri (Mansfield) displayed in an extremely tight white dress with a white fur stole, diamond jewelry, and waves of platinum hair falling to her shoulders. The fact that Mansfield does not even need to speak in the scene – her visual embodiment of female sexuality is enough to convince Miller to sponsor her – is only half of the joke. The crudeness of the representation is further underlined by the dialogue of the two men. When Miller suggests that "Rome wasn't built in a day," Fats counters, "She ain't Rome. What we're talking about is already built."

## II

The simultaneous fascination with class status and avoidance of class tension exemplified in postwar comedies like *Gentlemen Prefer Blondes* and *How to Marry a Millionaire* was consistent with American social

attitudes of the time. During an era ostensibly marked by a greater affluence and a growing sense of middle-class homogeneity, America became
intensely preoccupied with the particulars of class formation, as evi-
denced by the unprecedented number of articles, books, and textbook
anthologies devoted to the subject of social class. Led by C. Wright
Mills's famous 1951 study of the American middle class, *White Collar*,
books with titles like *Class, Status and Power*, *Social Stratification in the
United States*, and *Class and Society* documented in elaborate detail the
dynamics of social class in American life. This postwar obsession with the
subject of class was not simply the result of a growth in the field of academic sociology. It had its roots in an underlying sense of confusion and
anxiety about a social structure in the process of rapid transformation.
Despite a popular rhetoric of social homogenization, American society
was experiencing what Marianne Conroy has described as "a historically
specific class instability," an instability brought on by a "volatility and
complexity of class categories . . . and practices of class differentiation."[3]

Several interrelated factors contributed to changes in the perception
of class structures in the postwar United States. First, a significant
increase in educational opportunities for most Americans and a corre-
sponding increase in geographical, occupational, and social mobility led
to a breakdown of what had previously been more rigidly defined communities and allegiances based on class identification. Second, a significant shift from an industrial and production-based economy to a service
and consumption-based economy had established a greatly enlarged
cadre of "white-collar" urban professionals, whose position in the social
and corporate hierarchy was no longer easily defined in traditional class
terms. As C. Wright Mills put it, white-collar workers could no longer
"be adequately defined along any one possible dimension of stratification
– skill, function, class, status, or power."[4] Third, a shift away from the
direct ownership of property (characteristic of the traditional middle
class) and toward a greater dependence on occupational income meant
that the vast majority of middle-class Americans now depended on the
corporation or organization for their livelihood and for any chance of
socioeconomic mobility. While white-collar employees still retained
more prestige and generally higher incomes than wage-workers, the gap
in incomes had narrowed, and claims to prestige had become "vague and
fragile."[5] With respect to the class of owners and top executives, white-

collar workers had been placed "in exactly the same propertyless position as the wage-workers."[6] Like workers, white-collar employees had no financial tie to the means of production and no claim on proceeds from property and investment. Fourth, a consumerist ethos – made possible by a growing range of available commodities and encouraged by the rapidly expanding field of advertising – produced an increased reliance on commodified markers of socioeconomic status such as houses, cars, and clothing. These commodities came to replace more stable social factors such as education, religious affiliation, neighborhood, and family connections in determining class identity. Finally, the rise of "middlebrow" tastes and lifestyles as an alternative to either traditional high culture or localized working-class culture further eroded traditional cultural distinctions between the various class fractions, leading to what contemporary commentators saw as the spread of an undifferentiated and homogenized "mass culture." A new, culturally rootless middle class had emerged which, though still highly differentiated with respect to income, was much less clearly distinct with respect to cultural taste.

Such changes had important implications for the social psychology of the postwar United States. Americans of the postwar era may have been economically better off than their prewar counterparts, but they were increasingly experiencing what Mills called "status panic," a sense of the tenuousness of any claim to social status or class distinction in a world in which, to quote Conroy, "taste and consumption [had become] unmoored from a stable, class-determined system of social stratification" (117). According to Mills, white-collar workers were becoming especially sensitive to external marks of status or success, including a raise in pay or promotion, a change in job title, or a more desirable office. The emphasis on such distinctions led to a more general tendency in American society toward a reliance on symbolic measures of status. As Esther Milner put it in her 1955 book *The Failure of Success,* the postwar era saw a shift "toward judging personal worth on the basis of symbols external to the individual."[7] The "middle-class status struggle" was fast becoming the "middle-class ego struggle," as deep psychological anxieties were produced within middle-class workers and families. The struggle for social status also tended to discourage any form of group solidarity among employees, casting individual workers in direct competition with one another for rank and status within the corporation and further eroding traditional forms of class identification.

By the end of the 1950s, Vance Packard would publish his popularized sociological study of "class behavior in America," provocatively entitled *The Status Seekers*. Far from being the "classless society" some had claimed, Packard saw the United States as a society based on the constant search for meaningful "status symbols." It was a society of "status seekers," people "continually straining to surround themselves with visible evidence of the superior rank they are claiming" (7), and as a result highly susceptible to the messages of advertisers and other merchants of culture. The preoccupation of Americans with socioeconomic status and their need to display that status in ever more conspicuous fashion had become, Packard claimed, a vicious circle. As the "general diffusion of wealth" and the "crumbling of visible class lines" had convinced average Americans that they could surround themselves with the trappings of luxury – including consumer goods such as power boats, mink coats, new cars, and single-family suburban homes that had previously been available only to the rich – it would now become necessary to find new and more subtle means of creating class distinctions.

Hollywood films of the 1950s and 1960s were often allegories of American insecurities about class aspiration, status panic, patterns of consumption, and cultural taste. Although some of these allegories merely reproduced such insecurities, others, especially comedies, engaged in a form of metacommentary on the era's social contradictions that allowed them to take a greater critical distance from them. Just as some films of the 1930s simply reinscribed class differences while others actually critiqued their social effect, films of the 1950s and early 1960s positioned themselves in various ways with respect to questions of social status and status panic. While comic melodramas like Vincente Minnelli's *Father of the Bride* (1950) took a more conservative position in dealing with class issues, more subversive comedies such as those of Billy Wilder, Frank Tashlin, and Jerry Lewis used the comic form to invert power relations (including those based on class and gender) and to satirize class pretensions and status anxieties.

### III

Questions of class, status, and consumption are central to *Father of the Bride*. The marriage of Kay Banks, the event on which the film centers, is a display of the social status the Banks family has achieved. The film is in part a satire on the upper-middle-class commodity culture symbolized by the wedding, an event defined almost entirely as "the ostentatious accumulation and display of objects, of which the bride is the most expensive of all."[8] Spencer Tracy as Stanley Banks is a kind of middle-class Everyman, thrust into a situation over which he has no control. In the course of the film, he is humiliated in a number of ways: berated by his wife, insulted by the caterer, half-trampled at the wedding rehearsal, unable to escape mixing drinks in the kitchen during the engagement party, and even betrayed by his old tuxedo, which rips when he tries to put it on.

The wedding is an event fraught with status anxieties, reflecting the preoccupations of the status-conscious 1950s. Minnelli shows what Stephen Harvey identifies as his "keen eye for the subtle gradations of class snobbery" (160). From the beginning of the film, we see Stanley's capacity for the kind of "status panic" his daughter's wedding will inevitably bring out. In his opening monologue, in fact, the word "panic" occurs no less than three times. Although the alleged source of Stanley's panic is his daughter's interactions with the opposite sex, his use of the word sets up the context for a larger social panic as well. Stanley's preoccupation with socioeconomic standing is clear as he establishes in peremptory fashion the stability of his own middle-class lifestyle. As we see him getting out of his car and walking up the path to his house, we hear the following voiceover:

We own our own home in the suburbs, at least we almost own it.
Had it built when my law firm made me a full-fledged partner.

Stanley's fundamentally conservative approach to life depends on a firm relationship between home, family, and economic position; yet his use of the word "almost" and his emphasis on "full-fledged partner" betray the insecurities lurking just underneath his seemingly secure status. Stanley, in the jargon of the 1950s, "has it made" – a good job, a home in the suburbs, three "normal" children, and an attractive and loving wife. Yet throughout the film he seems almost existentially uncertain of his own good fortune and of his place in the world.

Stanley's status concerns first emerge at dinner that night, when Kay's sudden announcement that she intends to marry Buckley prompts a series of questions:

STANLEY: Who is this Buckley, anyway? And what's his last name? I hope it's better than his first one! And where the devil does he come from? And who does he think is going to support him?

Stanley is somewhat reassured when Kay informs him that Buckley conforms to his notion of appropriate socioeconomic status: he is not only a successful young businessman but the son of the respectable Dunstan family.

KAY: They're just as good as you and Mom. They're fine people, and they live in Westbridge. I guess you'll agree that Westbridge is just as good a place as Fairview Manor!

As it turns out, the Dunstans are slightly "better" than the Banks are, at least as measured by the terms of 1950s bourgeois ideology. The Banks's fear that Buckley will not be good enough for their daughter (perhaps even a "good-for-nothing" or a "confidence man") quickly shades into worries about their own relative social status. When they are invited to the Dunstans' house for dinner, the Banks are so nervous about the impression they will make that Ellie has to change her dress three times and Stanley needs to stop for a drink on the way. "I bet it's a shack," Stanley comments hopefully as they look for the house, which turns out to be larger and more luxurious than their own. Again, Minnelli brings out the subtle nuances of class: the Dunstans have a *white* maid, they speak with accents that are slightly more upper-class than those of the Banks and seem more at ease in the social situation, and they offer an aged Madeira instead of the usual cocktails. Mr. Dunstan is the consummate host. When he finds out that Stanley is a martini drinker, he is glad to oblige, moving a vase of flowers to reveal a well-stocked and cleverly hidden liquor cabinet. Stanley becomes so tense in the course of the evening that he makes a fool of himself, drinking several martinis as well as wine with dinner, and falling asleep over his after-dinner brandy.

As the wedding itself approaches, Stanley continues to exhibit anxieties about his ability to pay for an exorbitant wedding, and he worries that the costs will put him "in the gutter." The consumerism surrounding the wedding becomes obvious as Ellie and Kay, seemingly oblivious to Stanley's financial worries, go on a shopping frenzy, returning with boxes of clothes and other commodities. Furthermore, an entire room of the house is gradually given over to wedding presents, including a kitschy statuette of Venus de Milo with a clock in its navel.

Social and economic concerns also influence the guest list: Ellie has to invite her entire garden club to the wedding – "they're running me for president," she explains in her own version of status panic – and Stanley feels obliged to host all his important clients. Kay, offended by the aspect of the wedding as social performance, compares it to a "business convention." As if to confirm this notion, Stanley's secretary recommends thinking of each of the guests as "reception units" costing exactly $3.75 per unit.

The most extreme example of the social humiliation experienced by the Banks comes in the scenes with the caterer, a dandified fellow who epitomizes in exaggerated degree the kind of snobbery that makes the wedding such a social and economic ordeal. When the caterer shows them a cake that had been served at the wedding of a princess, Stanley declares that since "every Tom, Dick, and Harry" has a cake at weddings, he doesn't want one. Unfortunately, however, Stanley's attempt at saving money backfires. The caterer agrees that "very select weddings" no longer have a cake, and suggests something more elegant such as a long table covered with salmon and cold sturgeon and a huge ice sculpture filled with colored lights. When Ellie asks for a simple supper of sandwiches and ice cream, he archly informs her that such cuisine is usually reserved for "children's parties."

The most dramatic representation of the repressed social anxieties brought out by the wedding is Stanley's dream the night before the event, a transparent allegory of his own socioeconomic fears. In the dream sequence, the bourgeois community is seen as a crowd of voyeurs, displaying their disapproval of a socially humiliated Stanley. Arriving late to the wedding, Stanley attempts to walk up the aisle to join the rest of the wedding party and begins to sink through the floor; when he tries to escape, his clothes become caught and his pants and shirt are torn to shreds, while the superimposed faces of the wedding guests provide a silent commentary on his futile efforts to stay above the surface. Finally, Kay herself screams at the horrifying spectacle of her bedraggled father, whose failure to retain his respectability is a source of her social humiliation.

Of course, on the wedding day all nightmares are forgotten, and the event goes relatively smoothly, providing the utopian happy ending required of Hollywood social comedies of the era. Despite its underlying tensions, the film depicts no real disturbance of the social order, one that it in fact supports. We need only compare the film's virtually "perfect" wedding with the nearly disastrous effects of a working-class wedding in Richard Brooks's 1956 drama *The Catered Affair* to see what a rosy picture of the bourgeois ritual Minnelli presents. In Brooks's film, Bette Davis plays a working-class Bronx housewife who insists on a larger and fancier wedding for her daughter (Debbie Reynolds) than her taxi-driver husband (Ernest Borgnine) can afford. In *Father of the Bride,* Stanley's exaggerated fears of being financially ruined by his daughter's wedding are treated without the aura of social realism Brooks provides. Though a keen observer of the nuances of class difference, Minnelli is not a true satirist, since his comedies are not intended to undermine the institutions or lifestyles at which they poke fun. Audiences would have to wait until later in the decade for the kind of trenchant social satire provided by Frank Tashlin and Billy Wilder—two directors who would engage in a more meaningful critique of the system that produced the anxieties Minnelli identifies.

## IV

The status panic experienced by middle-class Americans was exacerbated by the marketing of consumer goods through direct appeals to social status. Advertisers continually encouraged consumers to improve their station in life by "upgrading" to ever fancier and more expensive products. As Packard suggests, the "upgrading urge" drove middle-class and working-class consumers to adopt "the consuming patterns of people in the higher classes":

> By striving to buy the product – say, wall-to-wall carpeting on installment – the consumer is made to feel he is upgrading himself socially. Or the limited-success-class housewife can achieve that feeling by paying a few cents more each day for the brand of cigarette that is puffed so elegantly by the genuine Park Avenue matron in the cigarette advertisement. (308)

The most important of the various commodities sold as status enhancers in the immediate postwar era was the automobile, a product that was explicitly linked to socioeconomic status through advertising slogans such as "You must be rich to own a car as big as this" (Dodge), "Let the people behind you know you're ahead of them" (Ford), and "They'll know you've arrived when you drive up in an Edsel." Car makers established a ready-made social hierarchy for their buyers, with Chevrolet, Ford, and Plymouth as the entry-level vehicles targeted for lower-middle-class consumers, the highly promoted Edsel as "the car for the young executive on his way up," the Buick as "the chic, sleek car for doctors and upward-mobile semi-upper-class people," and the Cadillac as the top of the line, "the ultimate symbol of success."[9]

Hollywood was well aware of the automobile's aura as preeminent 1950s status symbol. In Richard Quine's 1956 cross-class comedy *The Solid Gold Cadillac,* the working-class heroine Laura Partridge (Judy Holliday) ends up with the fairy-tale grand prize of the eponymous golden car at the end, after she marries the founder of International Projects Corporation and helps him rescue the company from a corrupt board of directors. Significantly, as Ed Sikov has noted, the shift from black-and-white to color in the final two shots of the film foregrounds the utopian fantasyland of 1950s cinema while contributing to the fetishistic worship of the Cadillac in the film's final image.

In another Hollywood comedy of the same year, Frank Tashlin's *Hollywood or Bust,* the primary objects of fetishistic interest are Anita Ekberg's body and a bright red Chrysler New Yorker convertible which the Jerry Lewis and Dean Martin characters win at a movie theater raffle. Lewis's Malcolm Smith, a delicatessen worker and obsessive movie fan using the car to reach Hollywood and meet Ekberg "in the flesh," seems equally in love with both the car and the actress. He writes a poem to the car and has written hundreds of fan letters to Ekberg. The car's streamlined and gleaming exterior – which Lewis polishes and caresses with almost sexual attention – and Ekberg's curvaceous physique become twin embodiments of the exaggerated postwar vision of the American Dream.

A more frightening image of the postwar automobile and its accessories occurs in Vincente Minnelli's *The Long, Long Trailer* (1954), a film that pairs up the popular television couple of Lucille Ball and Desi Arnaz. In the film, Tacy (Ball) convinces her husband-to-be Nicky Collini (Arnaz) to buy an enormous and well-equipped trailer in which to travel across the country. What begins as an innocent (though rather harebrained) scheme to allow Tacy to accompany her husband on his trips around the country as a geological engineer soon turns into a nightmare version of middle-class status panic.

From the beginning, the trailer is associated with the form of middle-class stability and comfort that Tacy wants for herself and her new husband. When Nicky first laughs at her idea of buying a trailer, she explains that given the nature of his job it is a reasonable option:

> We'll always be living out of suitcases and using other people's things, living in some stale little hotel or some grubby furnished room. But don't you see, if we had a trailer no matter where we went I could make a home for you.

Tacy and Nicky appear to be a typical postwar couple of the aspiring middle class. Tacy's vision of their lifestyle cannot include "stale little hotels" and "grubby furnished rooms," and while she agrees to an austere budget of $1700 for the first year of marriage, her real aspirations are much grander. Showing Nicky the picture of a trailer for "only $1800," she argues that they can save money while still deriving the advantages of buying a home. At the trailer show, however, we see the postwar "upgrading urge" in full swing. The "show" is itself a consumer spectacle dedicated to the good life, with neon lights, a live orchestra, and young men diving off a high board into a model swimming pool. But the "Bungalette" model Tacy has originally priced turns out to be smaller and dingier than she thought. While "it looked enormous in the ad," she claims, it is in fact so cramped that they can hardly fit past the other couples who are inside, and they have difficulty standing up straight. At that point, the viewer's gaze is turned to an enormous and gleaming yellow-and-chrome trailer while Nicky's voiceover proclaims, with a sense of consumerist fatality, "and then we saw it." Everything about the larger trailer indicates the kind of bourgeois luxury and prestige Tacy dreams of having: electric chimes ring as they open the door, and rather than the crowd of lower-middle-class types filling the "Bungalette," this trailer contains only a well-dressed salesman who informs Tacy of its exact price: "$5345."

Although the trailer costs nearly three times as much as the "Bungalette," Tacy convinces Nicky that since the down payment is only a third of the total price they can still afford it. In order to pull the enormous portable home, however, they must make additional purchases, including a bigger car (a fancy new convertible requiring another $1300 down payment) and a heavy-duty hitch ("the best on the market today") as well as various other accessories. By the end of all this, as Nicky informs us, they are saddled with a debt of $7000 before the honeymoon even begins. The Collinis' spiralling debt is symptomatic of a postwar trend toward a seemingly endless borrowing needed to fuel the consumption patterns of a status-hungry middle class.

As Betty Friedan argued in *The Feminine Mystique* (1963), postwar advertisers targeted women in particular for status appeals, based on the assumption that middle-class women would feel the instability of their class identity more intensely than their male counterparts and find in consumption a way of publicly affirming their class position. This is certainly the case in *The Long, Long Trailer,* where Arnaz provides an effective rendition of "male passivity," allowing himself to be "beguiled and trapped by the caprices of the energetic better half."[10] Tacy not only convinces Nicky to buy the larger trailer, but manages to fill it beyond capacity with their possessions. In the days before the wedding, Tacy and her friends stock the closets so full of dishes, cookware, towels, and linens that there is no room for Nicky's clothes, let alone his bag of golf clubs. The trailer is a site for Tacy's middle-class consumerist fantasies, outfitted with every conceivable household gadget – including a sleek refrigerator and a gas range with see-through oven door. When Nicky asks her why she couldn't do with just one casserole, she seems appalled by the very suggestion that having a trailer rather than a home would mean having to "rough it." Naturally, she replies, she will need one pan for soufflés, another for sauces, and so on.

The trailer signifies an American consumer's dream that is both literally and figuratively out of control. When faced with the spectacle of the overloaded trailer, Nicky comments sarcastically that "we need a trailer for the trailer." The spectacle of Tacy's consumerism is so stressful for Nicky that he is forced to leave the trailer after experiencing a crisis of nerves. As Harvey comments, "The forty-foot trailer is a farcically malevolent force, literally dwarfing its mortal owners" (167). The series of misadventures that follows the wedding only makes Nicky – and the film's viewers — all the more convinced of his mistake in buying it. Nicky and Tacy hold up traffic on the two-lane highway getting out of town; they make a wrong turn and have a terrible time turning around; they spend their wedding night among a fanatically neighborly group of busybodies at a trailer park; they destroy the garage of Tacy's cousins; they get stuck in the mud on a country road and lock themselves out of the trailer; and, in the climactic scene, they almost go over a cliff on a curvy mountain pass.

Not only is the trailer physically too large for the Collinis to handle (there is a running gag throughout the film about Nicky forgetting to apply the brakes on the trailer before he stops the car and nearly being rear-ended by the entire weight of the trailer), but the 40-foot monstrosity is an aesthetic joke as well. Tacy's dream of "a little place we could call our own where I could take care of [my husband]" soon becomes an absurd joke, as the "little place" becomes physically weighted down and looms ever larger as a source of friction between them. As if Minnelli's joke about compulsive consumerism were not obvious enough, he takes it further by having Tacy pick up a large stone from the various places they visit along the way, each carefully labeled, in order to display them when they reach Colorado and make the trailer their "permanent" home. These rocks accumulate to such an extent that Nicky insists they be jettisoned from the already overweight trailer before they attempt to cross an 8000-foot pass in the Rocky Mountains. When Tacy surreptitiously hides the rocks in the cupboards rather than leave them behind, their shifting weight almost causes the trailer to topple over the cliff, a near-catastrophe that threatens to end their marriage and shift this comedy into melodrama.

The rocks – seemingly rather ordinary objects that are transformed into aesthetic fetishes by Tacy – are the embodiment of 1950s middle-brow kitsch. Although it is not clear to what extent Minnelli's examination of Tacy's "taste class" is meant as a more general critique of postwar Americans' delusional obsession with social status, there are a number of indications that class is very much at stake in the film. The film does everything it can to thwart any attempts by the Collinis to achieve a more dignified sense of their own status, as if the middle-class American dream is a mirage constantly receding down the highway.

*The Long, Long Trailer* can be read as the more farcical revision of Minnelli's *Father of the Bride*, his early 1950s paean to the upper-middle-class suburban life. In its use of a television comedy team known for its slapstick routines rather than "classier" Hollywood actors like Spencer

Tracy, Joan Bennett, and Elizabeth Taylor, in its glaring use of color as opposed to the more restrained black and white of *Father of the Bride*, and in its more ridiculous, gag-propelled story line as opposed to the earlier film's gestures toward sophisticated social comedy, *The Long, Long Trailer* is *Father of the Bride*'s kitschier mid-1950s counterpart. Here we find the "newer, rootless middle class" (Harvey), a class that succumbs to the temptations of technology and mobility but never achieves the bourgeois stability represented by the Banks family in *Father of the Bride*.

Minnelli's keen awareness of such social distinctions may be a result of his own upbringing as a lower-middle-class Italian American. As a young child, he was either on the road with his parents' vaudeville theater company or shuttled between grandparents and boarding schools; as a teenager, he supplemented the meager pay of his father (a freelance musician) by working as an apprentice sign painter. Even as a boy, Minnelli's eye for the difference between the plush decor of his wealthier neighbors and the chintzier furnishings of his own house gave him a "vague hunger for sophistication" and a deep appreciation of class and social status.[11]

Despite certain similarities between *Father of the Bride* and *The Long, Long Trailer* – including versions of status panic in both cases – the Bankses are of an entirely different social order from the Collinis, a difference conferred by their WASP background, their beautiful and tastefully furnished suburban home (complete with black maid), their larger bank account, and their attractive and well-groomed children (including the fetishized "bride" herself played by the impeccably outfitted Taylor). Tacy and Nicky Collini, on the other hand, are attempting to negotiate themselves into the class to which the Bankses already belong. While the subject of class is never alluded to directly, it manages to rear its ugly head at various junctures.

Minnelli's treatment of the night spent in a "Breezeway Trailer Park" is a good example. The sequence is punctuated with shots of a large loudspeaker making announcements in a seemingly continuous fashion, as if to remind us of the routinized nature of daily life within the trailer park and the total lack of privacy it allows. Tacy and Nicky seem conspicuously out of place in this prototypically lower-middle-class community, a subculture of "trailerites," as one woman calls them, who identify themselves according to the kind of "rig" they own. Tacy calls one of the women "Mrs. Vagabond," mistaking her trailer model for her name and by suggestion identifying her with the social rootlessness that seems to characterize all the park's inhabitants. Without any overt reference to class difference, Minnelli makes the distinction between the Collinis and the trailer-park inhabitants patently obvious, from the clothing they wear (mostly checkered or Hawaiian shirts and fishing caps in contrast to Nicky's neatly tailored suit) to their slightly "hick" accents and their manic desire to be "neighborly."

Yet while Nicky and Tacy are somewhat appalled by the trailer park culture, they are not entirely rooted in the more stable middle class either. When they crash their trailer into the Victorian house of Tacy's very respectable extended family, they not only forfeit their wedding present but also symbolically rupture their ties to a certain form of traditional bourgeois stability. Tacy, however, remains undaunted by the incident, remaining as proud of her trailer as any bourgeois housewife of her suburban home. Later, when Tacy tries to cook her husband a gourmet dinner of "ragout of beef" in the trailer while Nicky drives them to their next destination – (for some reason they are both unaware that one should never ride in the trailer while it is moving, much less try to cook in it) – she winds up in a disastrous mess of food and utensils.

Though recalling the automat scene from *Easy Living*, this is not a food riot pitting man against man (reflecting the Depression era's more overt social conflicts) but a struggle of woman against machine. Ball uses her conspicuous talents as a slapstick comedian to render almost believable the epic battle with the dinner, while Arnaz drives blithely along, singing operatically about the meal he is about to consume and remaining totally unaware of his wife's troubles. The scene can be read in several ways. In the most general sense, it represents postwar America's coming to terms with rampant technology (from the space-age trailer to the space-age rocket). On another level, it suggests the situation of the postwar (female) consumer, unable to control her own consumption or to achieve her needs for material status. The humor of the scene is heightened by the gap between the pretentiousness and exacting requirements of the meal itself (the Caesar salad must contain "aged Parmesan cheese" rather than Roquefort, according to Tacy, and the lettuce must be torn rather than cut) and the disaster of its preparation. On a final level, the scene situates more specifically the plight of the postwar suburban housewife, experiencing a profound (and potentially hazardous) isolation as she tries desperately to please her oblivious husband.

## V

In Billy Wilder's 1960 film *The Apartment,* C. C. Baxter (Jack Lemmon) is the prototype of the low-level, white-collar male of the postwar era, immobilized by status panic and trying to use any means at his disposal to work his way up the corporate ladder of success. Baxter epitomizes the "average guy" often played by Lemmon, a sincere, confused, and insecure little man in search of the American Dream. An ambitious office worker and a junior member of the white-collar staff, Baxter agrees to lend his bachelor pad to higher-ranking executives in exchange for the promise of advancement in the firm. The ultimate trophy for Baxter – if he continues to play along with his superiors – is a promotion to the executive ranks. The perks that go along with such a promotion are considerable: a luxurious office on the twenty-seventh floor, an expense account, and the use of the executive dining room and executive washroom.

If Wilder's film is a deft satirical portrait of the angst-ridden middle-class urban male, Tashlin's *Will Success Spoil Rock Hunter* (1957) is an even more devastating satire of the 1950s success ethic, as well as an effective parody of postwar corporate America. Rockwell P. Hunter (Tony Randall) is a low-level advertising copywriter who suddenly achieves success in his firm when he has the idea of signing on glamorous film star Rita Marlowe (Jayne Mansfield) to endorse the product of their most important client, Stay-Put Lipstick. In exchange for her endorsement, however, Rita demands that Rockwell pretend to have an affair with her in order to make her muscle-man boyfriend Bobo Branigansky jealous. As Rita's unlikely "Lover Doll," Rock not only becomes a worldwide celebrity, but goes through a series of rapid promotions, eventually becoming president of the company. At the end of the film, Hunter rejects the success he had always thought he wanted, deciding instead to pursue another lifelong dream of owning a chicken farm and marrying his "plain Jane" fiancée Jenny Wells.

Rock Hunter represents the middle-class American male for whom status panic and what we might call "success anxiety" are the obsessive preoccupations. Though Harvard educated, Rockwell cannot earn enough from his job as a hack writer of television commercials to allow him to marry his fiancée. He dreams of one day moving up in the corporation – perhaps to the exalted level of vice president – and thereby of obtaining the all-important key to the executive washroom. At the same time that he is terrified of losing his job at the agency and having to return to his ignominious position as an editor for a fan magazine, he is also highly ambivalent about achieving success. Even smoking a pipe – a symbol of status he hopes will give him a "successful, Gregory Peck look" – is fraught with tension for Rockwell.[12] As his psychoanalyst tells him, he fails to keep his pipe lit because he doesn't know whether to inhale (signifying a desire for success) or to exhale. Furthermore, Rockwell suffers the indignity of being treated as a nonentity within his firm. When the company president Mr. LaSalle ("Junior") passes him in the hallway, he does not even acknowledge Rockwell's existence.

More than any other film of the 1950s, *Will Success Spoil Rock Hunter* points out the extent to which contemporary American culture had been infected by the language and messages of advertising. During the credit sequence, Tashlin presents a series of parodies of television commercials for consumer products such as refrigerators, beer, hair tonic, electric razors, breakfast cereal, peanut butter, and detergent. The satire of middle-class suburban life and of the susceptibility of middle-class consumers to ridiculous advertising claims is clear in several of the ads. In one, a woman holds a box of "Wow" detergent: "'Wow' contains fallout, the exclusive, patented ingredient." She goes on to explain that the product may be hard on the hands and fingernails, but with a clean kitchen, housewives won't feel the need to scratch themselves. In an advertising spot for the "Easy-Clean" washing machine, a housewife struggles to pull the clothes out of the washer as she delivers a monologue about the gentleness of the machine on each garment.

The ads are an ironic setup for the opening voiceover of the film itself in which Randall tells us about his job on Madison Avenue – "the street of Grey Flannel Dreams" – where he works at an ad agency with a name so ridiculously long it is generally known only by its initials: "L, S, J, R, P & C." Rockwell's friend Rufus, a fellow "Harvard man," is a vice president of the agency; the extent of his success is measured by the fact that he has a key to the Executive Washroom and takes his lunches in the form of martinis and tranquilizers rather than sandwiches. "Junior," it turns out, has an even more prestigious washroom, reserved for him alone.

The action of the film begins when Rufus tells Rockwell he needs to come up with an effective promotional campaign for Stay-Put Lipstick or else risk losing the account. When Rockwell tries to present his idea for the campaign at a board meeting, he is fired. Fortunately, one of the Stay-Put executives notices his plan to use Rita Marlowe and her "oh-so-kissable lips" to endorse the product. If Rock can sign Rita to a contract, he is told, he will instantly be transformed from expendable flunky to a major "success" in the company.

The high point in the film's satiric vision of corporate upward mobility comes toward the end of the film, in the scenes in which Rockwell receives his promotions—first to vice president and then to president. These scenes parody status panic and the success ethic at its most exaggerated. When Rock first sees his title of vice president on his new office door, he is understandably excited: "I never thought I'd live to see that; it makes everything that's happened seem worthwhile." But the predictable promotion scene turns to a parody of the "grey flannel dream" when Rock is given the key to the Executive Washroom. The Executive Washroom, with its "imported liquid soap," is a kind of temple to the success ethic. "This means I'm an executive," Rock declares fatuously, as Rufus, teary-eyed, hands him the key. Rock walks to the bathroom door, accompanied by background strains of "Hail to the Chief," and enters the inner sanctum while angelic singing is heard in the background. "Oh, the beauty of it all," he proclaims, overwhelmed by the fruits of his own success.

The over-the-top quality of Tashlin's gag is saved only by the fact that the Executive Washroom is connected to a more general motif of scatalogical references. When Rockwell is first fired by Junior, he tells his boss off in no uncertain terms: "You're just a little poop of a man, and that's the way the poop poops." Rockwell's language – simultaneously obscene and childish – seems to be emblematic of spoken discourse throughout the film. Rufus, for example, speaks in a jokey form of corporatese that often involves childish constructions such as "your problem can be solvie-solvie" or "we're on the gravy choo-choo," and he insists on infantalizing Rockwell as "Rocky-boy." Rita has an equally infantile tendency to think that any word of more than three syllables must be obscene. "Seclusion sounds so dirty," she titters during a television interview, and when Rockwell asks for her "endorsement," she admonishes him not to "start talking dirty." Both on Madison Avenue and in the entertainment industry, it seems, language has been reduced to the sanitized and infantilized discourse that can be used on television and in advertising. In one gender-bended euphemism, the Executive Washroom becomes the "Executive Powder Room."

If *Will Success Spoil Rock Hunter* has not achieved the status of classic Hollywood comedy in the same sense as the films of Capra, Hawks, Sturges, or Wilder, it is a hilariously transgressive romp through the postwar era, conflating class, sex, and language with more subversive abandon than any other film of the period. Tashlin takes a perverse delight in satirizing not only the middle-class success ethic, but also forms of class privilege, particularly those associated with an Ivy League background. The number of jokes at the expense of Harvard in the film suggests that the socioeconomic advantages automatically conferred by a Harvard education are on the wane in this faster-paced and more cynical postwar environment, and that a Harvard degree may even have become something of a liability in a world dominated by popular culture and television. The film's plot (and Rockwell's success) depends on both the creation of Rita Marlowe (the "goddess of love" with the "oh-so-kissable lips") by the popular media and the manipulation of the media (fabricating a "Lover Doll" for personal and promotional purposes) by Rita. As Rufus tells Rock, success no longer has anything to do with talent, accomplishment, or education. Rather, it is a matter of "being at the right place at the right time." When Rock reaches the executive rank, Rufus comments sardonically, "It's a miracle how you overcame your education." Much more valuable than Rockwell's Harvard diploma, which has so far only gotten him low-paying jobs as a copywriter and has given him an inflated sense of his own prospects in the world, is the serendipitous fact that his niece is president of the local chapter of the Rita Marlowe Fan Club.

Class consciousness is exhibited differently by the various characters in the film. Rita, for example, is impressed by Rockwell's vaguely upper-class name, which she thinks "sounds very influential." In order to impress her boyfriend Bobo with the social status of her new beau, she further inflates his name to the even wealthier-sounding "Rock Huntington" and represents him as "president" of the firm rather than merely an ad writer. "Junior," on the other hand, is embarrassed by his own background, having achieved "success by the dubious route of inheritance." Although such a route seems no more dubious than those of Rita or Rock himself, Junior feels that his inherited position in the company has been more of a burden than an asset. "Being the son of an illustrious parent is far from an easy road," he maintains, as the imposing portrait of his father and founder of the company (Mr. LaSalle Sr.) looks down on him from his office wall. Junior, as it turns out, is also a rather reluctant "big-shot." He would rather be a horticulturalist than an advertising executive, and his chief aspiration is to win first prize in a flower show. In a later scene, after handing over the reins of the firm to Rock, Junior receives him in his greenhouse, where the portrait of his father now hangs, partially covered over with ivy. As "Fair Harvard" plays in the background, Junior tells Rock mischievously that "Daddy was the first 'Ivy Leaguer.'"

The film is one of the few comedies of the period to address class relations in any direct way, and yet its irreverence about class background and class affiliation work against any attempt to posit a class-based social critique. Instead of the polarization of class positions we find in the comedies of the 1930s, the film presents a confusing array of class identities. It is significant in terms of the film's social economy that Rockwell, Rufus, and Junior are all Harvard graduates. Thus they are marked in at least one respect as occupying a more elevated class position, and yet they occupy very different positions on the social scale. Junior represents the established upper class with its patriarchal succession, its effete manners and hobbies, and its inherited wealth and economic power within corporate America; Rufus represents the midlevel executive, the quintessential "organization man" whose upper-middle-class existence is marked by a preoccupation with psychoanalysis, a penchant for cocktails and tranquilizers, and a simultaneously cynical and reverential attitude toward corporate "success"; and Rock is the middling middle-class male, barely able to keep his head above water in the corporate environment and torn between the hope of actually "making it" in the business world and the dream of retiring to a quiet life of chicken farming.

Rita, on the other hand, who has risen from what are presumably more humble social origins (her one true love was a man named George Schmidling) embodies the *nouveau riche* lifestyle of the entertainment world. She lives in a dream-world of material excess, moving from luxuriant bubblebaths to silky pyjamas, and she is literally able to change social reality by her whim. When she needs a new boyfriend, she transforms the unassuming Rock into her media-inspired image of the successful and upwardly mobile Rockwell Hunter, executive, "lover doll," and media darling.

Ultimately, both social status and corporate success are shown to be empty promises, and Rock himself – to answer the question posed by the film's title – will not be "spoiled" by his success. Rock's first night in Junior's old office as the new president of the firm convinces him that he is not cut out for the life of an executive. Although he is initially seduced by the power and prestige symbolized by the office (he dances around the room accompanied by the repeated refrain "you've got it made"), Rock remains unable to keep his pipe lit, suggesting that he may lack the requisite qualifications for the job. Rock's speech to Jenny on the following morning, however, is enough to convince her of his sincerity:

> ROCKWELL: I'm not a failure; I'm the largest success there is. I'm an average guy, and all us average guys are successes. We run the works, not the big guy behind the big desk. He's knocking himself out trying to please us, please you and me and all the other us's like us.

Rockwell's redefinition of "success" would appear to suggest some moment of social authenticity in the film, as he finally realizes the impossibility of assuming a class position other than that of "average guy." Yet Rock's realization, while it does lead to the film's inevitably happy conclusion, is a rather bathetic rendering of democratic social ideology, a parody of the Capraesque social "corn" of the 1930s. Just as in Preston Sturges's comedies – with which it shares its comic-book tendency to caricature and exaggeration – we see a deep cynicism behind the cheery resolution. "We've all learned that success is just being happy," the assembled characters pronounce in a final tableau of parodic averageness. Status panic has been replaced in mock-utopian fashion by a society apparently void of class difference, a world so antiseptically phony it appears as merely another Madison Avenue gimmick.

## VI

If Lemmon's and Randall's performances capture the plight of the "average guy," the insecure middle-class male caught between status panic and the anxiety of achieving success in the white-collar world, it is Jerry Lewis who more than any other comic performer of the 1950s and 1960s represents the social repression of the postwar era. Lewis epitomizes a more hysterical version of the same social anxieties found in Randall's and Lemmon's roles. Indeed, there are marked similarities between the roles played by the three actors. Lemmon's comic roles of the 1950s and early 1960s – like those of Lewis – embody motifs of domesticity and neurosis *(The Odd Couple)*, gender-switching *(Some Like It Hot)*, and demasculinizing passivity (*The Apartment* and *The Fortune Cookie*). Randall, who took over the Felix Unger role from Lemmon in the Broadway and television versions of *The Odd Couple*, specialized in the role of the sidekick/confidant to more "masculine" male leads, especially Rock Hudson. As a Jewish actor in postwar Hollywood, Randall (Leonard Rosenberg), does not overtly announce his ethnicity in his performances, yet his persona can be interestingly read in the context of Lewis's more ethnically marked characters. Furthermore, Randall's performances in films like *Pillow Talk*, the 1959 Rock Hudson/Doris Day comedy directed by Michael Gordon, are sexually ambiguous in much the same way Lewis's are.

In *Pillow Talk*, Randall plays Jonathan Forbes, a fastidious, whiny, and neurotic millionaire who is both the client and unsuccessful suitor of Jan Morrow (Day) and the best friend and patron of Brad Allen (Hudson). Jonathan, who talks constantly about his analyst and his failures with women, is coded as a closet gay, or at least an ambivalent heterosexual. He blames his problems with women (including three divorces) on unresolved feelings toward his mother; he is pathetically inadequate in his attempts to seduce Jan; he maintains a somewhat foppish appearance in distinction to Brad's more ruggedly masculine look; and he is physically dominated by Brad, for whom he has somewhat ambiguous feelings. Jonathan's feminized relations with Brad and his desexualized encounters with Jan (at one point they try an experimental kiss but no "rockets" go off) point to an identity that is, in the words of Cynthia Fuchs, "not quite gay and not quite straight."[13] As Fuchs suggests, Jonathan's status as "at once overtly queer and subversively straight" problematizes any attempt to place him in a particular category and destabilizes postwar gender roles in much the same way that Lewis's performances do. Randall's character, though never identified as Jewish, is also excluded from the normative middle-class WASP position occupied by both Brad and Jan in the film. At one point, Jonathan complains of his "oppression": "Some people are prejudiced against me because I'm a part of a minority." When Brad asks him, "What minority?" he answers, "Millionaires." While Fuchs reads this exchange as an embedded reference to Jonathan's "gay" identity, the more likely subtext in postwar America would be his Jewishness, which at that time was a more recognized "minority" status than homosexuality. Both sexuality and ethnicity – as possible subtexts for the joke – are mediated through Jonathan's class status as a dilettantish, ineffectual, and unproductive millionaire. Although Jan and Brad both work (Jan as an interior decorator, Brad as a songwriter), the only uses of Jonathan's inherited wealth appear to be redecorating his office and subsidizing Broadway shows.

The Lewis persona was, in an even more exaggerated way than Randall's character, "a glaring inversion of acceptable standards governing the body, maturity, and masculinity" during the postwar era."[14] In his effeminate mannerisms, protogay behaviors, and tendency to play nurturing, "feminized" characters, the Lewis persona inverts acceptable postwar models of male sexuality and gender roles. As the flagrantly incompetent "idiot," Lewis also subverts notions of mental and emotional normalcy in an era obsessively concerned with sanity and mental competence. And in his persona of "The Kid" – with his regressive childishness and reluctance to accept the responsibilities of adult life – he plays with contemporary ideals of psychic and sexual maturity.

What has been less often noted than these perhaps more obvious aspects of Lewis's performances is the function of social class in his films. In many of his roles, Lewis serves as an antithetical "other" to the complacently middle-class definition of mainstream America. In most of his films of the 1950s and early 1960s – both those in which he teamed with Dean Martin and in his solo career – Lewis plays some form of socially subordinate or marginalized role: a beleaguered army private in *At War with the Army* (1950), a comedy stooge in *The Stooge* (1953), a busboy in *Scared Stiff* (1953), a golf caddy in *The Caddy* (1953), a barber's apprentice in *You're Never Too Young* (1955), a delicatessen worker in *Hollywood or Bust* (1956), an apprentice janitor in *The Delicate Delinquent* (1957), another army loser in *The Sad Sack* (1957), a clumsy magician in *The Geisha Boy* (1958), an oppressed stepson and household servant in *CinderFella* (1960), a hotel bellboy in *The Bellboy* (1960), a film studio gopher boy in *The Errand Boy* (1961), the handyman at a girl's school in *The Ladies' Man* (1961), a dog-walker and department-store flunky in *Who's Minding the Store* (1963), a hospital orderly in *The Disorderly Orderly* (1964), a Hollywood bellhop in *The Patsy* (1964), and a meek bank clerk in *The Big Mouth* (1967).

Much of the humor in these films results from Lewis's social position, which usually involves a lower class status than that of the people around him. In *The Ladies Man,* for example, Lewis's character Herbert H. Hee-bert undergoes a downward social mobility after graduating valedictorian of his junior college class. (Lewis's use of funny names again places him in the American comic tradition of Fields, the Marx Brothers, and Preston Sturges.) Herbert takes a job as a houseboy at a Hollywood home for wayward young women, run by a wealthy widow and former opera singer. Here Lewis's subordination is simultaneously social and sexual – a confusion the title encourages – as both his servile status and his infantilized masculinity (the women insist on calling him "Herby") make him a totally unthreatening presence. Herbert's "need to be needed" (generally coded as a feminine quality) and his supposed hostility toward women (brought on by the loss of his college sweetheart to another man) are a cover for the era's containment of sexuality within an overtly sexual context (a man living among dozens of nubile young women). Even in films where Lewis plays a role with more ostensible sociocultural capital, such as that of Professor Julius Kelp in *The Nutty Professor,* he is placed in a subordinate position, bullied by both his superiors in the college administration and his students, such as the football player who stuffs him into a closet of his chemistry lab while calling him "naughty."

A less overtly stated level of Lewis's performances, but one that can be related to his social position within the films, is that of the ethnic (Jewish) other. Although Lewis's persona is not overtly coded as Jewish in the same sense as Woody Allen's or those of the Marx Brothers, his nerdy, dominated, physically inadequate, sexually complexed, and socially inept characters can be seen as playing on cultural stereotypes of the American Jewish male and anticipating Allen's more overtly coded Jewish characters. As Scott Bukatman suggests, *The Nutty Professor* is "easily understood as a discourse of Jewish self-hatred (in which Jerry Lewis is literally transformed into the Italian Dean Martin)."[15] And Robert Liebman reads Lewis's Julius Kelp as "a schlemiel to the extreme," a "meek, myopic, gawky chemistry professor" who epitomizes "the academically successful, socially retarded Nice Jewish Boy, complete with domineering mother, docile father, and *shikse* fixation."[16] In one outtake from the film, Lewis revealingly ad-libbed the line "Perhaps I was stupid" as "Perhaps I was a stupid Jew." Kelp's alter ego Buddy Love, on the other hand, is "a Jewish male's fantasy of the . . . goy perpetually indulging in sensual delights."[17] Even the transformation of the character's name from Julius Kelp to Buddy Love suggests a motif of assimilation to the exaggerated vision of a WASP playboy. (Lewis's own name was similarly anglicized from the more ethnic-sounding Joe Levitch.)

The intersection of class, gender, and ethnicity in Lewis's films of the 1950s and 1960s is unique among Hollywood comedies of the postwar era, expressing a profound discomfort with the era's dominant social ideology. But although Lewis's adoption of a subordinate socioeconomic and even ethnic position in many of his films would seem to indicate a level of meaningful social critique, the writers and directors of Lewis's films (including Lewis himself) generally seem more interested in producing verbal and physical gags than in engaging in a deeper exploration of the social issues the films, perhaps inadvertently, raise. Although a film like *The Delicate Delinquent* (Don McGuire, 1957) makes a gesture toward addressing class issues on a more overt level, most of Lewis's performances can be more usefully read as subverting the very possibility of coherent social constructions rather than as critiquing existing social structures.[18] In *CinderFella*, for example, Lewis plays "Fella," the poor stepson and lackey to his stepmother and two stepbrothers, who are less "evil" (in the terms of the original fairy tale) than simply greedy and socially ambitious. Lacking the class pretensions and social ambitions of his bourgeois stepfamily, who live in a Bel Air mansion and spend most of their time going shopping and playing tennis and polo, Fella is despised by them and treated as a menial servant. The film could be read as a commentary on the materialist greed of the postwar era, but its fairy-tale plot and its escapist resolution reduce the force of its potential as social critique. The ending – in which Fella gets both his father's money (from a hollow tree full of gold) and the princess – is more utopian than transgressive.

Lewis's films pose a challenge not so much to structures of social class as to the postwar construction of masculinity in all its social manifestations, enacting "a refusal to occupy any rigidly fixed subject position."[19] Lewis's treatment of social identity anticipates the postmodern treatment of social structures in the films of Woody Allen, Mel Brooks, and other comic film-makers of the 1970s and 1980s more than it approximates the level of social critique by such modernist film comics as Chaplin or the Marx Brothers. Films like *The Nutty Professor,* with its dual personality plot, and *The Family Jewels* (1965), in which Lewis plays seven different characters, may be the most clearly thematized version of what Bukatman calls Lewis's "elusive and elided self," but several of the films point in some way to the artificiality of social identity.[20] In *CinderFella,* for example, Lewis plays an updated and gender-switched version of the fairy-tale character. Lewis/Fella has a Fairy Godfather (played by Ed Wynn with obviously gay overtones) who makes sure that he not only gets the princess at the end but also discovers a large inheritance from his father. The film's destabilization of social categories is accompanied by a similar destabilization of fixed gender categories: Fella cooks, cleans, and waits on his stepmother and step-brothers in a role of highly feminized houseboy.

Lewis's emasculated social and sexual persona is also represented lin-guistically in many of his films, as his famous linguistic contortions prob-lematize his relationship to both gendered and class-based modes of speech. Lewis's speech is pathologically nervous. He stutters, stammers, places the emphasis on the wrong syllable, has trouble finishing sentences and pronouncing people's names, and is continually distorting verbal expressions and garbling syntax to the point of absurdity. Lewis talks at cross purposes to his interlocutors, ties himself into verbal knots, or speaks in guttural noises rather than words. The lack of verbal fluency and the pinched, nasal delivery of Lewis's typical characters can be read as infantile or imbecilic, but his characteristic form of speech can also be interpreted as a class-based form of linguistic habitus, particularly given the fact that Lewis's speech fails him most often in the presence of authority figures.

If a film like *The Nutty Professor* marks linguistically the resistance to fixed subjectivity through the juxtaposition of the nasal and faltering speech of Professor Kelp with the crooning, self-confident, and rhetori-cally persuasive speech (and singing) of his alter ego Buddy Love, the most extreme example of this bifurcation, *The Bellboy,* splits Lewis into the inept (and silent) bellboy and the successful entertainer. In this film, Lewis plays Stanley the bellboy at a hotel visited by the celebrity "Jerry Lewis." While Lewis as "Stanley" is denied the power of speech altogether (his silence, like Harpo's, also being a sign of his low socioeconomic status and lack of social power), Lewis as "Lewis" is the smooth-talking "star," surrounded by an enormous entourage and feted by the hotel management. The persona of "Jerry Lewis" – who as a stand-up and film comedian depends on his exceptional verbal abilities – is the linguistic and social antithesis of the tongue-tied Stanley, a character related explicitly to the comedian Stan Laurel of the Laurel and Hardy comedy team. Like Lewis, Laurel played the dominated member of a successful comedy duo; his performances were also marked by an imbecilic nature and a lack of verbal fluency. Thus the allusion to Laurel in Lewis's first self-directed comedy can be read as a commentary on his part in the Lewis/Martin team.

Lewis's disruption of language and linguistic convention enunciates the refusal of a coherent subject position, and it represents a rejection of the dominant male persona of the postwar era. The normative middle-class male – whether in the form of the executive in the grey flannel suit or the smooth operator exemplified by Cary Grant, Rock Hudson, Dean Martin, or the fictional Buddy Love – is the absence that defines Lewis's disturbing presence. Lewis, even with his social and sexual ambivalence, was the most successful film clown of the 1950s and 1960s because he epitomized all that was repressed by mainstream American society. Lewis's characters and performances put into question postwar Americans' normalized ideologies concerning work, money, social status, gender, and sexual identity. At the same time, Lewis's comedies helped set the stage for the postmodern comedy of Woody Allen, a form of comedy that would reinscribe Lewis's gag-based comedic performance within the more sophisticated tradition of American verbal comedy.

Lewis's films have a transgressive potential that reveals itself more clearly when they are read in the context of prewar comedies like those of the screwball genre, with their "unruly women" as subversive social agents. The figure of Lewis uses both gender and class to call into question a society that denied class difference even as it incited status panic. At the same time, however, the lack of *overt* references to class conflict in Lewis's films suggests that there are certain ideological patterns that even the most critical of the postwar comedies simply refused to engage.

# 6

# IS THERE A CLASS
# IN THIS TEXT?

## Woody Allen and Postmodern Comedy

The conflict is no longer about: Can I find work?
Can I cope with nuts and bolts in a factory?
It is: Can I stand the stress and pressure
of working in an affluent society?
Woody Allen

## I

The world depicted in the American comedies of the 1920s and 1930s underwent a radical shift in the postwar era, necessitating an equally fundamental change in the dominant modes of film comedy. While the Marx Brothers films engage in a certain amount of more open-ended parody (particularly in their more "anarchic" films like *Duck Soup*), the primary mode of their humor is satirical. It is directed at particular institutions, milieus, professions, and social classes. In Woody Allen's films, on the other hand, although a good deal of direct social and political satire remains, the dominant mode is parodic.

Allen's filmic *oeuvre* is often cited as the paradigmatic example of comic postmodernism, and Allen's work as an intertextual or metareferential filmmaker has attracted the attention of numerous commentators. From his first film, *What's Up, Tiger Lily?* (1967), a re-edited and redubbed version of a Japanese James Bond-type thriller, through more fully realized parodies such as *Take the Money and Run* (1969), *Stardust Memories* (1980), *Zelig* (1983), and *The Purple Rose of Cairo* (1985), Allen has made consistent use of parodic elements in his films.[1] Yet at the same time we can read Allen as a highly effective social satirist, a filmmaker determined to expose the hypocrisies and excesses of contemporary American life and to analyze the foibles of various cultural milieus. This satiric mode can be seen most clearly in films like *Bananas* (1971), *Sleeper* (1973), *Annie Hall* (1977), and *Manhattan* (1979), in which Allen exposes such aspects of modern life as the deadening effects of a uniformly affluent and technologized society, the sterile and hedonistic show business culture of southern California, and the misguided cadre of proto-yuppie intellectuals inhabiting contemporary New York City. In general, Allen's films criticize what he calls the "cultural junk food" of contemporary American culture, the ubiquitous falsity of a mediatized, commodified, and consumeristic society.

Allen's work, situated as it is on the margins of mainstream Hollywood comedy, exemplifies postmodern comedy's resistance to placement within any easily definable comic tradition. Neither art house films nor mainstream Hollywood products, his comedies defy simple cultural definition. Furthermore, Allen's films are generically hybrid. His own instantly recognizable comic persona, his use of sequences of "gags" to construct his films, and his frequent adoption of physical and slapstick elements, all tend to locate his films within the tradition of "comedian comedy" as exemplified by silent comics like Chaplin and Buster Keaton as well as comedians of the sound era like W. C. Fields, the Marx Brothers, Laurel and Hardy, Bob Hope, and Jerry Lewis. On the other hand, Allen's interest in exploring the intricacies of romantic plots, his predominant use of dramatic Hollywood actors rather than comics, his tendency to treat more "serious" themes or narratives within a comic frame, and his frequent reference to classical Hollywood and European cinema, seem to place many of his films within the genre of classical romantic comedy or social comedy as made by directors from Lubitsch to Wilder.[2]

Allen can also be identified as a typically postmodern filmmaker – in Fredric Jameson's terms – by virtue of his frequent use of historical pastiche or parody, both on the level of actual settings in the past and in relation to films and filmic conventions of the past.[3] *Bullets over Broad-*

*way* is set in the 1920s, *Purple Rose of Cairo* in the Depression-era 1930s, and *Radio Days* in the 1940s of his Brooklyn childhood. *Love and Death* is set in czarist Russia, and *A Midsummer Night's Sex Comedy* takes place in a turn-of-the-century country house. *Broadway Danny Rose* evokes Manhattan's theatrical past by presenting the world of small-time night-club acts that had largely disappeared by the time Allen began performing in the early 1960s. *Zelig* takes us through a range of historical moments, including the Roaring Twenties, the Depression, and the rise of Nazi Germany. Yet other films play with modes of nostalgia and historical pastiche in a variety of ways. *Take the Money and Run* spoofs the gangster film genre of the 1930s; *Stardust Memories* evokes the rarified cultural atmosphere of the 1960s; *Sleeper,* while it is set in the future, re-creates the filmmaker's present (the early 1970s) as a nostalgic past, with references to health food restaurants, Richard Nixon, Norman Mailer, and Charles de Gaulle; *Play it Again, Sam* parodies the more romantic world portrayed by Hollywood films of the 1940s; and even *Manhattan,* though set in the present, uses black-and-white cinematography and a musical score composed of Gershwin songs to create a highly nostalgic vision of New York City.

What I will refer to in the final two chapters of this book as "postmodern comedy" – a genre exemplified by the work of such filmmakers as Woody Allen, Mel Brooks, Joel and Ethan Coen, John Waters, Susan Seidelman, Albert Brooks, Hal Hartley, Jim Jarmusch, and Whit Stillman – is perhaps less thematically determined than films of other genres, such as science fiction, but it nevertheless exhibits many of the same features of postmodern cultural production as a whole. Unlike the vast majority of Hollywood comedies – which continue to rely on the conventional structures of romantic comedy, domestic comedy, or farce – postmodern comedy uses devices such as parody or pastiche, citation, and the self-conscious or self-reflexive play with standard genres and traditions of Hollywood film, in order to ironize both contemporary social codes and more specific codes of Hollywood production. An early example of the postmodern comedy would be a film like Woody Allen's *Sleeper* (1973), which combines these various elements in a series of parodic styles: the relationship of Allen's character Miles Monroe with Diane Keaton's Luna introduces the romantic comedy trope of a screwball sparring match; the use of Chaplinesque silent sequences and

Keystone Kops chases serves as an *homage* to the masters of silent comedy; and the parody of science fiction and dystopic films introduces a postmodern play with noncomic genres. In the process, Allen also uses his futuristic setting to satirize various aspects of contemporary social life: the robot servants and sterile luxury of the living spaces function as a parody of the postmodern "yuppie" lifestyle. In *Sleeper,* Allen presents a vision of human society that has fallen into a kind of hedonistic apathy. Sex is a subject studied at university (everyone is frigid, though Luna has a Ph.D. in oral sex), while physical human contact has been replaced by a cubicle known as the "Orgasmatron."

Allen's comedy may be less overtly satirical than that of the Marx Brothers and less tied to a particular class dynamic, but it nonetheless participates in a complex form of ideological commentary and critique. Allen's comedies take as their starting point the postmodern culture inhabited by the affluent and educated urban dweller – from artist and yuppie to would-be artist and ersatz yuppie. Allen views this culture from the perspective of the perennial social outsider, a figure who is at once part of the urban demographic he critiques and separated (or alienated) from it. For both ethnic and sociocultural reasons, Allen's persona feels excluded from certain class positions and affiliations. Although his films are not as obviously concerned with issues of social class as the comedies of Capra and Sturges, they are deeply concerned with a diagnosis of certain tendencies in contemporary American society.

Over time, Allen's comic persona has remained remarkably consistent. The neurotic, neurasthenic, sexually tormented, angst-ridden, death-obsessed character established in his early films has become a defining postmodern antihero for the late twentieth century, just as Chaplin's tramp was a representative antihero for the early decades of the century and Lewis's hysterically spastic nerd was an antiheroic icon for the postwar era. The Allen figure is, as Graham McGann suggests, a character "disaffected by the acquisitive consumer society . . . wary of convention . . . [and] dwarfed by the monsters of industry, science, business, and government."[4] Excluded by what he perceives to be the WASP-dominated establishment, Allen's persona is socially inept and highly self-conscious about his own ethnicity. He is in fact an updated version of the *schlemiel* figure, the helpless little man engaged in a ceaseless struggle against every conceivable natural and human obstacle.

Yet at the same time, Allen's persona is intellectually and culturally sophisticated in a way the Marx Brothers could never be in their films. Even when Groucho successfully dupes the middle-class WASP society he frequents, the audience and at least some of the characters are always aware of his true social identity. Allen, on the other hand, has a more difficult time convincing *himself* of his own right to belong than he does convincing other people. He is a social misfit not because of his class position, but because he is unable to overcome a combination of ethnic anxiety and a sense of physical, psychological, and cultural inferiority. Both Groucho's and Allen's characters live in fear of being "found out," of being revealed as phonies by the society that surrounds them. For Groucho the insecurity that motivates him is linked primarily to socioeconomic status (a status that is often a cover for an unassimilated and "unacceptable" ethnic identity). In contrast, for Allen the insecurity is linked to a fundamental fear that despite his superficial ability to play the game required by upwardly mobile urban society, his real intellectual and cultural capital are inadequate to both social and sexual success in a highly educated, culturally sophisticated milieu.[5]

Groucho and his brothers were the product not only of a different age and sensibility, but also of a less assimilated ethnic milieu. The urban Jewish ghetto of the early twentieth century was very different from the Flatbush, Brooklyn of Allen's youth, a relatively assimilated, though still predominantly Jewish, lower-middle-class neighborhood.[6] Nevertheless, Allen's identification of himself as Jewish is clear in virtually every film. As Gerald Mast has suggested, "Allen, unJewish, is as unthinkable as Chaplin without his cane, Groucho without his cigar, or Fields without his nose."[7] Although he may claim never to have suffered direct ethnic discrimination, he is acutely aware – at times to the point of paranoia – of the cultural differences between Jews and non-Jews. Allen's work is filled with references to Nazism, the Holocaust, and antisemitism. In one of the most famous scenes from *Annie Hall,* Allen's character Alvy Singer envisions himself sitting at the Halls' WASP dinner table in the guise of an Hasidic Jew, complete with beard, black hat, and coat. As Mast remarks, this vision of "the most extreme form of unassimilated American Jewry" calls on the stereotype of "the freaky, tacky foreignness of Jews, strangers in the strange American heartland of the clean, bright, open, tasteful, stylish, normal Halls" (132). In a film so deeply concerned with the crossing of ethnic and other social barriers (Jewish vs. WASP; intellectual culture vs. popular culture; New York vs. southern California), it is significant that Allen twice repeats Groucho's joke about not wanting to belong to any club that would have someone like him as a member. Whereas Groucho was subject to pressures that were predominantly socioeconomic, Allen is subject to the generic pressures of life in a commodified and mediatized postmodern society, as well as the particular social pressures deriving from his ethnic identity and family background. The pressures within a middle-class Jewish household to finish a conventional education and accept a conventional career are a dominant motif in Allen's films.

Allen's Jewish references can be read in class terms as well as ethnic terms. As Eric Lax suggests, "under different circumstances of birth [these references] could just as easily have been those of a lower-middle-class Irish Catholic in Boston who saw prettier women and a more interesting life across the river and set out to get there."[8] Perhaps the most overt comic reference to his own class anxieties can be found in the first sketch of *Everything You Always Wanted to Know about Sex (*but were afraid to ask)*. In the short film, entitled "Do Aphrodisiacs Work?", Allen plays a court jester named Felix who tries unsuccessfully to have sex with the queen, played by the statuesque Lynn Redgrave. In a parody of *Hamlet*, Felix is ordered by his father's ghost to seduce the queen but replies that it is impossible for a "baseborn" court fool to have sex with a queen: "I can't screw above my station." Here the fool can be seen as an allegorical representation of Allen himself: a social misfit who is not only of low social standing but also an obvious anachronism (a modern Jewish stand-up comic in a medieval setting), he is an ironic outsider misunderstood by his society.[9] The fact that the fool's comic routine is not especially funny and is in particularly poor taste (he makes jokes about the black plague in the midst of an epidemic) is only part of the problem. We have the sense that even with the world's best material, his humor would not be understood by this audience. Felix does succeed in getting the queen's sexual interest when he slips her an aphrodisiac potion, but his attempts to break open her chastity belt with an enormous pike wake the king, who discovers him with the queen and orders his beheading. The moral of the film is one that will be thematized in several of Allen's works, from *Play it Again, Sam* to *Annie Hall* to *Manhattan:* a "baseborn" social misfit like Allen has no business trying to sleep with a WASP queen, even if he is lucky enough to find an effective means of seducing her. We see this same tendency to identify ethnicity with class in Allen's noncomic film *Interiors* (1978), where the lower-middle-class and ostensibly Jewish character of Pearl is contrasted with the family of upper-middle-class New England WASPs into which she marries. And we see it again in the semiautobiographical *Radio Days,* in which the lower-middle-class Jewish Brooklyn of Allen's youth is contrasted with the glamorous dwellings and social clubs of the non-Jewish radio performers to whom they listen.

## II

In *Take the Money and Run,* the first film that Allen wrote and directed himself, Allen plays with conventions of both narration and historicity as he presents the life of his humorously criminal protagonist Virgil Starkwell. Throughout the film, cinema verité footage of a contemporary setting (the late 1960s) is mixed with black-and-white footage from earlier eras, while the voiceover narration, performed in mock-newsreel style by "March of Time" narrator Jackson Beck, provides a false sense of documentary realism. The film also contains parodies of prominent films from very different eras – from 1930s crime films like *I Am a Fugitive from a Chain Gang* and *You Only Live Once* to films of the 1960s such as *West Side Story, Bonnie and Clyde, The Hustler,* and *Cool Hand Luke.* Virgil Starkwell's name may evoke the gangsters of the Depression era (it was actually suggested by the famous 1950s murderer Charles Starkweather), but his experience is filled with clichés of modern life such as sessions with a Freudian psychiatrist and a job interview where he is asked if he has experience working with high-speed computers.

Allen's parodic use of Virgil's criminal "career" anticipates the more radical assumption of different identities by the protagonist of *Zelig.* Virgil's life, as Maurice Yacowar suggests, is "a pastiche of films whose values, illusions, and life styles he has absorbed as if by osmosis."[10] Virgil's recurrent failures appear to be based primarily on images from the movies. Whether it is a botched bank robbery or a blundered prison escape, Virgil is constantly measured against the standard of Hollywood gangsters and the plots of Hollywood films. That Virgil is fundamentally unsuited to a life of crime – both physically and temperamentally – never seems to occur to him, though he does attempt to legitimate himself by inventing identities at the other end of the social spectrum: first as a musician (a cellist with the "Philharmonic") and later as an obstetrician.

The film parodies both the social realist crime film – providing through Beck's voiceover commentary the details of a childhood of poverty and violence – and the American success ethic. Virgil is the quintessential *schlemiel*, repeatedly failing to prosper within the world of crime. He robs a butcher shop of veal cutlets but then has to steal the bread crumbs to go with them; he carefully cuts a pane of glass out in order to rob a jewelry store but then steals the pane of glass instead of the jewels; he is reduced to mugging old ladies but gets beaten up by their crutches. When he tries to tell a man in a restaurant booth behind him about a plan for a bank robbery, he fails to notice that the man has left and that he is in fact talking to two policemen. In planning the robbery, he shows his gang a secret film of the bank they are about to rob (filmed with a camera hidden in a loaf of rye bread, another ethnic reference), but he has to show the obligatory short feature ("Trout Fishing in Quebec") first. When another gang arrives at the same time to rob the same bank, Virgil makes an inappropriate appeal to a sense of fair play: "we were here first," he tells the much tougher rival gang.

The film makes a brilliant use of verbal comedy to emphasize the futility of Virgil's criminal career, as well as his more basic alienation from the society that surrounds him. In one of the most effective verbal gags, Virgil goes to rob a bank and decides to write out his request for the money rather than speaking it. His plan backfires when his handwriting turns out to be so illegible that the cashier has to show the note to a series of different bank employees, during which time Virgil is arrested and sent back to prison. Virgil's inability to write a legible robbery note (he writes "abt natural" for "act natural" and "I have a gub" for "I have a gun") suggests the limited education more commonly associated with the criminal population, an interpretation supported by the fact that the bank employees all speak with highly educated accents. Yet at the same time Virgil's inarticulateness suggests a more basic problem with even the most rudimentary form of human communication, a kind of metaphysical estrangement from his own language.

Language is also used throughout the film to parody Virgil's desire for a more respectable middle-class lifestyle. At one point, he and his wife

Louise discuss what he should wear to a bank robbery. Virgil worries that wearing a beige shirt would be "in poor taste" (a cultural distinction hardly befitting such an activity), and Louise suggests calling up the other members of the gang to see what they are wearing. This verbal gag goes with a more general theme of socioeconomic confusion throughout the film. When the gang comes over to the house for meetings, Louise puts out "little trays of pretzels and bullets." At one point, Allen parodies conventional bourgeois attitudes toward both crime and more "respectable" professions by literalizing the cliché that crime doesn't pay. Sounding more like a travel agent or an insurance agent than a career bank-robber, Virgil tells the interviewer: "I think that crime definitely pays: the hours are good, and you're your own boss, and you travel a lot, and you get to meet interesting people." Louise also embraces the success ethic, turning the infamous "Most Wanted" list of dangerous criminals into a desirable badge of career status: "I think if he'd been a successful criminal he would have felt better. You know, he never made the '10 Most Wanted' list. It's very unfair voting: it's who you know."

Even as a criminal, Allen's persona is that of the misfit, out of step with the low-level hoodlums he encounters. Allen's film can be seen as a wry joke on the idea of the criminal as social outcast: Virgil is a metaphysical outcast, a misfit among misfits. Allen consistently undercuts any sociological explanation for Virgil's status, as if satirizing the tendency to identify class and social background as the cause of all society's ills. Virgil himself seems to be a gentle and rather articulate person, hardly fitting the profile of the typical criminal. His accent (Brooklyn Jewish) and vocabulary (relatively educated) are both in marked contrast to those of the other criminals who surround him. Even his quintessentially WASP name is belied by his obviously Jewish identity. As if to accentuate an identity from which Virgil cannot escape, his parents use stereotyped Jewish accents and mannerisms and wear Groucho Marx noses and moustaches in their on-camera interviews. Virgil himself is transformed by a prison medical experiment into an orthodox rabbi.

A kind of Zelig *avant la lettre*, Virgil is a mess of social contradictions. A sensitive and romantic soul, he adopts a life as a career criminal; he takes cello lessons, but he steals the money to pay for them; he wants to be a good provider for his family, but the only way he can think of doing so is by robbing banks. Finally, Virgil cannot be placed as a social subject. His is a subjectivity that is continually dispersed and displaced; his is a postmodern world that is based on a media-produced simulacrum of reality.

## III

Like Virgil Starkwell, Fielding Mellish in *Bananas* is a version of the perennial outsider or *schlemiel* figure, and again it is his use of language that works against him. If Virgil is incapable of writing a legible holdup note, Mellish is plagued by his often ludicrous attempts to master the verbal discourse and the air of sophistication necessary to gain entrance to a more desirable cultural milieu. In an attempt to impress Nancy (Louise Lasser), a prospective date who is a student at City College and something of an intellectual as well as a political activist, Mellish remarks fatuously: "I love yoga. I love eastern philosophy. It's metaphysical and abortively pedantic." When Nancy asks Mellish to proclaim his love for her in French, he has to admit to his cultural deficiency of not knowing French, offering to tell her in Hebrew instead.[11] Once again, a lack of the appropriate cultural capital is conflated with an inappropriate ethnic status, leaving Allen's character doubly deficient.

*Bananas* contains several references to Mellish's lack of what others deem an appropriate level of education. When Mellish goes to see his parents in the operating room where his mother is assisting his father in an operation, they repeatedly berate him for not finishing college and becoming a doctor. In a brilliant allegory of the child's nightmare of being pressured into a career by his parents, Fielding's father asks him to take over the operation for him even though he has no medical training or experience. The motif of Mellish's insufficient education occurs throughout the film. He once claims his college major was Black Studies but misunderstands the title ("by now I could have been black"). At another point, he claims to have majored in philosophy but admits he spent a total of two days in college before dropping out. In San Marcos, he is treated as a highly educated intellectual, although, as one of the rebels tells him, he achieves that distinction simply by knowing how to read in a country where the vast majority of the population is illiterate. Once again, any pretensions to intellectual achievement are deflated by the reality of the situation.

At the same time that it presents Mellish as the ethnic and sociocultural outsider, *Bananas* also satirizes the distinction between the "inside" and the "outside." Allen's character is at once an outsider who has come in (to the tiny Latin American dictatorship of San Marcos) and an insider (American) who has gone out (to the Third World). Furthermore, the entire idea of political revolutions satirized in the film is a matter of outside replacing inside and then being replaced in turn by another outside once it has become the inside. Mellish begins the film as a classic Allen outsider. He has trouble getting a date, he works at a job for which he is physically and temperamentally unsuited, and when he does find a girlfriend, she unceremoniously dumps him for a variety of reasons, including social, psychological, and sexual immaturity. Mellish briefly becomes an insider when he works his way up the ranks of the San Marcos rebel movement to become the country's new president, but he becomes an outsider again by the end of the film. When the U.S. government tries him for treason, his sentence is to promise that he will never move into the judge's neighborhood, a prohibition that can be read simultaneously in ethnic, political, and socioeconomic terms. *Bananas* is a film that stands on the border between satire and parody, a "culture-clash" comedy that uses the clash between the United States and San Marcos as a substitute for the ethnic clash between the Jewish Allen and the WASP-dominated American culture.

The film also engages in a sharp critique of the consumerist and commodifying tendencies of the dominant American culture, a theme that will reappear in several of Allen's films. The first instance of this tendency is the invasion of everyday life by the clichés of television. The story begins with Howard Cosell doing a "Wide World of Sports" coverage of a presidential assassination, and much of what happens in the film is mediated through television. A "News at Six" broadcast covers Mellish's trial; a telegenic Miss America testifies against Mellish; and Cosell reappears at the end of the film for a live-action broadcast of Mellish and Nancy's wedding night as a boxing match. As invasive as these television broadcasts are, Mellish's own job reveals the consumer product as an equally invasive fact of modern life. Mellish is a products-tester, whose products include the "Exec-U-Sizer," a machine designed for executives who need exercise but are too busy to leave their desks. This contraption, reminiscent of the feeding machine in Chaplin's *Modern Times,* represents the tendency in postmodern consumer culture to create unnecessary products that only serve to create more anxiety for their owners. Such products, along with the vapid and overly hyped television programming, epitomize modern-day America at its worst, a dystopic vision that Mellish can escape only by going to an equally dystopic but much poorer Third World country.[12] Yet even here the spread of American culture has taken hold. When given the assignment of going to town to get food for the rebels, Allen orders thousands of take-out lunches, complete with deli sandwiches, soft drinks, and cole slaw; when he eats dinner with the dictator at the presidential palace, he pays for his meal with a credit card.

Such gags are updated versions of the Marx Brothers' socially irreverent form of comedy, but rather than shady art dealers, upper-class heiresses, gangsters, and real estate swindlers, the object of Allen's satire is more global in nature: the sleaze, conformism, and mediocrity of an Americanized commodity culture that has spread its tentacles throughout the entire world. Allen may have claimed that *Bananas* was only "coincidentally political," but its political implications are just as clear as those of the Marx Brothers' *Duck Soup*. Mellish (whose name itself suggests a kind of weak muddle) is an American Everyman (he first appears in a red-and-white-striped shirt). Undereducated and ineffectually middle-class, he is victimized by his government and its imperialist politics, and he is manipulated by the various factions within San Marcos itself. Allen's film satirizes not only such political targets as Third World dictators and the interventions of the American government in San Marcos, but also the effects of a more general form of cultural imperialism, including the inescapable American media.

Allen's film is a dire warning for the postmodern information age, an age in which society receives its news from Howard Cosell and its politics from Miss America. In this world, misinformation and miscommunication are rampant. In a commercial for "New Testament cigarettes," it is suggested that even God uses the brand ("I smoke 'em; He smokes 'em"); a conversation between Mellish (as president of San Marcos) and the U.S. ambassador is carried out in perfect English but is "translated" by an interpreter who repeats everything they say with a heavy Spanish accent; Vargas mistakenly asks for aid from the UJA (the United Jewish Appeal) instead of the CIA. Mellish himself participates in such misinformation. He believes that by majoring in Black Studies he can become black, and he tells Nancy that he once visited the Vatican in Denmark ("they did so well in Rome, they opened in Denmark"). Within this world, a character like Mellish is a hopelessly lost soul, a figure only one step away from Chaplin's tramp. What Chaplin described as the "accumulating complexities of modern life . . . gigantic institutions that threaten from all sides" have become even more bewildering in the postmodern era. Whether the entire world has gone "bananas," as the film's title suggests, or has merely become a kind of "banana republic" under the cultural control of the American media, Mellish's position within it is a frighteningly tenuous one.

## IV

As its title implies, *Manhattan* is as much about a milieu as about any individual character. Allen defines a world circumscribed both geographically (Manhattan's East Side) and socially (a cadre of fortyish proto-yuppies with intellectual and artistic leanings). In a self-described satire of the "cultural junk food" of contemporary American life, Allen portrays an upper-middle-class society characterized by cultural hubris, intellectual pretension, and lack of personal discipline. The film's upscale New Yorkers move in the charmed world of downtown art galleries, Museum of Modern Art parties, the Stanhope Hotel, Zabar's, Bloomingdale's, and carriage rides through Central Park.

The protagonist of *Manhattan* is Allen's character Isaac Davis ("Ike"), a TV comedy writer who quits his job in order to become a writer of serious fiction. Ike is no longer the *schlemiel* figure represented by characters like Virgil Starkwell and Fielding Mellish, but a successful New Yorker whose life seems to typify the upwardly mobile Manhattanite of the late 1970s. Ike eats at Elaine's, takes his son to lunch at the Russian Tea Room, owns stocks, has an accountant, and, for the first half of the film at least, lives in a spacious Manhattan apartment. Ike is surrounded by a group of characters who epitomize the confused values and aspirations of his class: his best friend Yale Pollack (Michael Murphy), a married English professor more interested in buying a vintage Porsche and in pursuing affairs with other women than in finishing his book on Eugene O'Neill; Mary Wilke (Diane Keaton), a neurotic, insecure, and competitively intellectual freelance journalist who churns out novelizations of screenplays rather than finish a review of Tolstoy's letters; and Jill (Meryl Streep), Ike's ex-wife, a humorless and self-righteous bisexual who left Ike for another woman and who has written a tell-all book with the pretentious title *Marriage, Divorce, and Selfhood,* revealing the most intimate details of their marriage and breakup. The most mature character in the film is arguably Tracy (Mariel Hemingway), a 17-year-old student and Ike's lover for the first two-thirds of the movie. Tracy, though clearly from a privileged socioeconomic background – she lives in Gramercy Park and attends the Dalton School – has not internalized the worst aspects of contemporary urban culture. As she says toward the end of the film, "not everyone gets corrupted." The "corruption" of Ike by other members of New York society, the hypocrisy he displays in leaving her to enter a relationship with Mary, and his ultimate return to Tracy at the end of the film constitute the main trajectory of the film's plot.

Like many of Allen's films, *Manhattan* is characterized by a high degree of self-consciousness about writing and language. Authors and authorship are very much at issue. Ike is a writer, whose reworking of the opening lines of his novel at the beginning of the film sets the self-consciously literary tone of the film as a whole. The film's references are also often literary. Ike warns Yale that Mary is the winner of the "Zelda Fitzgerald Emotional Maturity Award," and Ike tells her that her self-esteem is "a notch below Kafka's"; he characterizes his own record with women as meriting "the August Strindberg Award." The film's other main characters with the exception of Tracy – Yale, Jill, and Mary – are all writers of one kind or another. Even Tracy, as an actress who is about to go to London to study Shakespeare, is involved with language. And it is surely no mere coincidence that Tracy is played by the granddaughter of Ernest Hemingway. Ike's rewriting of the sentences at the opening reminds us of Hemingway's own care for the precision of language, and his search for "individual integrity" amidst "the decay of contemporary culture" might recall Hemingway's alienated individualism. Furthermore, Ike himself can be seen as the ironic opposite to Hemingway's prototypically masculine and heroic persona. In the first dialogue scene of the movie, Ike claims pompously that "the most important thing in life is courage," but he immediately disqualifies himself in a discussion of whether he would jump into freezing water to save a drowning man by saying he can't swim.

Ike's tendency toward corruption and hypocrisy is even more exaggerated among the other characters in his circle. Yale, whose name can be associated with Ivy League, WASP, old-moneyed privilege, is a relatively shallow hypocrite. He tells his wife Emily that he isn't ready to have children because he has to finish his O'Neill book and start a magazine, but as Ike tells him later in the film, he would really rather buy a Porsche than put the effort into his writing.[13] Yale tells his wife that Ike is "wasting his life . . . writ[ing] that crap for television," but Yale himself is in fact no more directed than Ike is. By the end of the film, we see that Ike and Yale have changed places. Ike is well on his way to having his new book published by Viking, while Yale's only accomplishment is having bought a car. Furthermore, Yale's discussions of art and philosophy are full of facile catch-phrases such as "Gossip is the new pornography," or vacuous pseudo-statements such as "I think the essence of art is to provide a kind of working through the situation for people, you know, so that you can get in touch with feelings that you didn't know you had."

Throughout the film, Yale and Mary place faddishness above what Allen considers to be real artistic integrity; nothing is experienced for its own sake without being filtered through inside cultural references or the pseudo-academic jargon of art criticism. When Ike first meets Mary after seeing a show at the Castelli Gallery, she dismisses a photography exhibit he and Tracy have enjoyed as "straight out of Diane Arbus," and praises a steel cube (which Ike hated) as "perfectly integrated" and having "a marvelous kind of negative capability." The most egregious aesthetic misjudgments come in the form of Yale and Mary's "Academy of the Overrated," a list of writers, composers, painters, and filmmakers they have compiled in order to make themselves feel more intellectually sophisticated than those around them. The fact that names like Walt Whitman, Gustav Mahler, Ingmar Bergman, and Vincent Van Gogh (which Mary insists on pretentiously pronouncing as "Van Goch") appear on the list is appalling to Ike, who sees these artists as "all terrific."[14] When Ike suggests that Bergman is "the only genius in cinema today," Mary counters vapidly that Bergman's films are too "Scandinavian": "Real adolescent, you know, fashionable pessimism." At the same time, Mary considers the television program Ike writes for, a comedy called "Human Beings—Wow!" which Ike himself considers "empty" and "antiseptic," to be "brilliantly funny." Mary's hypocrisy – or simply her lack of cultural discrimination – is apparent in her actions as well as her words. While presenting herself as an intellectual committed to the arts, she writes novelizations of screenplays because "it's easy and it pays well." The novelization, according to Allen's system of values, is the quintessentially debased postmodern form, a simulacral adaptation of a form that is most often of little value in the first place.

The perverse inversions of aesthetic and cultural value enacted by Yale and Mary act as a cover for their underlying sociocultural insecurities. At the end of their first meeting, Mary says to Ike by way of explanation for what might be seen as aggressive or pretentious behavior: "I don't even want to have this conversation. I mean . . . I'm just from Philadelphia. You know, I mean, we believe in God." Mary's phony claim to innocence should be read in contrast with the real innocence – or the total lack of cultural pretension – represented by Tracy. Whereas Mary feels the need to experience "legitimate" culture by attending a symphony concert, play, or gallery opening almost every night, Tracy enjoys the simple pleasures of eating Chinese food in bed and watching W. C. Fields movies on the late show. While Ike is intimidated by Mary and displays his sexism in dismissing her as a "little Radcliffe tootsie," it is clear that Mary harbors insecurities about her own background. Unlike Ike, Yale, and Tracy, she is not a native New Yorker (an important distinction in a movie called *Manhattan*) and feels the need to overcompensate for being "just from Philadelphia." Mary uses her intellectualism to cover for a lack of inherited cultural capital, fetishizing intelligence and "culture" at the expense of emotional maturity and ethical responsibility. Mary even conflates intelligence and sex: "I could go to bed with the entire M.I.T. faculty if I wanted to," she tells Yale in a burst of self-righteous indignation. As it turns out, Mary is overly impressed by the apparent sophistication of others around her, whom she continually overrates. She calls her friend Helen a "genius" and describes her former teacher and ex-husband Jeremiah as an "oversexed brilliant kind of animal" and "a very brilliant, dominant man." Yet when Ike meets Jeremiah later in the film, he turns out to be a small, balding, and apparently unexceptional character. In another example, Mary's psychoanalyst calls *her* at three in the morning to tell her his problems, yet she insists that he is a "highly qualified doctor."

Mary epitomizes the cultural decay Allen locates in the late 1970s. She is part of a well-educated and affluent but intellectually and morally hollow culture, a culture of narcissism best exemplified by her psychobabble pronouncement, "I'm beautiful, I'm bright, and I deserve better." Read in class terms, she is the epitome of upward sociocultural mobility in the information age. Mary's "pseudointellectual garbage," as Ike calls it, is particularly galling to him because he remains ambivalent about his own intellectual and cultural status. Whereas Yale and especially Mary exemplify the postmodern emphasis on information as an index of cultural mobility (at one point, Mary begins pedantically naming the satellites of Saturn), Ike at least *attempts* to deal with ideas at a deeper and more sincere level. Although he claims half-seriously that the brain is the body's "most overrated organ" (ironically echoing Mary and Yale's own list of "overrateds"), Ike is every bit as identified with an intellectual life as they are. In fact, Ike's ex-wife Jill accuses him of exactly the kind of solipsistic self-involvement of which he accuses Yale and Mary: "He had complaints about life but never any solutions. He longed to be an artist but balked at the necessary sacrifices. In his most private moments, he spoke of the fear of death, which he elevated to tragic heights when, in fact, it was mere narcissism." Ike breaks through his narcissism at the end of the film, however, when – in a scene reminiscent of Benjamin Braddock's race to the church at the end of *The Graduate* – he runs through the streets of New York to catch Tracy before she flies off to England. As in the Mike Nichols film, where Benjamin's escape with Elaine Robinson symbolized an escape from suburban affluence and its distorted values, Ike's realization of his love for Tracy allows him to reject the moral and cultural relativity represented by the world of Yale and Mary.

In *Zelig,* Allen creates a multiply divided protagonist who can move, chameleon-like, between one identity and another. A more successfully adaptive misfit than Virgil Starkwell or Fielding Mellish, Zelig transgresses boundaries of politics, culture, and religion, as well as class. As Ruth Perlmutter suggests, "*Zelig* represents Allen's most exhaustive transgression of American Gentile culture by a Jew . . . and a comic" (208).

Through a unique comic metamorphosis, Zelig becomes a figure unidentifiable by ethnicity, profession, or class status, and thus no longer subject to the limitations placed on the socially defined subject.

Zelig's hybridization and sociocultural assimilation can also be seen as a reference to Allen's Jewish background. The Jewish immigrant was by necessity at least bilingual, speaking both Yiddish and English, while often having at least some knowledge of both Hebrew and other European languages. As Robert Stam comments, Zelig is an exaggeration of this sociolinguistic tendency, "a walking polyphony of ethnic personalities [who] mimics the appearance and impersonates the voices of the diverse synecdochic cultural figures with whom he comes into contact, representatives of the various ethnic communities of New York City and its environs."[15] Zelig differs significantly from Allen's previous projections of himself as a Jew in a WASP world, or even as a more general misfit or outsider. Zelig's narrative parodies and ultimately deconstructs the fantasy of assimilation itself. "Eager to be absorbed into the dominant culture," Perlmutter observes, "he epitomizes the dilemma of the American Jew who wants to change his or her ethnic envelope in order to be socially integrated" (214). And yet Zelig's assimilation goes beyond any normal process of social integration. In the course of the film, he not only marries his *shiksa* psychiatrist Dr. Fletcher (Mia Farrow), but at one point goes through an outrageous transformation into one of Hitler's antisemitic claque. Zelig's assimilation anxiety, and his resultant changes in identity, are precipitated by two events that have marked him as un-American: not having read the great American novel *Moby-Dick,* and not wearing green on St. Patrick's Day. It is clearly ironic, however, that at least one of the instances of his failure to assimilate to the "dominant culture" involves his not adopting another ethnic identity (Irish-American) in place of his own Jewish-American identity.

As Allen himself has stated, the film was intended not as a utopian "fantasy of metamorphosis," but rather as a dystopian analysis of "the kind of personality that leads to fascism."[16] At the end of the film, however, Zelig does achieve both psychic integration and social assimilation by marrying Dr. Fletcher, thus defusing both his sexual inadequacy and his ethnic guilt. The film also depicts a dissolution of class boundaries, and it can be read as an allegory for the postmodern breakdown of class identification. Zelig is no longer subject to a deterministic grid of class identity, but is defined only in relation to those with whom he comes into contact. By almost immediately taking on the social characteristics, speech patterns, and opinions of the people around him, Zelig becomes the avatar of a classless society.

This social mimicry is demonstrated most clearly in an early scene, in which we find an account of Zelig at the Long Island estate of "Mr. and Mrs. Henry Porter Sutton, socialites, patrons of the arts." At a party, reminiscent of the upper-class house party in the Marx Brothers' *Animal Crackers,* "politicians and poets rub elbows with the cream of high society." Zelig is first described (in the notebook of another class-conscious guest, F. Scott Fitzgerald) as seeming "clearly to be an aristocrat and extoll[ing] the very rich as he chatted with socialites." Zelig "spoke adoringly of Coolidge and the Republican party, all in an upper-class Boston accent." But only an hour later, Fitzgerald notes a total transformation: "I was stunned to see the same man speaking with the kitchen help. Now he claimed to be a Democrat, and his accent seemed to be coarse, as if he were one of the crowd."

Zelig has no trouble switching political allegiances or even accents. For him, the difficulty is in maintaining *any* fixed identity, *any* stable sense of self. Yet Zelig is only an exaggeration of tendencies latent in all Americans. His stunning social metamorphosis highlights the fact that social identities are artificial constructs, assumed by their users in order to "fit in" with a particular group or class. Zelig's popularity among the American people can be largely explained by the fact that he mirrors typical American desires, including the desires for both an upward social mobility and an ultimately classless society. As Richard Feldstein suggests, "By being the quintessential symbol of adaptability, Zelig helps to perpetuate the notion that the American dream is achievable."[17] In his fluid and unidentifiable class position, Zelig spans the entire range of possible social identities. Zelig reconciles the extremes of Allen's own career-long cinematic attempt at social self-definition; at the same time, he serves to delineate the postmodern comic hero, a classless exemplar of the information age.

## VI

In the metafictional *The Purple Rose of Cairo,* Allen makes reference both to the historical past of Depression-era America and to the cinematic past of 1930s Hollywood film, with its glamorous lifestyles and settings and its cross-class plots. When one of the upper-class characters from a Hollywood movie ("Tom Baxter") descends from the screen to attempt a romance with the real-life working-class woman Cecilia (played by Mia Farrow), he throws into relief the distinction between two forms of nostalgia: a historicized (though still fictional) filmic vision of life in the 1930s (complete with reference to the social problems of poverty and joblessness), and a parodic vision of the Hollywood film which provided an alternative fantasy life for many Americans. If the film is a quintessential example of postmodern pastiche, it is also a parody of the 1930s cross-class fantasy. When the film's protagonist, Cecilia, enters romantic relationships with both the fictional character of the film and the actor who played the character, the relations between "real life" (working-class New Jersey in the 1930s), commodified fantasy structures (the Hollywood system of actors and producers), and utopian fictional narratives (the film itself with its romance and exotic adventure plots) become very complex indeed.

Social and economic relations are important in the film as well. Cecilia has taken a job as a waitress in a diner in order to support her husband, whose factory has been closed by hard times. The town's movie theater (appropriately named "The Jewel") provides her with an alternative fantasy life, a place where she can escape her oppressive world and participate vicariously in the lives of the rich and famous. In one scene, she discusses a Hollywood wedding between Lew Ayres and Ginger Rogers with her sister while working at the diner: "They got married on a boat off the island of Catalina. They live in Beverly Hills and sometimes holiday in Spain." Yet Cecilia's reverie of Hollywoodesque upward mobility is rudely interrupted by the plebeian facts of a customer asking for his toast and her boss telling her and her sister to work faster: "Ladies, there's a depression on. There are a lot of other people who would like this job if you can't handle it." Cecilia's fantasy life, it turns out, has important consequences for her real-life existence. She ultimately loses her waitressing job because her obsession with movies and movie stars makes her absent-minded on the job, and her decision to leave her unemployed, alcoholic, and abusive husband results at least in part from the false dreams of a more romantic life provided by Hollywood films and characters.

The fictional society of Tom and the other characters in *The Purple Rose of Cairo* is, in contrast to Cecilia's working-class existence, a wealthy "smart set" that lives in Art Deco apartments and drinks champagne at the Copacabana. In this rarified world, no one has to work, and there is seemingly no Depression. Tom Baxter (an "explorer-poet-adventurer" of the "Chicago Baxters") is not only objectively "perfect" but is also an embodiment of nonethnic WASP identity. He is therefore the antithesis not only of Cecilia and her husband Monk but also of Allen himself. Tom is tall, classically handsome, brave, unemotional, totally without sexual desire, apparently without class prejudices, and unaware of unemployment, poverty, disease, death, or God (none of which has been written into his character). The characterization of the romantic and virtuous but ultimately bland Tom represents not only the typical hero of Hollywood in the 1930s, but also the homogenization of American life portrayed by Hollywood films until the 1970s. Tom is an empty cypher for the American Dream rather than a real embodiment of it.

Tom's descent from the screen to woo Cecilia, however, offers only an empty promise of utopian fulfillment. When it becomes apparent that his impressive-looking wad of money is fake, he and Cecilia are forced to flee the restaurant where they have eaten dinner. On the other hand, when Cecilia enters the film by crossing through the screen with Tom, it is clear that she will always be an outsider, socially as well as ontologically. Tom introduces her to his upper-class set, but even there she is treated as an "extra" (a second-class citizen within the Hollywood system) who messes things up by changing the party of six into an uneven party of seven and who looks totally out of place among the fashionable women in her modest clothes and plain hairstyle. One character calls her a "skirt," and even the maitre d' refers to her disdainfully as "this person." When Tom tells Cecilia that the New York skyline displayed before them is "[hers] for the asking," the reality is that it is only a painted backdrop of the city, something she can never possess in her actual life. This gap between utopian fantasy and reality is made explicit in the metaphysical structure of Allen's film. When one of the characters on screen suggests that they redefine themselves as the "real world" and the external audience as "the world of illusion and shadow," he is quickly disabused of this notion. After all, the projector could be stopped at any minute and their "illusory" existence would end.

The utopia of Cecilia's stay on the other side of the silver screen is to be extremely short-lived. When the actor who plays Tom in the movie,

Gil Shepherd, calls her name from offscreen, he interrupts the fictional space in which she and Tom are interacting. Gil convinces her to leave Tom and come with him to Hollywood, but it is only a manipulative gesture designed to get Tom to go back into the film. Realizing that Tom, despite being "perfect," will never be a real man, Cecilia returns to her apartment to pack her things in order to leave with Gil. Gil, however, more concerned with his acting career than with the feelings of a working-class woman like Cecilia, leaves and flies back to Hollywood without her, leaving her to pick up the pieces of her broken life. The film ends with her once more in the theater, immersed again in the Hollywood fantasy of an Astaire and Rogers movie.

Allen's creation of a character like Cecilia demonstrates yet again his empathy for the outsider, the "little person" who is left behind by the callous world represented by Gil, an upwardly mobile and ambitious actor who has his sights set on the role of Lindbergh (another heroic WASP type) in his next film. Just like her attempt to enter the glamorous fictional world of a Hollywood movie, Cecilia's vision of a romance with an actual movie actor (even if a relatively minor star within the Hollywood system) is doomed to failure and disillusionment, a disillusionment rectified only by the utopian dream supplied in other films. "Heaven, I'm in heaven," sings Fred Astaire in the movie she watches at the end, epitomizing Cecilia's star-struck desires as he serenades the glamorous and enraptured Ginger Rogers. Allen's portrayal of Cecilia remains sympathetic, even though the movies are only a narcotic that allows her to dull the pain of an otherwise unbearable existence. On one level a postmodern parody of Hollywood cinema, *The Purple Rose of Cairo* is on another level a film of social statement that can be read within the tradition of American comedy from Chaplin and Keaton to the Marx Brothers and Frank Capra.

In *The Purple Rose of Cairo* – perhaps more poignantly than in any other film he has made – Allen displays an acute sense of the reality of class relations, of class divisions, and of class struggle. In one scene, the on-screen characters in the film within the film take on a social existence of their own and begin to speak to each other, thus providing a meta-commentary on the social relations in the "real world" outside the film. A "communist" appears and urges the characters to rise up against the "fat cats in Hollywood" who are "getting rich on our work": "We're the ones who sweat," he shouts. Allen exploits the interaction of fantasy and social realism here, using the evocation of social relations among the film's characters to mirror the real-life social relations of the Depression.

Along with *Zelig* and *Radio Days, The Purple Rose of Cairo* completes a triumvirate of socially engaged films from the mid-1980s. Since the middle of the 1980s, Allen has moved away from this kind of class-based film, focusing on a narrower spectrum of American society: the lives of successful and often wealthy New Yorkers. If the films from the first half of Allen's career look back to the more socially oriented comic tradition of filmmakers like Chaplin, Keaton, and the Marx Brothers, his later films gravitate toward the genre of bourgeois domestic comedy. In *Hannah and Her Sisters* (1986), for example, we see a shift in Allen's approach from the satiric mode of *Annie Hall* and *Manhattan* to a more celebratory or elegiac portrait of the urban middle class. Indeed, *Hannah and Her Sisters* can be read as a lament for a kind of urban, middle-class domesticity. Much of the action takes place in the family home of the film's title character, played by Mia Farrow – a spacious and comfortable apartment on Central Park West – and Hannah herself is married to a successful financial advisor.[18] This trend toward anatomizing the lives of the contemporary urban middle class continues in most of Allen's comedies of the 1990s. In *Alice* (1990), Farrow plays the pampered consumer Alice Tate, a New York woman married to a man from a wealthy WASP family; *Husbands and Wives* (1992) concerns two well-to-do New York couples (Allen's character is a successful novelist and creative writing professor at Columbia); in *Mighty Aphrodite* (1995) we find another middle-class New York couple living in a comfortable Upper East Side apartment (he is a sports writer, she an ambitious gallery owner); *Everyone Says I Love You* (1996) is the story of a bourgeois family living in a Park Avenue penthouse (Allen's character is a writer living in Paris); and *Deconstructing Harry* (1997) once again depicts a successful New York novelist.

The subject of class, though it continues to be present on some level in these films, seems to be of less importance to Allen than a general portrait of a Manhattan milieu, a milieu ranging from the intellectual or artistic sector of the middle class to its more conspicuously bourgeois manifestation. The upwardly mobile urbanites and upper-middle-class WASPs who would have been the subject of satire in his earlier films are treated with a kind of affectionate humor. In *Everyone Says I Love You,* even the mildly critical viewpoint of a film like *Alice* has disappeared, leaving us with an appreciation of the good life but little distance from the comforts that only a substantial inheritance can buy. Attempts to portray life on the other side of the class divide are neither wholly convincing nor, one suspects, totally sincere. Alice Tate in *Alice*, for example, despite her growing dissatisfaction with her protected bourgeois lifestyle and consumeristic values, decides to make a change only in the final minutes of the film. Her decision to leave her husband, travel to Calcutta to meet Mother Theresa, and take care of her children on her own (without the aid of a cook, housekeeper, or nanny!) is only presented as a brief epilogue rather than as an integral part of the narrative. In *Mighty Aphrodite*, the cross-class plot is treated more as a comic gag than as a vehicle for social comment. When Lenny Weintraub (Allen) finds out that the biological mother of his adopted son is the prostitute and porn star Linda Ash (Mira Sorvino), we have the potential for a revealing meeting of the classes. Yet despite the obvious attraction of Lenny for the lively world of Linda as opposed to the rarified artistic milieu of his wife, the portrait of the working classes (Linda and the redneck boxer from upstate to whom Larry introduces her) is more a caricature than a fully realized portrait. Ultimately, no class tensions are allowed to exist, and no cross-class romance is allowed to blossom. The cultivated Manhattan bourgeoisie will stay on its side of the class barrier, and the good-hearted but somewhat feeble-minded denizens of the blue-collar community on the other.

If Allen could be accused of socioeconomic insensitivity in his recent films, or at least of a more conventional attitude toward certain forms of social inequality, it is important to remember that Allen is essentially an autobiographical or self-referential filmmaker. As he has himself become older and more successful, his characters have reflected that change by becoming more successful and more culturally sophisticated in their own right. No longer the *schlemiel* figure of his early career, Allen now appears in his films as the successful but conflicted artist (usually a writer), a character more comfortable with his upscale middle-class surroundings than with the working-class Brooklyn of his childhood.

# 7

# YUPPIES AND OTHER STRANGERS

## Class Satire and Cultural Clash in Contemporary Film Comedy

---

Do yuppies even exist? No one says "I am a
yuppie." It's always the other guy who's a yuppie.
I think for a group to exist somebody has to
admit to be part of it.

Dez, in *The Last Days of Disco* (Whit Stillman)

## I

For the "baby-boom" generation of the 1980s and 1990s, the figure of the
"yuppie" – the young, urban, upwardly mobile professional – served as an
iconic representation of the aspirations, tensions, and anxieties that characterized American socioeconomic life. The economic growth of the 1980s,
and in particular the boom in financial markets and services, led to what
David Harvey has identified as "a whole new Yuppie culture . . . with its
accoutrements of gentrification, close attention to symbolic capital, fashion,
design, and the quality of urban life."[1] Although yuppies represented only a
fraction of the overall population of "baby boomers" born in the postwar
era, they exercised an inordinate influence on cultural patterns of the 1980s
and 1990s, both through their own buying power and through their influence on a larger number of would-be yuppies who attempted to imitate
aspects of their lifestyles and consumption patterns.[2]

For yuppies and pseudo-yuppies alike, the most important status symbols were cultural commodities rather than consumer products. Yuppies were urban rather than suburban in lifestyle and orientation, and they were generally well informed about current trends in culture and the arts. Although they may have worked as stockbrokers, accountants, lawyers, advertising executives, publishing editors, computer programmers, and investment bankers, they were as likely to collect art, discuss books and films, and participate in urban nightlife as to buy expensive cars and homes. As consumers, they were the primary fuel for the growth of postmodern culture, providing the primary market for postmodern cultural forms based on nostalgia, pastiche, and kitsch.

American film comedies of the past two decades have represented the figure of the yuppie in a variety of ways.[3] As Douglas Kellner and Michael Ryan point out, films of the Reagan era – much like films of the Depression years – often involve either the desire for class transcendence or the thematization of class conflict and difference.[4] Although such films do not overtly advocate a leveling of class differences, they often return to the Depression-era model of socioeconomic difference overcome by cross-class romance.

One of the most popular comic subgenres of the 1980s was the comedy of cultural dislocation or "culture-clash comedy," a genre in which the experiences or expectations of a middle-class (most often yuppie) protagonist come into conflict with a "wilder" or more marginalized environment. In these films, the yuppie world is placed in juxtaposition with a very different chronotope, an initially seductive but ultimately dystopic alternative to the safe and protected existence of the middle-class urban or suburban professional. The non-middle-class "other" is figured in several ways: as the world of urban nightlife rather than the daytime working world; as the artistic, bohemian, or marginally criminal subculture rather than the typically "square" mainstream inhabited by the yuppie characters; and as a socially disenfranchised population in opposition to the more upwardly mobile yuppies.

The 1980s comedy of cultural clash or cultural dislocation can be seen as a commentary on the economic excesses, social dislocations, and internally divided national psyche of the Reagan era. These films function as warnings about the inherent dangers of attempting to escape a stable and comfortable middle-class existence in search of more adventurous alternatives. They represent an attempt to come to terms with the dark underside of the nation's social fabric, while at the same time signaling a deep ambivalence about the status of the middle class and the new yuppie cadre. The disenchantment of many middle-class Americans with the materialist version of the American Dream they had been able to achieve at a relatively young age was counterbalanced by real fears of life on the other side of the socioeconomic divide. As James Harvey suggests, the socioeconomic reality of life for many Americans was the inverted image of the fashionably upscale lifestyle of the young urban professional. The deindustrialization, high unemployment, and increasing social inequality of the Reagan years were marked by the physical signs of homelessness, disempowerment, and impoverishment that "engulfed many of the central cities" (332). During the 1980s, despite Reagen-era promises of a "trickle-down economy," the poor became significantly poorer, and the number of children living in poverty increased dramatically. The mentally ill were released from their institutions – greatly increasing the homeless population – while racial divisions became more apparent and addictive drugs became a major national problem, especially for those of lower socioeconomic status. It may have been a good time to be a yuppie, but it was not such a good time to be a laid-off factory worker, a single mother living in the urban projects, or, for that matter, nearly any member of the working class or the unemployed "underclass." As Kellner and Ryan point out, it was workers and blacks who suffered disproportionately from the economic changes of the early 1980s, their "wages . . . cut, their social power demolished, and their work menialized" (134).

It is with the growing complexity and increasingly contradictory nature of social relations during this period that the most self-reflective films of the era, including comedies, had to struggle. If mainstream Hollywood comedies of the period largely abandoned any pretense of meaningful social commentary – insisting instead on the kind of slick irreverence found in popular films from *Ghostbusters* to *Beverly Hills Cop* to *Big* – other comedies continued to offer more trenchant insights into the contemporary sociocultural experience.[5]

**II**

Martin Scorsese's mid-1980s comedy *After Hours* (1985) begins with a seemingly innocuous date between the computer programmer Paul

Hackett (Griffin Dunne) and a socially marginal and emotionally disturbed young woman named Marcy (Rosanna Arquette). Paul's date with Marcy, however, involves him in a night-long series of misadventures among the inhabitants of lower Manhattan. When Paul, the embodiment of middle-class normality, leaves his neatly ordered existence, he becomes literally and figuratively lost within the artists' lofts, bars, and kinky nightclubs of Soho and TriBeCa. Mistaken for a thief who has been responsible for a rash of robberies in the neighborhood, he is pursued by a gang of hostile residents and only escapes by being turned into a living papier-maché statue – symbolically bound and whitewashed into his original role as middle-class professional – which is in turn stolen by the real thieves who dump it in his own uptown neighborhood. On one level a comedy about class and cultural difference, *After Hours* is on another level a warning about the dangers of crossing to the other side of a growing social divide. Unlike the screwball comedies of the 1930s, this is not a film that envisions romance as a crossing of class boundaries, but one that warns against the attempt to leave one's own class parameters.

Two other comedies of the mid-1980s have very similar themes. In Jonathan Demme's *Something Wild* (1986), the ultrastraight yuppie Charley Drigges (Jeff Daniels) gets more than he bargains for when he enters a relationship with a sexy punkette (Melanie Griffith) from the wrong side of the tracks. When Charley, an upwardly mobile executive recently promoted to vice president of his firm, tries to sneak out of a Manhattan luncheonette without paying, he is caught in the act by a young woman calling herself "Lulu" who takes him in her car to a New Jersey motel for a sexual encounter. The portrayal of social relations in this film is somewhat more complicated than in *After Hours,* since both Lulu and Charley are something other than what they appear to be. While Charley maintains the persona of a happily married man, we learn that his dream of middle-class suburban tranquility had already been destroyed when his wife ran off with the family dentist, taking their two children with her. On the other hand, while "Lulu" plays the role of the dangerous rebel, her real desire is for the kind of middle-class stability Charley represents. When Charley goes to Lulu's high school reunion, he meets her mother and discovers Lulu's real identity as "Audrey," a rather sweet and unexotic young woman of lower-middle-class background. He also crosses paths with her former husband Ray (Ray Liotta), a seedy and violent hood and recently paroled ex-con who will stop at nothing to get Audrey/Lulu back in his life. After a dramatic sequence of the film in which Charley accidentally kills Ray, order is restored when Charley and Audrey meet at the same luncheonette and are reunited. Rather than the nightmarish vision of cultural crossing represented by *After Hours,* this film presents the socially marginal and criminal "other" as a desired, though somewhat dangerous, complement to the stable middle-class world. Charley is liberated from his overprotective middle-class life by Lulu and is able to discover another part of himself, while at the same time the "something wild" embodied in Lulu (the sexually and socially dark side of life repressed by Charley's middle-class value system) is "tamed" by the traditionally middle-class man. Despite the film's generic hybridity – combining elements of the crime thriller with the romantic comedy – its ending returns to something like the cross-class reconciliation of the screwball comedy, suggesting that while crossing out of yuppiedom can be risky it can also be rewarding.

Susan Seidelman's *Desperately Seeking Susan* (1986) involves an upper-middle-class suburban housewife, Roberta Glass (Rosanna Arquette), whose life changes dramatically when she becomes obsessed with the life of a stylish vagabond, Susan (Madonna). Roberta is totally bored in her routinized suburban existence (symbolized by her automatically timed oven and her regular trips to the beauty parlor) and her marriage to the financially successful but self-involved and culturally unadventurous hot-tub salesman Gary (Mark Blum), a man so oblivious to Roberta's needs that when she buys Susan's elaborately embroidered leather jacket his only reaction is to ask her why she has to buy a "used" jacket rather than a new one. Roberta escapes her middle-class routine by reading the personal ads and living vicariously through Susan, an independent woman who lives outside the conventions of bourgeois society and on the boundary of its legalized order. As in *After Hours,* the non-middle-class "other" is placed in lower Manhattan, seemingly a world away from Roberta's suburban New Jersey. Roberta begins as a voyeur, fantasizing about Susan's life, spying on her at Battery Park, following her around the city, and buying her jacket. But when she is mistaken for Susan and knocked unconscious, she forgets her identity and becomes enmeshed in a totally different lifestyle when she is rescued by Des, the best friend of Susan's boyfriend Jim. Ultimately, Roberta is arrested on a mistaken charge of prostitution, but she regains her memory and her husband Gary comes to pick her up. The film ends with a cross-class resolution as Roberta, instead of returning to her bourgeois husband, stays with Des, the penniless projectionist who takes care of her during her amnesia. Here, the satire of bourgeois life is more pronounced than in the other two films, and it is the bohemian lifestyle of downtown musicians and projectionists that is made to seem the more appealing (if more risky) alternative to a deadening life in the suburbs.

I conclude this summary of the culture-clash comedy with a somewhat longer analysis of what I consider to be the most interesting film of the genre, Albert Brooks's *Lost in America* (1985). In this film, David Howard (Brooks) is an ambitious midlevel advertising executive who has been working for eight years at a large advertising agency in Los Angeles. For the last two years he has earned a six-figure salary as "creative director" of the agency, and now he expects a promotion to vice president of the firm. Along with his wife Linda (Julie Hagerty), who works as a personnel manager, he has moved up the ladder of yuppiedom to the point of buying an expensive new house and shopping for a new Mercedes. His biggest concerns in life, other than his promotion, are whether to pay extra for the car's leather upholstery and whether they should buy a house with a tennis court. David and Linda suffer from what is represented as a typical middle-class angst. On the one hand, they worry that they are "a bit too responsible" – that their drive to socioeconomic security has taken away their spontaneity and enjoyment of life. On the other hand, David is convinced that he will be happy as soon as he gets a promotion to the executive level and begins to own stock in the agency. When he learns that he is to receive a transfer to the New York office instead of the expected promotion, however, David's life is turned upside down. He becomes irate in his boss's office, gets himself fired, and convinces Linda to quit her job as well. After exploring various options, they decide to invest in a motor home and go on the road "just like [in] *Easy Rider.*" They will start their lives over, leaving behind their yuppie lifestyle and "finding themselves."

Ironically, however, David and Linda remain a world apart from the antisocial renegades of *Easy Rider.* If anything, their disastrous cross-country journey is closer to that of Lucy and Desi in *The Long, Long Trailer* than to that of the 1960s motorcyclists in Dennis Hopper's film. While they have been experiencing a deepening anxiety about the overly programmed direction their upwardly mobile lives have taken, David and Linda are completely attached to their money (the fetishized "nest egg" of $145,000 which is to see them through the coming years) and to their middle-class prerogatives, including a luxurious new motor-home equipped with all the latest conveniences.

From the time they arrive in Las Vegas, where they plan to have a second wedding and inaugurate their new lives, things go steeply downhill. Linda, unable to relinquish her middle-class prerogatives, insists on spending the night at a Las Vegas hotel rather than "sleeping under the stars," and when David tips the check-in clerk $100 to get a bridal suite they are given the "Junior Bridal Suite," a rather ordinary single room with diminutive heart-shaped beds. That night, while David is asleep, Linda goes down to the casino and loses their entire life savings in a few crazed hours of gambling. After an unsuccessful attempt to convince the casino to return their money as a public relations stunt, they drive on to Hoover Dam with only $802 of their nest egg left. In an angry outburst, David accuses Linda of not understanding the "nest-egg principle":

> DAVID: It's a very sacred thing, the nest egg. . . . The egg is a protector like a god, and we sit under the nest egg, and we are protected by it. Without it, no protection.

David's vision of the nest egg as a kind of middle-class security blanket that will protect them from all socioeconomic harm reveals his fundamental inability to "drop out of society," or even to comprehend what such a dropping out would mean in actual socioeconomic terms. As Linda reminds David, "if you really want to drop out, you start with nothing." But Linda's vision of an authentic "drop-out" also proves to be naive. After attempting to hitchhike and being picked up by an angry ex-con who threatens to beat up David, Linda realizes that the gap separating their protected middle-class existence from the precarious situation of the rest of the world is a very large one indeed. In an effort to make their limited resources last as long as possible, they pull into the sleepy town of Sanford, Arizona, where they resolve to look for new jobs.

It is in this section of the film that the cultural clash between the Howards and the working-class world of small-town America takes on its most bitingly satirical aspect. It soon becomes clear that the only work available in Sanford is in the form of low-paying service jobs for which David and Linda are vastly overqualified. When David fails to get a job as a delivery-man for a pharmacy, he visits the town's employment agency, where the discrepancy between David's expectations of a job commensurate with his previous $100,000 salary and the reality of the local job situation – a position as a school crossing-guard at $5.50 an hour – creates a satiric commentary on the yuppie's total ignorance of the economic situation faced by the average American.

Brooks uses language throughout the film to emphasize the gap between David Howard and the other America he tries to "discover." Although David has a job that depends on his skills in language and communication, the absurdist joke of the film is that he finds himself incapable of communicating effectively with people outside of his narrowly defined middle-class existence. Even before David and Linda leave the confines of Los Angeles, David's "Easy Rider" fantasies of "dropping out" are deflated. When David gives the thumbs up to a passing motorcyclist, he is given the "finger" in return. This brief sight gag foreshadows more extended failures in communication, beginning at the Las Vegas hotel where they spend the night and lose their "nest egg." After David's story about "dropping out of society" fails to procure them the "best bridal suite," he is forced to bribe the receptionist. David's linguistic abilities fail him once again the following morning when he tries to convince the casino manager to give them their money back.

> DAVID: As the boldest experiment in advertising history, you give
>   us our money back.
> MANAGER: I beg your pardon?
> DAVID: Give us our money back. Think of the publicity. The
>   Hilton Hotel has these billboards all over Los Angeles where
>   the winners of these slot machine jackpots . . . their faces are
>   all over LA . . . and I know *that* works. I've seen people at cor-
>   ners look up and say, "We'll go to the Hilton!" Give us our
>   money back. I don't even know now because I'm just talking
>   off the top of my head, but maybe a visual where we had a
>   billboard, and the Desert Inn handed us our nest egg back.
>   This gives the Desert Inn . . . really . . . Vegas is not associated
>   with feeling.
> MANAGER: Well, first of all, those people on those billboards,
>   they won. You *lost*.

DAVID: But that's it! That's the campaign!

MANAGER: What's the campaign?

DAVID: You give my wife and I our money back because you reviewed our situation and you realized that we dropped out of society and we weren't just gamblers, and we made a mistake and you gave our money back. You couldn't get a room in this place for ten years!

MANAGER: Then everyone will want their money back. All the gamblers will say, "Hey, let's go to the Desert Inn and get our money back."

DAVID: Not gamblers. You keep all the money. My wife and I aren't "gamblers." That's what I'm saying. That's the distinction. My wife and I represent the few people . . . and I'll tell you something, there's nobody else that's ever going to come here and have that happen, but it happened . . . and we're the few people who have "taken the chance." And we took it and the Desert Inn corrects it and gives it back. There is a warm feeling here.

MANAGER: But don't you think that everyone will want their money back?

DAVID: No, no! In the campaign, there's a distinction between the "bold," which would be my wife and I, and all the other schmucks who came here to see Wayne Newton.

MANAGER: I like Wayne Newton.

DAVID: Did I say "Wayne Newton"?

MANAGER: What are you talking about? I heard you: "Schmucks see Wayne Newton."

DAVID: Oh no, no. I'm stupid to use an entertainer as a dividing point. I just meant all the people who came here carefree on the way to see a show and my wife and I who, if you knew us, believe me, you would, believe me . . .

MANAGER: You're "bold"?

DAVID: Yes. So what do you think?

MANAGER: I don't think the sign is going to work, and giving the money . . .

DAVID: The sign is wrong. A jingle. A television campaign. "The Desert Inn has heart. The Desert Inn has heart. The Desert Inn has heart."

David attempts to sell his idea as he would an advertising campaign, but the pitch that might work in a corporate boardroom has no credibility in a Las Vegas casino, and David's desperate attempts to convince the casino manager (played brilliantly by Garry Marshall) become increasingly absurd. David's slick presentation – peppered with slogans about "the boldest experiment in advertising history," "taking the chance," or creating a "warm feeling" – is meaningless in an environment such as the Desert Inn, where the bottom line is the earnings from its gambling operations, not the "warm feeling" promoted by advertising campaigns. In his desperate effort to make his case, David only ends up displaying his own cultural elitism, referring to "the schmucks who come to see Wayne Newton" and suggesting that he and Linda are somehow different from all the others – the "gamblers" – who come to the casino. Even the fact that his wife has just spent all night at the roulette table does not convince him that they are in fact "gamblers." For him, there is a basic sociological distinction that supersedes even the grim reality of their situation. David's class-based sense of superiority has no standing here, however. As the manager reminds him, in Vegas there are only winners and losers.

The second scene in which David displays his sociocultural insensitivity is the dialogue with the employment officer in Sanford, another *tour de force* of comic miscommunication. Despite the clear signs that Sanford is a one-horse town with little in the way of positions suitable for David and Linda, David seems unable to conceive of a place where high-paying white-collar jobs simply do not exist.

> DAVID: Do you have anything at all? Can you rack your brains, something maybe in the executive file, or maybe you have a "white-collar box" or something?
> OFFICER: What sort of box would that be?
> DAVID: Just a box of higher-paying jobs.
> OFFICER *(sarcastically)*: Oh, I know, you mean the "$100,000 box"!

While David agrees to take the available position of crossing-guard job (whose benefits package consists of a ride to and from the school each day), Linda has only slightly better luck than her husband, finding a job as the "assistant manager" of a Der Wienerschnitzel fast-food restaurant. Her inflated job title is ironized when the manager himself appears, a local teenager of limited intelligence and even more limited socioeconomic prospects. Linda and David immediately realize that their lives in Sanford will never allow them to replace the nest egg, and they decide to swallow their pride and drive the motor-home to New York, where David can beg for his old job.

The film is resolved happily, though with a heavy dose of irony. Significantly poorer for their brief escapade, but also wiser and more deeply connected to each other for the experience, the Howards realize that even with all its stresses and responsibilities the middle-class rat race is a far better alternative than the dead-end lives of many Americans. Although David and Linda are a yuppie couple temporarily "lost in America," the film has a darker social subtext as well. It depicts a Reagan-era America divided between haves and have-nots, split between those who can afford to drive Mercedes automobiles with leather seats and those forced to take jobs as crossing-guards and fast-food servers.

## III

I turn now to more detailed readings of two comedies of the 1980s and early 1990s: *Raising Arizona* (1986), by Joel and Ethan Coen, and *Metropolitan* (1990), by Whit Stillman. Both comedies deal with issues of class, but while the Coen brothers' film adopts a self-consciously working-class or marginalized perspective on bourgeois existence in the American 1980s, Stillman's film explores the upper-class proto-yuppie milieu of New York City in the 1970s.

If culture-clash comedies like *Desperately Seeking Susan* and *Lost in America* provide an effective satire on the norms of yuppie existence, the form of parody adopted by the Coens attempts a more radical destabilization of language in an effort to dislocate the social position of the audience, placing the viewer outside of the conventions and culture of the classical Hollywood film. In *Raising Arizona,* the twist on the culture-clash comedy involves a reversal of the protagonists' socioeconomic category. Here, rather than the middle-class characters attempting to escape their predictably bourgeois lifestyles, it is the marginalized lower-class characters who attempt to adopt the culture, values, and attitudes of the dominant middle class. Thus the film is not simply a satiric view of yuppies out of their element, but a deeper and more transgressive commentary on the self-absorbed yuppie values of the 1980s and on the materialist aspirations of the middle-class American family.

As Jeff Evans suggests, *Raising Arizona* employs a number of different rhetorics and generic conventions in order to suggest "the confusion of definitions and values at the base of the American dream(s)."[6] The movie's parody of different films and film genres and its continual play with language disturb the audience's traditional cultural assumptions, making possible a more flexible play with social and cultural definitions. The film's pastiche takes the form of citing film genres like the chase film (from the Keystone Kops to *The French Connection*), the post-apocalyptic "road warrior" film *(Mad Max, Road Warrior),* and the outlaw film *(Bonnie and Clyde),* as well as the culture-clash comedy.[7] The film also makes reference to various levels of social class through the use of familiar cultural icons both of working-class life – trailer homes, fast food, and convenience stores – and of a generic form of middle-class existence – the suburban home, the furniture outlet.

The film's protagonists are Edwinna ("Ed"), an Arizona policewoman (Holly Hunter), and H. I. ("Hi") McDonnough (Nicholas Cage), a frequently arrested petty thief specializing in holding up 7-Elevens. Now paroled, Hi's only stabilizing influence is his marriage to Ed and their desire to start a family. Although Ed and Hi are, as Evans suggests, "characters of limited education, background, and promise" (41), they clearly aspire to the American middle class, with its promise of family life, economic security, social stability, and safe distance from a life of crime. Promising to go straight, Hi marries Ed and they settle down to what appears to be the relatively comfortable lifestyle of a lower-middle-class couple. Ed's father stakes them to what is euphemistically referred to as a "starter home in suburban Tempe" (actually a trailer in the middle of the Arizona desert), Hi gets a job in a machine shop which gives them "a paycheck at the end of the week," and they spend their evenings sitting in front of the trailer watching the sunsets. Ed's and Hi's efforts to construct a middle-class existence for themselves and their future family – though made heavily ironic by the discrepancy between their inflated visions and the constant intrusion of social reality – is a sincere if somewhat naive attempt to capture the American Dream.[8] Hi's voiceover informs us of their aspirations, as we see him watering their minuscule patch of front lawn while Ed knits a booty: "Seemed like nothing could stand in our way now. My lawless years were behind me; our child rearin' years lay ahead."

Yet even as the rising tide of the couple's success makes this period feel like "the happy days, the salad days," their circumstances and social backgrounds conspire against them. After numerous attempts to get pregnant fail to produce a child, the couple are informed that Ed is "barren," and they are turned down by an adoption agency because of Hi's criminal record. Ed becomes so depressed that she quits her job with the police force, and Hi begins thinking about robbing convenience stores again. It is at this point that two events occur that will radically change the lives of Ed and Hi. First, they decide to kidnap and raise as their own one of a set of quintuplets born to Mrs. Nathan Arizona, the wife of a successful local furniture salesman. Second, two of Hi's friends from prison, Gale and Evelle Snopes, escape and try to convince Hi to join them in a life of crime. These two events represent not only two complications within the film's plot, but also two ends of the social spectrum that frames Ed's and Hi's universe.

The kidnapped Arizona child ("Nathan Jr.") represents a version of the American Dream of fertility, (over)production, and material promise. As Evans comments:

> The film's title . . . nominally suggests correspondence between an individual and her state or country and, by extension, suggests the tendency for individual dreams to mimic popularizations of national ones. "Raising," as in ascension, initiates the film's satiric depiction of the American cultural virtue of progress, improving the quality of life. (41–42)

The birth of the "Arizona quints" – whose last name also happens to be the name of the state where they live – is a public spectacle (Ed first hears about it on the television news) that is associated within the film's symbolic economy with selling, consumerism, and the creation of economic wealth. Just as the television newscast "sells" the story of the quintuplets by presenting news footage of nurses holding the babies before the camera, Nathan Arizona sells his "Unpainted Arizona" furniture on late-night television commercials. Arizona has become something of a local celebrity as "the owner of the largest chain of unpainted furniture and bathroom fixture outlets throughout the Southwest," but he is now even more famous as the father of quintuplets. Pictured in the ads wearing a white polyester suit and white cowboy boots and gesturing toward a huge warehouse store with an enormous parking lot, Arizona epitomizes a working-class vision of middle-class success and abundance, just as his five perfect children (the unexpected result of his wife's use of fertility pills) constitute an exaggerated version of the idealized American family, and his suburban house – with a large living room dominated by an oil portrait of Nathan and Florence – represents the idealized American home.

The analogy between the Arizona children and the Arizona furniture is visually foregrounded in the scene where Hi kidnaps the baby. The "unpainted" crib bears the name of each baby – Harry, Barry, Larry, Garry, and Nathan Jr. – burned "Bonanza-style" into the headboard. The rhyming names of the babies themselves represent their virtual interchangeability. Only their mother can tell them apart, and even she is not completely sure which of the babies has been kidnapped. Like the thousands of sets of unpainted furniture sold by Nathan Arizona's warehouse (and famous for their low prices), these are babies produced and raised on a mass scale. When Hi brings the kidnapped baby to the car where Ed is waiting, she asks him, "Which one ya get?" "I dunno," Hi replies, "Nathan Jr., I think." Like a consumer convincing himself that he has chosen the one "special" piece of furniture from among the identical models in the warehouse, Hi argues for the superiority of "their" baby: "He's awful damn good. I think I got the best one." And just as the buyer needs a set of directions in order to assemble the product, Hi takes a copy of Dr. Spock's *Baby and Child Care,* which he hands to Ed, saying "Here's the instructions."[9]

The Arizona babies can also be read as a metaphor for the socioeconomic disparities that separate people like Nathan Arizona and his wife from people like Hi and Ed. When he describes the birth of the babies, Hi says that "[Florence] and Nathan hit the jackpot," and he goes on to use the terms usually applied to economics to justify the kidnapping: "we thought it was unfair that some should have so many while others should have so few." Later, when Ed has second thoughts about the kidnapping, Hi makes explicit the parallel of "robbing" the Arizonas to his previous career of robbing 7-Elevens: "She's got four little babies almost as good as this one. It's like when I was robbin' convenience stores." According to Hi's logic, the Arizonas, like the convenience stores, have "more than they can handle"; a single missing baby, he reasons, like a little missing cash from the register, won't cause undue harm to anyone.

At the other end of the social spectrum from the nouveau-riche middle class of the Arizonas are Hi's two prison buddies – Evelle and Gale – who pay Hi and Ed an uninvited visit soon after the "adoption" of Nathan Jr. The appearance in the film of the Snopes brothers reenacts another "birthing" parallel to that of the quintuplets. Their escape from prison involves tunneling their way out of the muddy ground (passing through the main sewer on the way) in a grotesque analogy to the voyage down the birth canal, and their primal bellowing resembles the crying of a newborn infant after its delivery. The two escaped cons — their last name an allusion to William Faulkner's infamous "white trash" southern family – represent an uneducated working-class background, though they have learned in their prison counseling sessions how to effect a more educated demeanor. When they first arrive at Hi and Ed's door, Ed asks them whether they had "busted out of jail":

EVELLE: We released ourselves on our own recognizance.
GALE: What Evelle means to say is, we felt the institution no longer had anything to offer us.

Evelle's and Gale's euphemistic attempt to manipulate the kinds of legalistic and psychological jargon they learned in prison does not fool Ed, who wants them out of the house as soon as possible. In informing them that "this is a decent family now," Ed casts aspersions on their class position (they are not the kind of middle-class role models she wants for her husband and child) as well as on their status as escaped convicts. Later in the film, however, the Snopes's decision to go on a robbery spree "across the entire Southwest proper" reminds us of Nathan Arizona's aggrandizing language of advertising. Despite their more marginalized social position, Gale and Evelle claim a work ethic not far removed from that of Nathan Arizona – the only difference being that theirs involves a career in crime rather than in marketing and sales. "Work is what's kept us happy," Evelle says in one counseling session. When they try to get Hi to join them in a bank robbery, they appeal to an inverted version of American capitalist initiative:

GALE: I know you're partial to convenience stores, but H. I., the sun don't rise and set on the corner grocery.

EVELLE: It's like Doc Schwartz says: you gotta have a little ambition.

Gale and Evelle even find themselves influenced by the domestic ideology that seems to run rampant through the film. After they steal the baby from Hi and Ed, they decide to keep it rather than return it for the ransom money:

EVELLE: Promise we ain't never gonna give him up, Gale! We ain't never gonna let him go!

GALE *(choked up with emotion)*: We'll never give him up, Evelle. He's our little Gale Jr. now.

Evelle's and Gale's decision to "raise Arizona" themselves functions as a further parody of the already parodic attempt of Ed and Hi to create a family through kidnapping. The Coens' multiple layers of parody enact a radical destabilization of a middle-class domestic ideology founded on ideas of security and material progress.

As Gale's and Evelle's manipulation of linguistic codes makes clear, the socially defined use of language is significantly at issue in *Raising Arizona.* But what makes the Coen's parodic use of language different from that of previous Hollywood comedies is the difficulty in assigning specific speech habits to characters from particular social backgrounds. In this film, *all* the characters appear to use a debased form of language, one filled with clichés, characterized by banality, and indebted to the effects of popular culture and the mass media. We have already seen the use of advertising language and pop psychology by Nathan Arizona and the Snopes brothers. Similarly, Hi himself makes use of a jumbled and indiscriminate form of language that appears to lack any clear social origin. After he and Ed bring Nathan Jr. home to their trailer, Hi gives the baby a verbal tour of his new home:

HI: Lookahere, young sportsman. That-there's the kitchen area where Ma and Pa chow down. Over here's the TV, two hours a day maximum, either educational or football so's you don't ruin your appreciation of the finer things. This-here's the divan, for socializin' and relaxin' with the family unit.

Here we find contradictory forms of language, representing the confused form of linguistic habitus associated with a mediatized postmodern culture. The hypercorrect or affected diction of words like "divan" and terms like "the kitchen area" and "the family unit" clash with the use of a seemingly incongruous colloquialism – "chow down" – as well as with less refined or educated speech patterns: "that-there," "this-here," "so's you don't." These linguistic discrepancies are highlighted by a similar collapse of cultural categories: "either educational [television] or football." Later in the same scene, Hi himself adopts the language of television advertising, sounding like a Kodak ad: "Let's us preserve the moment in pictures!" Hi is also fond of a pretentious form of pseudoliterary language, punctuated by such archaisms as "I crept in yon window," "I cannot tarry," and "never the twain shall meet." When describing the doctor's diagnosis of Ed's infertility, Hi extemporizes in a quasi-biblical style that "her insides were a rocky place where my seed could find no purchase." Later in the same monologue, he "preminisced [*sic*] no return of the salad days."

Just as Hi's language reveals his aspirations to a form of upward sociocultural mobility, Ed's language suggests her burning desire for a stable middle-class existence. Her frequent use of the word "decent" – as in "decent people" and "decent home" – and her constant invocation of concepts such as "home life" and "family life," make clear a social agenda very different from Hi's. Ed's model of "decent friends," however, turns out to be a frightening parody of the middle-class family. Hi's foreman Glen and his wife Dot appear to have achieved the kind of middle-class stability Ed desires, complete with life insurance, college savings accounts, and regular pediatric care for their children. But their seemingly more elevated class status is ironically undercut in the scenes in which they appear. Glen is a rather brainless and boorish character who enjoys "Pollack" jokes and wife-swapping ("What they call nowadays Open Marriage"). Dot is completely obsessed by the minutiae of raising children and planning against disastrous scenarios: "You gotta get [the baby] dep-tet boosters yearly or else he'll get lockjaw and night vision," she tells Ed. Later, she admonishes Hi for not having life insurance: "What would Ed and the angel do if a truck came along and splattered your brains all over the interstate? Where would you be then?" Worst of all are Glen and Dot's six children, unruly brats who appear to be the antithesis of the kind of well-mannered and intelligent children their parents think them to be. Glen and Dot maintain their middle-class pride in their children's actions, no matter how offensive. When one of the children writes "FART" in crayon on the wall of Hi and Ed's trailer, Glen comments proudly that he "already knows his ABCs."

The presence of Glen and Dot makes Hi profoundly uncomfortable as he begins to realize that the role of the middle-class family man goes against his very nature. As Hi tells Ed after robbing another 7-Eleven when he temporarily reverts to his criminal behavior, he "never postured as the three piece suit type," and he cannot envision their life together as "Ozzie and Harriet." While Hi's final dream at the end of the film involves a comfortably domestic (though still trailer-bound) existence, surrounded by grandchildren and Thanksgiving dinner, it still represents an uneasy and highly ironic relation to middle-class life. Certainly, as Hi suspects, such a dream represents "wishful thinking" on his part, an attempt to "flee reality." It is also a dream that can be achieved only outside of Arizona: in "a land, not too far away," that he thinks may possibly be "Utah."

## IV

To move from the world of the Coens's *Raising Arizona* to that of Whit Stillman's *Metropolitan* (1990) entails a shift from one end of the American social spectrum to the other. Stillman's dialogue-based comedy of manners can be read as a continuation of the tradition of verbal comedy extending from the early sound films of Lubitsch to the comedies of Woody Allen. *Metropolitan* was the first in a trilogy of films exploring the American upper bourgeoisie, from the preppies of the 1970s to the yuppies of the 1980s. Stillman's subjects are the sons and daughters of an East Coast elite class – the old American social establishment that feels its own dwindling importance within contemporary American financial and cultural life. Even more than Allen's, Stillman's work engages in an extremely detailed analysis of a particular social milieu. His films are comedies of manners in the most interesting sense, exploring the act of cultural reading and misreading within a relatively closed arena of society. In *Metropolitan*, we find the charmed circle of New York debutantes and their "preppie" male contemporaries in the 1970s; in *Barcelona* (1992), we see the American yuppie abroad during the Reagan era, attempting to negotiate cultural differences in a European city; and in *The Last Days of Disco* (1998), we find a group of characters from much the same social background transplanted into the upscale urban club scene of the early 1980s.

Like Allen's *Manhattan,* Stillman's *Metropolitan* focuses on the lifestyles, concerns, and romantic attachments of a particular subset of New York society. Set at a time before the invention of the term "yuppie," but made with a hindsight refracted through the yuppie New York culture of the 1980s, the film involves its characters' endless and humorously naive attempt to define their own class position. When familiar terms like "preppies" and "New York social types" prove inadequate, they attempt to coin a new acronym, "urban haute bourgeoisie" or "UHB." Much of their conversation is taken up with a narcissistic speculation on their own social situation, one that they feel to be in decline even though they have no definitive proof of such a change. Like the narcissistic individuals depicted in Allen's *Manhattan,* this is a social group defined by the shallowness of its moral and cultural values. In this sense, both films can be read as ambivalent morality plays that seek to establish an ironic distance from their subject while at the same time engaging in a subtle examination of class-based lifestyles and attitudes.

The protagonist of *Metropolitan,* Tom Townsend (Edward Clements), is, like Ike in *Manhattan,* simultaneously a participant and an outsider in the society depicted in the film. Tom is a young man of "limited means" who lives with his divorced mother in a small apartment on the Upper West Side. Much of the action of the film takes place in the spacious East-Side apartment of a young debutante, Sally Fowler, who hosts after-parties for the "Sally Fowler Rat Pack" (or "SFRP") during the Christmas debutante season. Tom is immediately defined as socioeconomically distinct from (and inferior to) the group's other members. He lives on Manhattan's West Side rather than the more upscale East Side, and he sleeps in a narrow "maid's room"; he avoids taking taxis (less out of reverse snobbism than out of economic necessity); he has to rent his tuxedo rather than buy one; and he lacks a decent winter coat, shivering conspicuosly in a thinly lined raincoat. Later in the film, Tom receives another blow to his socioeconomic status when he is "disinherited" by his father, who moves with his new wife to Santa Fe. The rat pack discovers that Tom's "resources are limited," as they euphemistically put it, when they see him board a crosstown bus after one of the after-parties. One of the more established members of the rat pack, Nick Smith (Chris Eigeman), announces to the others what appears to be a sufficient explanation for Tom's class difference: "That explains it . . . a Westsider among us."

Tom's "Westsider" status, and the other differences in his social and economic position, are made to explain a great deal within this film of finely calibrated class distinctions. Tom, for example, claims to be a socialist (or even more pretentiously, a "Fourierist") and an admirer of the social critic Thorstein Veblen, whose seminal studies of the "leisure class" serve as a model for his own class attitudes. When he first begins attending the debutante parties, Tom claims to be interested in them in a purely sociological way:

> TOM: I think it is justifiable to go once, to know at first hand what it is you oppose. I'd read Veblen, but it was amazing to see that these things still go on.

Tom's outwardly critical attitudes, however, soon appear to be of little relevance to his social behavior, and he turns out to be less of an outsider than he pretends to be. Although he is not wealthy, he does have a trust fund – at least until his father's decision to abandon him – and he has attended elite schools all his life (Pomfret Academy and now Princeton). While he claims that his trust fund "wasn't that much money" and that he "never really counted on having it," he admits to having experienced the "big load of guilt that went with it." Furthermore, he is clearly "in" with the very exclusive Sally Fowler crowd, and he continues to attend the parties despite his reservations, even buying his own tuxedo by the end of the film.

As the film progresses, it is increasingly clear that Tom's rhetoric about the upper classes is more a cover for his own social insecurities than any profoundly held set of social beliefs.[10] As Nick points out to him, Tom's rhetoric is somewhat falsified by his own "inferior" social situation. When Tom claims to be against the after-parties "on principle," Nick ridicules his guilt about enjoying a conspicuous upper-class lifestyle at the expense of the "less fortunate":

> NICK: Has it ever occurred to you that *you* are the less fortunate? . . . Do you want some richer guy going around saying, "Poor Tom Townsend doesn't even have a winter coat. I can't go to any more parties"?

As Nick suggests, class and class privilege are measured on a relative and not an absolute scale. Tom's guilty conscience about those further down the social ladder is no less patronizing than the attitudes the wealthy hold about Tom himself. As it turns out, even Nick, a solid member of the New York bourgeoisie, has his own class axe to grind. Nick's nemesis is Rick Von Sloneker, an arrogant and rather unsavory member of the highest class fragment of all: the "titled aristocracy." Nick's intense dislike of Von Sloneker – which turns out to be an important element of the film's story line as well as a factor in its social symbology – is founded in part on his more general resentment of a social elite that by virtue of a title can claim a superiority to members of the nonaristocratic upper bourgeoisie. When Von Sloneker makes his first appearance in the film, Nick calls him "riff-raff" and claims that "titled aristocracy are the scum of the earth." Later in the film, when called upon to defend his repeated attacks on Von Sloneker, Nick invents the story (a "composite" based on similar instances) of a girl named "Polly Perkins" whom Von Sloneker supposedly seduced and submitted "to the most disgusting abuse," eventually causing her suicide.

Nick's antipathy for the aristocracy – a class he views as not only arrogant but totally without the kind of personal and moral scruples that define the rest of society – is not shared by all the members of the preppie set, but it does appear to have at least some legitimacy within the context of the film's overall depiction of social relations. The preppies, or "UHBs," have been made to feel inadequate and ineffectual both from above and from below. As a class, they are unable to enjoy either the privileges conferred by an aristocratic title or the ability to compete effectively in the marketplace with the less privileged sectors of the middle class. Charlie Black (Taylor Nichols), another member of the rat pack who spends much of the film engaged in sociological speculation about the situation of the preppie class, explains that the urban upper-middle class operates at a disadvantage with respect to the aristocracy. While the social position of the aristocracy is "publicly acknowledged and secure no matter what they do," members of the "UHB" are obliged "to at least appear to act productively and responsibly." Even the most overt public display of the preppie class (the "deb season") is in jeopardy, according to Nick and Charlie, who continue to attach a great deal of importance to the dances and after-parties as a vanishing symbol of their class distinction. "This is

probably the last deb season as we know it," Nick melodramatically proposes, as Charlie identifies a number of factors – including "the stock
market, the economy, [and] contemporary social attitudes" – that spell
the end not only of deb seasons but more generally of the kind of lifestyle
and socioeconomic expectations enjoyed by the urban bourgeoisie.

The film's satire comes in part from the discrepancy between the conspicuous material comfort enjoyed by members of the preppie class –
upscale Manhattan apartments, summers in Easthampton, elegant
dances and parties – and their obsession with their declining status and
limited opportunities. Nick, Charlie, and the others can take no critical
distance from their own class situation, and thus they lack any sense of
humor concerning its hypocrisies. In one scene, a discussion of Bunuel's
satirical film *The Discreet Charm of the Bourgeoisie*, Stillman satirizes their
myopic self-seriousness:

> CHARLIE: When I first heard the title, I thought, "finally some-
> one's going to tell the truth about the bourgeoisie." What a
> disappointment! It would be hard to imagine a less fair or
> accurate portrait.
> SALLY: Of course: Bunuel's a surrealist – despising the bour-
> geoisie's part of their credo.
> NICK: Where do they get off?
> CHARLIE: The truth is, the bourgeoisie does have a lot of charm.
> NICK: Of course it does. The surrealists were just a lot of social
> climbers.

Nick and Charlie's responses to the Bunuel film represent the typical
defenses of an upper class whose social prerogatives are called into question. Both the assertion of their own distinction ("charm") and the
impugning of the social motives of their attackers ("a lot of social
climbers") are given a wonderfully parodic treatment in the context of
Bunuel's surrealist film, a work whose complex ironies Nick and Charlie
are entirely incapable of reading.

Both Nick and Charlie are dyed-in-the-wool "UHBs," but while
Charlie spends most of his time in a funk about the declining opportunities for the upper classes, Nick takes an almost perverse delight in rel-
ishing the decadent privileges he enjoys. In one scene, when Tom

dismisses playing bridge as "a bourgeois cliché," Nick responds: "That's exactly why I play. I don't enjoy it one bit." Later, when preparing to attend the "International," a garish televised debutante ball in which each debutante is escorted both by a uniformed cadet and an upper-class civilian, Nick remarks: "It's vulgar – I like it a lot."

Nick is the contrarian, always finding the silver lining in any situation, whereas Charlie is the pessimistic rationalist. Charlie expresses his own sense of class paralysis at several points in the film. At one after-party, Charlie lectures the other rat packers about their "downward social mobility":

> CHARLIE: We hear a lot about the great social mobility in America, with the focus usually on the comparative ease of moving upwards. What's less discussed is how easy it is to go down. I think that's the direction we're all headed in. And I think the downward fall is going to be very fast, not just for us as individuals but the whole preppie class.

Although their fathers may have gone to elite schools and had respectable careers, Charlie reasons, their elevated class positions made it more difficult for them to compete in the workplace. As a result, the advantages they enjoyed are even less available to members of the current generation. "We are all almost certainly doomed to failure," Charlie bathetically concludes.

Charlie's obsessive determination that the "UHB" class is "doomed to failure" is one of the cultural clichés that is somewhat playfully examined in the film. In one scene toward the end of the film, after the season's parties have dwindled, Tom and Charlie encounter a fortysomething preppie, Dick Edwards, in a bar. At first, Edwards's world-weary attitude and uninspiring career seem to exemplify Charlie's fears about the decline of his class:

> EDWARDS: I'm not destitute. I have a job that pays decently. But it's all mediocre and unimpressive . . . You start out expecting something much more and some of your contemporaries achieve it – you start reading about them in the papers or seeing them on TV.

When Charlie tries to press Edwards to admit that the preppie class as a whole has failed, however, the older man refuses to share in Charlie's pessimism: "You'll have to accept it – not everyone from our background is doomed to failure." But Charlie remains unconvinced: either the successful members of the class were not "typical UHBs," or "the failure could still be to come."

Although the definition of social class is at the center of this film, the questions it raises are never entirely resolved. Instead, Stillman offers a view of the complexities of class identification in contemporary American society, using the subtly delineated social world of Jane Austen's novels as an intertext for his own depiction of class relations. Austen is an appropriate analogue for Stillman's film, not only in her close attention to nuances of social class, but also in her emphasis on language, conversation, and verbal wit. Austen is only one of the literary and filmic intertexts employed by Stillman. The world of Stillman's films, like that of Woody Allen's, is filled with both literary and popular texts, as well as readers, writers, and interpreters of various kinds. In addition to Austen's novels and Bunuel's film, we find allusions to Tolstoy's *War and Peace,* as well as to different kinds of cultural texts. Nick's "composite" story of Polly Perkins acts as a kind of sensationalist novel in miniature – an embedded story within the story of the film as a whole – and Tom's letters to his girlfriend Serena, later given to Audrey, become a source of fascination as Audrey uses them in an attempt to "read" Tom's character.

The most pervasive use of language in the film, however, is in the form of talk. Dialogue of various kinds provides the very texture of the film to an extent that we find in few American comedies (those of Lubitsch and Wilder come most quickly to mind). The action of the first two-thirds of the film is based almost entirely on idle conversation, social gossip, or intellectually pretentious verbal analysis of social and cultural trends. If the language of *Raising Arizona* represents the debasement of discourse within various segments of contemporary American society, the language of *Metropolitan* is largely made up of the vapid or trivial speech of the urban upper class. It is a form of speech that is as self-conscious as that of *Raising Arizona* is lacking in self-consciousness. Although the characters appear to be highly articulate members of American society, they suffer from the same tendency as Allen's characters in

*Manhattan* to hide behind their language, composing eloquent-sounding but ultimately empty speeches or making meaningless verbal distinctions. Charlie, for example, spends much of the film worrying about the correct terminology for his social class:

> CHARLIE: I don't think "preppie" is a very useful term. It might be descriptive for someone still in high school or college, but it's ridiculous to have to refer to a man in his seventies – like Averell Harriman — as a "preppie." And none of the other terms people use – WASP, PLU, et cetera — are much use either . . . That's why I prefer to use the term "UHB."

The self-aggrandizing and somewhat silly attempt to fix a class position in language, the pretentious use of acronyms, and the punctilious "et cetera" all suggest the language of a group or social class that has lost its ability to find a meaningful sense of social identity. Charlie's overly fussy language — the language of a highly educated but socially isolated class — represents the deep sense of insecurity at the heart of Stillman's "urban haute bourgeoisie."

In another scene, Tom uses sophistic arguments to defend Fourierism against Charlie's charge that it was a "failed" movement:

> TOM: That it ceased to exist, I'll grant you. Whether it was really a failure, I don't think can be definitively said.
> CHARLIE: For me ceasing to exist is failure. That's pretty definitive.
> TOM: Everyone ceases to exist. That doesn't mean everyone's a failure.

As usual, the two characters talk at cross purposes: in Charlie's hyperrationalist schema, everything that ceases to exist must by definition be a failure, while for the more idealistic Tom, "failure" is a concept that is difficult to define in absolute terms. The theme of failure, one that is taken up again in the scene with Edwards, resonates in important ways throughout the film. Central to Stillman's vision is the question of what it means to be a failure – or, on the contrary, to be a success – within a variety of domains: political, economic, social, cultural, ethical, interpersonal. Stillman's ironically detached cinematic style, and the difficulty in any meaningful communication between the different characters, leaves ambiguous the ultimate definition of success, both individually and as a social group.

## V

The work of filmmakers like Stillman and the Coen brothers, though it displays an awareness that an entity such as class exists, expresses a profound uncertainty about how class demarcations relate to the American success ethic or the American Dream, and about what class definitions can mean in a society increasingly dominated by the media and popular culture. While a 1930s romantic comedy like *It Happened One Night* typifies the classical paradigm of Hollywood comedy – one in which personal integrity can be reconciled with material wealth and prosperity – American comedies have become increasingly cynical about such utopian resolutions. In the later comedies of Capra, with their more ambivalent resolutions of class conflict, we already find a rejection of the social ideology promoted by the Hollywood studio system. In the still more cynical films of Sturges and Tashlin, we see an intensified critique of this same ideology. By the 1980s and 1990s, we find the depiction of an America in which no attempt at social self-definition – whether it is the "Easy Rider" ideal in *Lost in America,* the televised debutante ball in *Metropolitan,* or the "Unpainted Arizona" television commercials in *Raising Arizona* – remains free of the omnipresent influence of the media and its representations. In *Lost in America,* we find a couple frustrated by the limitations of the middle-class culture it has worked so hard to construct, and yet unable to break out of the confines of that culture and achieve a larger vision of American life. In *Raising Arizona,* we find a culture confused about its definitions of the success ethic, the American Dream, and class mobility. In the haute bourgeoisie trilogy of Stillman, we find a class that attempts either to deny its own existence (as in its reluctance to accept the label of "yuppie" in *The Last Days of Disco*) or to perpetuate itself through a reliance on ritualized behaviors and the creation of meaningless labels.

The film with which I will conclude both this chapter and this study of American film comedy is one that goes beyond the implicit critique of the contemporary media to engage in a more explicit satire of a television-crazed culture. Ben Stiller's *The Cable Guy* (1996), starring comedian comic Jim Carrey, is one of the most provocative comedies of the 1990s, though it was largely rejected by audiences and critics alike.[11] Along with other "dark" comedies of the decade, such as Quentin Tarantino's *Pulp Fiction* (1993), John Waters's *Serial Mom* (1993), Gus van Sant's *To Die For* (1995), the Coen brothers' *Fargo* (1996) and *The Big Lebowski* (1997), and Peter Weir's *The Truman Show* (1998), the film displays a mastery not only of the American comic tradition but also of various other film and television genres, any of which are fair game for its brilliant postmodern pastiche. For Carrey, whose masterful comic performance dominates the film, *The Cable Guy* was a departure from the genre of outrageous comedian comedy he had already exploited in films such as *Ace Ventura: Pet Detective* (1993), *The Mask* (1994), and *Dumb and Dumber* (1994).

The story, about an obsessively needy cable installer who "stalks" his customers in order to gain their friendship, is both a bitter satire of contemporary American culture and a postmodern hybrid. Stiller calls the film a "satiric thriller," a comedy on the border between a thriller and a parody of a thriller (just as *Pulp Fiction*, for example, is simultaneously a crime film and a parody of one).[12] In the movie, Carrey plays the "cable guy," a pathetic and overbearing lout who is so desperate for affection that he insinuates himself into the life of his customer Steven Kovacs (Matthew Broderick). If the plot is inspired by "stalker" films such as *Cape Fear* and *Fatal Attraction*, the cinematography of Robert Brinkmann – with its dark tones and active camera movement – owes a debt to the gothic genre, particularly the horror films of Roman Polanski.

Although we never learn the real name of the "cable guy" – who uses a series of aliases taken from popular television programs of the 1960s – he is known throughout most of the film as "Chip Douglas" (one of the characters from the series *My Three Sons*). Chip's obsession with television began at an early age. Like many others of his generation, he spent far more time in front of the television than with his parents, and he feels that he was raised by virtual television families such as those of *The Brady Bunch*, *The Cosby Show*, and *Happy Days* rather than by a real family: "I'm the bastard son of Clare Huxtable. I'm the lost Cunningham. I learned the facts of life from *The Facts of Life*."

Chip's choice of these particular television families – all exemplifying the middle-class American ideal – is significant given his own socioeconomic background. A psychotic n'er-do-well who as we later discover has been fired from his job as a cable installer, Chip lacks all the appurtenances of middle-class life: a job, a family, and a home of his own. In a speech near the beginning of the film, Chip tells Steven that he never met his real father and that his mother worked nights, leaving him in front of the television. His life is the antithesis of that portrayed on a television sitcom: "Reality isn't *Father Knows Best* anymore; it's a kick in the face on a Saturday night with a steel-toed Kodiak work boot, and a trip to the hospital for reconstructive surgery."

Steven, on the other hand, a thirtysomething yuppie from a middle-class background, has a promising career with a large architectural firm. When the film opens, we see Steven's furniture being moved into a new apartment; as we soon find out, he has just entered a period of trial separation from his girlfriend Robin. Chip's attempt to befriend Steven, and later to take over his life, can be seen not only as the quest for human contact by a desperately lonely individual, but also as his attempt to affiliate himself with a class to which he can never otherwise belong. The class subtext of the film was partially informed by Carrey's own life experience. When his father lost his job as a company controller, the family was forced to work as janitors and security guards in a factory and lived for a time out of a Volkswagen van and a tent.

*The Cable Guy* can be linked with other comedies of the "culture-clash" mode, especially the darker examples of the genre such as *After Hours* and *Something Wild*. But rather than the case of the middle-class character crossing the line into a marginal world, it involves the invasion of middle-class or yuppie space by the working class or socially unacceptable "other." The film revolves around a number of symbolic social spaces within which the characters interact, the two most important of which are Steven's apartment (invaded in increasingly literal ways by Chip) and the huge satellite dish to which Chip takes Steven and later Robin. Whereas Steven is associated with several "homes" – his own apartment, Robin's apartment, and his suburban family home – Chip is apparently homeless; he sleeps in his cable delivery truck, and the closest thing he has to a home is the satellite dish deep in the woods. The dish represents a place of security for Chip, who takes his new cable customers there to impress them with the futuristic technology of cable TV. The return to the dish also represents a symbolic return to the mother. Chip has visions of his childhood while there, and he tries to kill himself at the end of the film by jumping into the center of the circular dish from its phallic control tower.

Chip's desire to belong to the middle class and to deny his own working-class identity can be seen throughout the film. While Steven attempts to distance himself from the "cable guy" by discouraging discussions of his personal life ("I certainly don't want to talk about it with *you*," he pointedly tells him), Chip insists on a more personalized relationship with his customer. Not only does he rearrange the furniture for the installation, but he gives Steven his personal pager number, leaves repeated messages on his answering machine, invites him to see the satellite dish, takes him to dinner at his favorite restaurant, and shows up uninvited at his basketball game. Chip is blind to the social implications of his job, which he sees as far more significant than that of a low-level service worker. Not satisfied to be merely the "cable guy" (already a term whose jokey familiarity brands it with a sense of professional marginality), he wants to be treated as a friend and a social equal. "You'd be surprised how many customers treat me like snot," he tells Steven, "like I'm a plumber or something." Yet at the same time his attitude toward his profession is something between self-aggrandizement and self-parody. He asks Steven to mail him a comment card when he has finished the installation, and he initially acts shocked when Steven suggests slipping him $50 for free cable channels ("You mean 'illegal cable'"?). He ends up giving him the extra cable for free (a service he apparently provides for all his "preferred customers").

The class distinctions in the film are clearly marked by cultural taste and differences in cultural capital. Steven's world is one of slick architectural presentations to clients, white wine tastefully sipped on the couch with his girlfriend, and the occasional friendly basketball game with his friends. Chip's idea of fun is dinner at the tacky theme restaurant "Medieval Times" ("the finest restaurant in town," he proudly claims), a ride in his "fun van" (the cable company van which he has apparently kept after being fired), or an all-night karaoke party. Yet at the same time that he embodies a kind of tacky and outmoded culture, Chip is able to change, Zelig-like, to fit each of the film's different social situations. He is, in this sense, an exemplary postmodern figure, simultaneously identifiable by class and able to manipulate its semiotic markers.

Chip is also able to insinuate himself into the lives of Robin and Steven's family. His maniacal perfectionism makes him a perfect chameleon: he comes to the karaoke party perfectly outfitted as a 1960s hippie (wide belt and fringed suede jacket); in a scene where he impersonates a bathroom attendant, he dresses in 1970s polyester slick; at "Medieval Times," he orders his food in faux medieval English; at Steven's family house, he dresses and acts like the perfect boy next door, even sporting a V-neck sweater. Chip is a nightmare on both a social and a personal level, embodying the social repression of the upwardly mobile middle class. When he comes to play basketball with Steven and his friends, he literally destroys their friendly game, playing with such ferocious abandon that he alienates the other players and breaks the backboard. A staged fight between Chip and Steven at "Medieval Times" – using fake medieval weapons and armor – becomes a grudge match that Chip transforms into a realistic "battle to the death." When Chip hears that Steven is unhappy about Robin seeing other men, he beats up her date in a restaurant bathroom. Later, he orchestrates getting Steven arrested and put in jail (framing him on the charge of receiving stolen goods) and then manages to get him fired from his job by playing a tape on the office computer system of Steven insulting his boss. By the time Chip visits Steven in jail, he has succeeded in reversing their social roles: Chip now wears a suit and tie, and Steven is in prison garb. On Steven's release, Chip gets himself invited to dinner at Steven's family home, where Chip is accepted by Robin and Steven's parents while Steven is treated as the outsider.

Chip's performance (and Carrey's performance as Chip) can also be read in terms of the Bakhtinian carnivalesque. The carnival is invoked in Chip's taste for excess (exemplified by the "home entertainment system" he gets for Steven, complete with big-screen TV, professional sound system, and karaoke machine), his transgression of decorum and aesthetic rules (hiring a prostitute to spend the night with Steven), and his bawdy humor (he enjoys playing "Porno Password" with Steven and his family and watching Steven squirm as he gives the clues for "vagina" and "nipple" to his mother). As opposed to the uptight and somewhat humorlessly yuppie Steven, Chip at times appears to be a welcome change. Steven himself starts to loosen up around Chip and ends up enjoying both the evening at "Medieval Times" and the karaoke party.

Ultimately, however, the carnival is not invoked in the service of a liberating subversion of social norms. Instead, it represents a loss of control stimulated by a media-obsessed culture. What unites each of Chip's social performances – whether it is the perfectly simulated Altamont concert at the karaoke party, the fake medieval combat with Steven at "Medieval Times," the backboard-breaking slam dunk in the basketball game, or the ritualized assault on Robin's date – is their debt to media-tized popular culture. Often, these scenes cite several cultural references at one time. When Chip and Steven stage their fight at "Medieval Times," Chip suddenly warps into a battle on *Star Trek* between Spock and Captain Kirk; Chip's attack on Robin's date in the men's room com-bines references to pro wrestling, Dizzy Gillespie, and the actor Eric Roberts; and the climactic scene at the satellite dish contains allusions to Kevin Costner's *Waterworld,* the *Spiderman* series, and the James Bond film *Goldeneye.* Chip lives his life through a haze of film and television culture. As he says in the final scene, "the trouble with real life is there's no danger music."

Like Chip's social identity, his use of language is a hybrid of various speech genres: TV-speak, colloquialism, cliché, and psychobabble, as well as more formal discourse. His lisp, a psychophysical deformity of speech that is symptomatic of a much deeper problem, makes his manic use of language all the more jarring, as if an overcompensation for a social and personal lack. Like Virgil Starkwell in *Take the Money and Run,* another social and metaphysical misfit, Chip is constantly using speech in ways that are inappropriate to the social situation. And like the characters in *Raising Arizona,* Chip's language is filled with clichés, the only "truth" he has learned from a life of watching television. His speech is sprinkled with expressions such as "cleanliness is next to godliness," "necessity is the mother of invention," and "what doesn't kill us makes us stronger." His speech is annoying to an almost maniacal degree, punctuated by grating colloquialisms and adolescent expressions ("Stev-ie, time to leav-ie"). At the same time, he has mastered the "soundbite" of television broadcasting: "the future is now," "a ride on the information superhighway," "sending entertainment and information to millions of satisfied citizens." In Carrey's nonstop verbal performance, Chip is like a television with the volume constantly turned up, incapable of silence and constituted by a seemingly limitless repertoire of language.

At times, Chip seems capable of an eloquence that is surprising, until we realize that his speech is almost always a simulation of something heard on television. At one point, he gives Steven lines of pop psychology taken directly from *The Jerry Springer Show* to use with Robin. Not surprisingly, they work. Chip is not the only character in the film affected by television culture; he is simply the most exaggerated case of this malaise. As the film opens, Steven is seen alone in his apartment channel-surfing through a series of talk shows, game shows, sitcoms, and soap operas. Like Chip, he compares his own situation to that of a television character: "I feel like Felix Unger," he says, referencing the character thrown out by his wife at the beginning of *The Odd Couple*. If Steven is Felix Unger, Chip is his Oscar Madison, the other half of an updated and far more dysfunctional "odd couple." The postmodern version of the original uncultured slob is no longer a cigar-smoking sports writer but a dystopic "cable guy," a receptor and transmitter of all the violence and noise, the pathos and banality, the inflation and stylized excess of the televised world.

Like cable television itself – a form of radical heteroglossia that has been sanitized of all relation to material and social difference – the character we know only as "Chip Douglas" or "Larry Tate" or "Ricky Ricardo" is a transmission without a fixed source or a meaningful social reality. And just like the content of television – a mode of information or entertainment that invades our consciousness without telling us anything we really need to know – "Chip" is an arbitrary and endlessly floating signifier without a meaningful link to the past, present, or future in the real (social or linguistic) world. As Mark Poster puts it in his analysis of television ads, each ad comes to represent "an unreal made real, a set of meanings communicated that have no meaning . . . a simulation of a communication" that is made to seem "more real than reality."[13] This analysis can be extended to all aspects of television, from talk shows and infotainment programs to reruns of *Star Trek*, *The Odd Couple*, and *I Love Lucy*. "Chip," as his name suggests, is at once an overgrown child whose psychic progression has never moved beyond the television programs he watched in the 1960s and an interchangeable component (the computer chip) in a vast information system. As such, he can only be satisfied in the midst of what Jean Baudrillard calls the "hyperreal," the state of simulated and artificially heightened reality that predominates in the postmodern world, and his speech is a virtuoso performance with no real communication behind it.[14] Chip experiences human emotions (loneliness, anger) and human needs (friendship, human contact), but they are so filtered through a system of media-inspired references that he can never achieve the condition of a full human being. For that reason he cannot be killed, only interrupted or temporarily "turned off." Significantly, he survives his dramatic suicide attempt at the end of the film and will live on to torment anyone else who comes into contact with him. The film takes a final comic turn as the medic in the helicopter taking Chip to the hospital calls him "buddy." "Am I really your buddy?" Chip asks, thus setting into action another, untold narrative.

As exemplified in each of the films discussed in this chapter, the continuing success of American film comedy has been due in large part to its capacity to renew itself, to find new life with each generation of comic actors and directors and with each modification of its generic conventions. If lines of continuity can be drawn from Groucho Marx to Jerry Lewis to Jim Carrey, from Preston Sturges to Frank Tashlin to Woody Allen, or from Ernst Lubitsch to Billy Wilder to Whit Stillman, we also see the emergence of important differences in each successive era.

Where comedies at the beginning of the sound era focused explicitly on issues of class and social difference, these issues inform recent American comedies in more subtle ways. With the spread of the middle class to include all but the very poorest and most marginalized members of society, "class" has been an increasingly elusive category both in American society and in American film. Nevertheless, the differences in socioeconomic status, cultural capital, and educational background that constitute social class are a permanent feature of modern capitalist (and even "postcapitalist") society. As this study has shown, comedies not only provide entertainment or suggest utopian solutions to social problems; they also explore the underlying tensions and contradictions that exist within any modern society. If the subject of class at the end of the twentieth century no longer provides the generating impulse behind comic films as it did in the 1930s, American comedies continue to display an acute awareness of social realities, an awareness that often reveals itself through language. At their best, comedies continue to use language as a means of transgressing or challenging the rules of normalized social discourse. In doing so, they provide important insights into the increasingly complex web of social relationships by which we define our lives.

# NOTES

## INTRODUCTION

1. Quoted in Charles Musser, "Work, Ideology, and Chaplin's Tramp,"in Robert Sklar and Charles Musser, eds., *Resisting Images: Essays in Cinema and History* (Philadelphia: Temple University Press, 1990), 43.
2. Steven Ross, *Working-Class Hollywood: Silent Film and the Shaping of Class in America* (Princeton, NJ: Princeton University Press, 1998).
3. Amy Schrager Lang, "The Syntax of Class in Elizabeth Stuart Phelps's *The Silent Partner*," in Wai-Chee Dimock and Michael Gilmore, eds., *Rethinking Class: Literary Studies and Social Formations* (New York: Columbia University Press, 1994), 268.
4. Lary May, *Screening Out the Past: The Birth of Mass Culture and the Motion Picture Industry* (New York: Oxford University Press, 1980), 257.
5. See Miriam Hansen, *Babel and Babylon: Spectatorship in American Silent Film* (Cambridge, MA: Harvard University Press, 1991), 64.
6. Ross takes an essentially negative view of these cross-class fantasies, which he feels "reveal an extremely conservative and patronizing attitude toward class relations" (201). Ross's characterization may by and large be accurate, although if we read these films in Richard Dyer's terms as "utopian" forms of entertainment rather than simply as reactionary fantasies, we can see them as socially liberating as well as politically deadening forms of cultural production. See my discussion of Dyer below.
7. Margaret Thorp, *America at the Movies* (New Haven: Yale University Press, 1939), 271–72.
8. Richard Pells, *Radical Visions and American Dreams: Culture and Thought in the Depression Years* (New York: Harper and Row, 1973), 267.
9. Richard Dyer, *Only Entertainment* (New York and London: Routledge, 1992), 18. Dyer's categories for utopian solutions to social tensions, inadequacies, or absences include abundance as a response to poverty or scarcity, energy as a

response to exhaustion, intensity as a response to dreariness or monotony, transparency as a response to social manipulation, and community as a response to social fragmentation. Although all of these utopian elements can be found in Hollywood comedies of the 1930s, other aspects of Depression-era comedy such as irony, satire, and parody frequently work against them.

10. It would be difficult to characterize as utopian the perspective of such films as the Marx Brothers' *Duck Soup* (1933) or Fields's *It's a Gift* (1934), or in more recent decades Stanley Kubrick's *Dr. Strangelove* (1963), Mike Nichols's *Carnal Knowledge* (1971), Woody Allen's *Sleeper* (1973), Martin Scorsese's *After Hours* (1986), the Coen brothers' *Raising Arizona* (1986), or Robert Altman's *The Player* (1992), even though all of them are essentially comic. Instead, these comedies involve a vision that is at once liberating and anxiety-provoking, a form of anarchy that is always on the edge of going *too* far beyond social norms.

11. Steve Neale and Frank Krutnik, *Popular Film and Television Comedy* (New York: Routledge, 1990), 4.

12. Robert Stam, *Subversive Pleasures: Bakhtin, Cultural Criticism, and Film* (Baltimore, MD: Johns Hopkins University Press, 1989), 45.

13. Pierre Bourdieu, *Language and Symbolic Power,* ed. John Thompson, trans. Gino Raymond and Matthew Adamson (Cambridge, MA: Harvard University Press, 1991), 86.

14. Kathleen Rowe, *The Unruly Woman: Gender and the Genres of Laughter* (Austin: University of Texas Press, 1995), 150. Also see Patricia Mellencamp's discussion of the musical comedy *Gold Diggers of 1933* for an analysis of the intersection of class and gender in classical Holywood film. In *Gold Diggers,* Mellencamp argues, the union of three working-class chorus girls with upper-class men can be read as a figure for the restoration of American capitalism during the Depression. These marriages defuse both the economic woes of the Depression and the unbridled sexuality of the young women, "collapsing the inequities of both class and gender into marital salvation." See "The Sexual Economics of *Gold Diggers of 1933*," in Peter Lehman, ed., *Close Viewings: An Anthology of New Film Criticism* (Tallahassee: Florida State University Press, 1990), 180.

15. In *Bringing Up Baby,* for example, it is Susan's capacity for wordplay, storytelling, and lies, along with her complete lack of concern for middle-class decorum and the patriarchal rules of the working world, that allows for her social transgressiveness. In *The Lady Eve,* it is Jean's storytelling abilities, along with her capacity to take on an entirely new social identity as easily as a new set of clothes, that enables her to exercise her power over "Hopsie" Pike and the world of assumed masculine privilege he represents. And in *Ball of Fire,* it is Sugarpuss's ability to exploit her own vulgarity and her streetwise vernacular that allows her to seduce Potts and disrupt the orderly work of the Totten Foundation.

## CHAPTER I

1. Quoted in Pells, *Radical Visions,* 264.

2. In *The Dialogic Imagination: Four Essays,* ed. Michael Holquist, trans. Caryl Emerson and Michael Holquist (Austin: University of Texas Press, 1981), Bakhtin defines the heteroglossic or dialogic mode of the novel as one in which

the author presents the reader with a series of "heterogeneous stylistic unities" (261) rather than a unified voice or style.

3. "Comedian comedy" is a term used to denote a form of comedy characterized by "its self-consciousness and artificiality, its constant disruption of a 'fictional universe' in order to acknowledge the comedian's status as a performer." See Henry Jenkins, *What Made Pistachio Nuts?: Early Sound Comedy and the Vaudeville Aesthetic* (New York: Columbia University Press, 1992), 10. In comedian comedy, a tension exists between the comedian's (or comedy team's) position as a recognized performer and the need to integrate that performance into a classically linear narrative. There is also a tension between the comedian's disruptive, eccentric, or countercultural behavior and the social, cultural, or narrative conformity represented by other characters in the film. Examples of comedian comedy would be the films of Laurel and Hardy, W. C. Fields, the Marx Brothers, Burns and Allen, Jerry Lewis, Peter Sellers, and Mel Brooks. More recently, films featuring comedians such as Steve Martin, Chevy Chase, John Belushi, and Jim Carrey could be located within the comedian comedy genre.

4. Gerald Mast, *The Comic Mind: Comedy and the Movies,* 2nd ed. (Chicago: University of Chicago Press, 1979), 219.

5. See Kael's introduction to *Three Screen Comedies by Samson Raphaelson* (Madison: University of Wisconsin Press, 1983), 17.

6. In addition to *Trouble in Paradise,* Milner was to shoot some of the most successful comedies for both Lubitsch and Preston Sturges, including *Design for Living, The Lady Eve, The Palm Beach Story,* and *Unfaithfully Yours.* He was known for an elegant but restrained cinematographic style.

7. *Language and Symbolic Power,* 66.

8. The film made money on its initial release, even in the difficult year of 1932, and was on the list of box-office leaders for the month of November.

9. James Harvey, *Romantic Comedy from Lubitsch to Sturges* (New York: Knopf, 1987), 53–54.

10. Despite the apparent differences in style, Lubitsch was interested in working with the Marx Brothers on a film in the early 1930s. Paramount announced the film (an early incarnation of *Duck Soup*) as a burlesque of mythical kingdoms to be titled *Oo La La.* When the time came to make the film, however, Lubitsch was unavailable, having begun work on *Design for Living.* It is difficult to imagine what a Marx Brothers film directed by Lubitsch would have looked like, or how his highly controlled directing style would have fit in with their more "anarchic" approach to filmmaking. Leo McCarey, another distinguished Hollywood director who ultimately directed the Marx Brothers in *Duck Soup,* found working with them a very frustrating experience, even though he contributed to what many believe was their best picture.

11. The later MGM films are less subversive and anarchic than the Paramount productions, though they also contain important elements of class satire. I have chosen to focus on the Paramount pictures both because of the period during which they were made and because of the stronger contrast they offer with other Hollywood comedies of the 1930s.

12. Henry Jenkins, *What Made Pistachio Nuts?, 185.* The objects of political satire in these films include the machinations of German munitions manufacturers,

wars between small European states, American foreign aid grants, and the lack
of substance in American politics.

13. Joe Adamson, *Groucho, Harpo, Chico and Sometimes Zeppo: A History of the
Marx Brothers and a Satire on the Rest of the World* (New York: Simon and
Schuster, 1973), 212.

14. Allen Eyles, *The Marx Brothers: Their World of Comedy* (New York: A. S. Barnes,
1969), 30.

15. Amy Lawrence, *Echo and Narcissus: Women's Voices in Classical Hollywood Cinema* (Berkeley: University of California Press, 1991), 98.

16. See Michel Marie, "The Poacher's Aged Mother: On Speech in *La Chienne* by
Jean Renoir," *Yale French Studies* 60 (1980): 227.

17. Gerald Weales, *Canned Goods as Caviar: American Film Comedy of the 1930s*
(Chicago: University of Chicago Press, 1985), 60.

18. Allen Eyles, *The Complete Films of the Marx Brothers* (New York: Citadel Press,
1992), 92.

19. In a revisiting of the same comic motif, *At the Circus* ends with another example of a high cultural performance being replaced with a mass cultural spectacle.
At the party thrown by the wealthy Mrs. Dukesbury for the high society of the
"Newport 400," Groucho replaces the symphony orchestra to be conducted by
the famous French maestro Jardinet with a performance by the circus owned by
the film's hero, Jeff Wilson. In a brilliant closing sequence, the orchestra is
placed on a floating bandstand tethered near the shoreline of Mrs. Dukesbury's
Newport mansion. Chico and Groucho cut the rope attaching them to land,
and the members of the orchestra continue to play, oblivious to their surroundings as they drift further and further out to sea.

20. See Michel Chion, *The Voice in Cinema*, ed. and trans. Claudia Gorbman (New
York: Columbia University Press, 1999).

21. Mark Winokur, *American Laughter: Immigrants, Ethnicity, and 1930s Hollywood Film Comedy* (New York: St. Martin's, 1996), 139–40.

22. Groucho usually lacks the patience to deal with Harpo, whereas Chico can com-
municate with both Groucho and Harpo and often serves as intermediary between
them. Chico is usually in a subservient position to Groucho but is a more "civilized" and less purely destructive physical and social force than Harpo.

23. The use of pretentious WASP names has an interesting biographical parallel with
the case of Groucho's mother Minnie, who changed her name in the 1920s to
Minnie Palmer, capitalizing both on the name of a popular vaudeville star and on
the high-class status of Chicago's Palmer House. See Wes Gehring, *Groucho and
W. C. Fields: Huckster Comedians* (Jackson: University of Mississippi Press, 1994),
45–46. Also note the recurrence of the socially pretentious initial in the names of
Groucho's characters: Jeffrey T. Spaulding, Rufus T. Firefly, Hugo Z. Hackenbush,
Otis B. Driftwood, Wolf J. Flywheel, J. Cheever Loophole, and S. Quentin Quale.
Similarly, in W. C. Fields's comedies like *It's a Gift* and *The Bank Dick*, we find the
satirical use of socially pretentious names. *It's a Gift* features the Bissonette family
who insist on the faux-French pronunciation "Bis-o-nay." In *The Bank Dick*, an
even more pointed joke is based on the name of the Fields character, Egbert Sousè,
who is constantly having to remind people of the "accent *grave* over the e" in order
to prevent them from using the more accurate but inelegant "Mr. Souse."

24. The only one of the films in which all the Marx Brothers appear as poor immigrants is *Monkey Business,* where they are stowaways on an ocean liner headed for New York. Even here, however, Groucho quickly assumes the identity of the ship's captain, if only temporarily.
25. These foils continue in the MGM films, most notably with the characters of Herman Gottlieb in *A Night at the Opera* and Whitmore in *A Day at the Races.*
26. As Winokur suggests, "The Marx Brothers' satire of the wealthy is always a satire of the pretensions of upward mobility and a denial of the existence of authentic gentility. Culture is always only veneer, the attempt to escape the consequences of a self that is neither genteel nor refined" (128).
27. Groucho Marx, *Groucho and Me* (New York: B. Geis/Random House, 1959), 23.
28. Quoted in Hector Arce, *Groucho* (New York: Putnam, 1970), 34.
29. Glenn Mitchell, *The Marx Brothers Encyclopedia* (London: Batsford, 1997), 126.
30. Arthur Marx, *Life with Groucho* (New York: Simon and Schuster, 1954).
31. Charles Musser, "Ethnicity, Role-Playing, and American Film Comedy: From *Chinese Laundry Scene* to *Whoopee* (1894–1930)," in Lester Friedman, ed., *Unspeakable Images: Ethnicity and the American Cinema* (Urbana: University of Illinois Press, 1991), 71.
32. While some film historians and critics have made the point that the Marx Brothers never played explicitly Jewish characters in their films, and Groucho himself claimed that they were not identified by contemporary audiences as Jewish, it seems clear – as both Charles Musser and Mark Winokur have observed – that their Jewish identity as performers is crucial to an understanding both of their ethnic humor and their relationship to a normative WASP culture.
33. In *A Night at the Opera* he is Otis B. Driftwood, personal business manager to the wealthy Mrs. Claypool; in *A Day at the Races* he is the "horse doctor" Hugo Z. Hackenbush, who pretends to be a psychiatrist; in *The Big Store* he is a struggling private detective (Wolf J. Flywheel) who is hired as a bodyguard for the department store heir Tommy Rogers; in *At the Circus* he is a shady lawyer (J. Cheever Loophole) who in one scene claims he has been disbarred; in *Go West* he is an east coast con man seeking rather unsuccessfully to make his fortune in the west.
34. Another example from an MGM film would be the end of *At the Circus,* when Mrs. Dukesbury, the "richest widow in America" and a particularly snobby version of the Dumont persona, becomes an unwilling part of the circus act. In this scene, Dumont is fired from a canon, loses her skirt, is forced to hang from Harpo's legs in a trapeze act, and suffers the final indignity of having a gorilla walk over her before finally being allowed to fall into a net. The social implications of placing the "three-ring circus" in the midst of a Newport house party are obvious, but the social humiliation of Mrs. Dukesbury in front of her guests is taken further than would be necessary to make the point.
35. The film contains at least two unambiguous references to the Brothers' Jewish identity. One of Groucho's lines in "Hooray for Captain Spaulding" is "Did someone call me 'schnorrer'?" and after the Brothers appear singing "My Old Kentucky Home" Groucho announces, "This program is coming to you from the House of David." Chico and Harpo's prior acquaintance with Chandler in Czechoslovakia would also seem to place all their origins in the Jewish ghetto.

The Chandler connection was an even more specific Jewish reference in the stage version of *Animal Crackers,* in which Chandler's original name was not "Abe Kabibble" but "Rabbi Cantor." According to *The Marx Brothers Encyclopedia,* the figure of Chandler was intended as a satire on the Jewish financier and art connoisseur Otto Kahn, who regularly attempted to downplay or deny his ethnic heritage. The change in Chandler's name was only one of several deletions of Jewish references from the filmed version.

36. Mitchell, *The Marx Brothers Encyclopedia,* 13.
37. In the stage version, there were additional references to the stock market, which was obviously very much on the minds of both the Brothers and their audiences.
38. Many of the most ridiculous of these pronouncements are collected in Edward Apley's 1931 compilation *Oh Yeah?* (New York: Viking, 1931). Hoover, for example, predicted in March 1930 that the worst effects of the crash would have passed within sixty days; by May 1930 he was declaring (prematurely by several years) that the worst had already passed. Executives in the film industry were no less sanguine: Adolph Zukor suggested in August 1930, just before the release of *Animal Crackers,* that "if we all buckle down to our jobs, prosperity will be back again before we realize it." Members of Hoover's cabinet, as well as prominent executives from the steel, automobile, and banking industries, made similar statements.
39. In the original play, Arabella was "a more spoiled, immature character than her film counterpart" (Mitchell, *The Marx Brothers Encyclopedia,* 13), another indication of the more biting social satire of the stage version as compared to the film.
40. In addition to personal insults regarding Mrs. Rittenhouse's looks and age, Spaulding also insults the condition of Mrs. Rittenhouse's home, calling it "one of the frowsiest-looking joints I've ever seen," questioning the condition of her wallpaper, and suggesting that she is "no longer attracting the class of people she used to."

## CHAPTER 2

1. Rita Barnard, *The Great Depression and the Culture of Abundance: Kenneth Fearing, Nathaniel West, and Mass Culture in the 1930s* (New York: Cambridge University Press, 1995), 15.
2. Mike Cormack, *Ideology and Cinematography in Hollywood, 1930–39* (New York: St. Martin's, 1994), 106.
3. Ed Sikov, *Screwball: Hollywood's Madcap Romantic Comedies* (New York: Crown Books, 1989), 28.
4. Stanley Cavell, *Pursuits of Happiness: The Hollywood Comedy of Remarriage* (Cambridge, MA: Harvard University Press, 1981).
5. Brian Neve, *Film and Politics in America: A Social Tradition* (New York: Routledge, 1992), 1.
6. Giuliana Muscia, *Hollywood's New Deal* (Philadelphia: Temple University Press, 1996), 67.
7. In the first category we find *It Happened One Night, Holiday, The Philadelphia Story, Libelled Lady,* and *Bringing Up Baby;* in the second are *Midnight, Hands Across the Table, Easy Living, Fifth Avenue Girl, The Lady Eve, The Palm Beach Story, Bachelor Mother,* and *You Can't Take It with You.*

8. Interview in Pat McGilligan, ed., *Backstory: Interviews with Screenwriters of Hollywood's Golden Age* (Berkeley and Los Angeles: University of California Press, 1986), 221.
9. These forces included a national moral crusade by the Catholic Church, the establishment of the National Recovery Administration that created more direct regulation of the movie industry by the government, and the publication of a series of books on the harmful effects of the movies on children. See Gregory Black, *Hollywood Censored: Morality Codes, Catholics, and the Movies* (New York: Cambridge University Press, 1994).
10. Black, *Hollywood Censored,* 173.
11. The film is listed in Ed Sikov's filmography of screwball pictures, but this may have more to do with its release date and the identity of its director than with the film itself. Jack Conway also directed the screwball comedies *Libelled Lady* and *Love Crazy.*
12. The title appears to be a late addition, since the only reference to Eadie's place of origin, a speech by Tom to his father, gives it as Kansas rather than Missouri.
13. *It Happened One Night,* released some six months earlier, was not particularly successful at the box office in its initial release, grossing only about $1 million, but it achieved far more critical success than *The Girl from Missouri* and it made an unprecedented sweep of the five major Academy Awards. *The Thin Man* was extremely successful both critically and commercially, grossing over $2 million and receiving four Academy nominations.
14. Andrew Bergman, *We're in the Money: Depression America and Its Films* (New York: New York University Press, 1971), 138.
15. Even the title of the magazine for which she works, *Boys' Constant Companion,* suggests a sexual innuendo in that Mary is assumed to be Ball's "companion" (i.e., his mistress).
16. Elizabeth Melosh, *Engendering Culture: Manhood and Womanhood in New Deal Public Art and Theater* (Washington, DC: Smithsonian Institution Press, 1991), 184.

**CHAPTER 3**

1. Leland Poague, *The Cinema of Frank Capra: An Approach to Film Comedy* (South Brunswick, NJ: A. S. Barnes, 1975), 57.
2. At the age of six, Capra emigrated with his family from Palermo, Sicily, settling in Los Angeles. Capra's father worked in a bottle plant, and his mother labeled olive cans, while Frank stuffed newspapers and waited on tables to help support the family.
3. Vito Zagarrio, "It is (Not) a Wonderful Life: For a Counter-Reading of Frank Capra," in Robert Sklar and Vito Zagarrio, eds., *Frank Capra: Authorship and the Studio System* (Philadelphia: Temple University Press, 1998), 85.
4. Lee Lourdeaux, *Italian and Irish Filmmakers in America: Ford, Coppola, Capra, and Scorsese* (Philadelphia: Temple University Press, 1990), 142.
5. At least some of the credit for this social vision must go to Capra's screenwriter Robert Riskin, though it is a matter of some debate to what extent Riskin's scripts contributed to Capra's conception of his projects.

6. Joseph McBride, *Frank Capra: The Catastrophe of Success* (New York: Simon and Schuster, 1992), 305.

7. See William Kittredge and Steven Krauzer, eds., *Stories into Film* (New York: Harper and Row, 1979), 34.

8. Roger Maltby, "*It Happened One Night:* The Recreation of the Patriarch," in Sklar and Zagarrio, *Frank Capra,* 149.

9. Rita Barnard and Barbara Ching comment very persuasively on the social symbolism of King Westley: "With his cane, tails, bow-tie, and self-satisfied demeanor, he clearly represents old money; he is a lounge lizard, reeking by 1934 of the departed glamour of the 1920s. Further, he is a celebrity aviator, a man of style who would make the silly gesture of arriving at this wedding in his autogyro … Representing an older generation, and an older socio-political dispensation, he will be legitimately and almost inevitably replaced by a man of a new, more vital, and more just order." See Barnard and Ching, "From Screwballs to Cheeseballs: Comic Narrative and Ideology in Capra and Reiner," *New Orleans Review* 17.3 (1990): 56.

10. Barnard and Ching, "From Screwballs to Cheeseballs," 54.

11. Elizabeth Kendall, *The Runaway Bride: Hollywood Romantic Comedy of the 1930s* (New York: Knopf, 1990), 42.

12. Charles Wolfe, *Frank Capra: A Guide to References and Resources* (Boston: G. K. Hall, 1987), 107.

13. Other important parallels between the two films establish them as versions of essentially the same story. Johnny Case in *Holiday,* like Dan Brooks in *Broadway Bill,* is a young working-class man of rising fortunes who has to decide between a marriage to a daughter of the wealthy Seton family — and the economic and social prestige associated with a successful career in business — and the "black sheep" daughter who represents the freedom to explore his own dreams.

14. Wolfe *Frank Capra,* 5.

15. Capra had worked at MGM on a film called *Brotherly Love* while on loan from Columbia in the late 1920s, and in 1933 he was again loaned to the studio to make *Soviet,* a film about life in the Soviet Union. Both of these experiences with the largest and most prestigious Hollywood studio were failures. Capra was fired by MGM in 1928, and the *Soviet* project was terminated after four months of work. According to Joseph McBride, Capra found the MGM environment constricting, despite larger budgets and higher production values than he was used to at Columbia. Like the Higginsville sons-in-law, MGM directors were well paid, but they were prohibited from gaining full control of their product. Forced to do extensive retakes on most pictures, directors were discouraged from developing "personal styles" (197) in the way they could at a smaller studio like Columbia.

16. Capra's use of music as a social marker is a motif that will continue throughout his comedies of the 1930s. In *Broadway Bill* we find the repeated song about the "split-pea soup and the succotash" that links the plebeian Dan Brooks to the upper-class Alice Higgins; in *Mr. Deeds Goes to Town* the tuba Longfellow Deeds plays in the town band serves as an emblem of small-town community life in opposition to the corrupt social world surrounding the opera; and in *You Can't Take It with You* the harmonica duet between Grandpa Vanderhof and Anthony P. Kirby represents their reconciliation – and that of their two families and social classes – at the end of the film.

17. Capra acknowledged this change in calling *Mr. Deeds* the "first of a series of social-minded films." Such a characterization is not altogether accurate, however, since nearly all of Capra's films of the Depression era – including the highly topical dramatic film *American Madness* as well as such comedies as *Platinum Blonde, Lady for a Day, It Happened One Night,* and *Broadway Bill*—are significantly engaged with social issues. By indicating that *Mr. Deeds* marks a departure from his previous work, however, Capra suggests that it was with this film that he began using his work as a vehicle for explicit political statement.

18. Raymond Carney reads *Deeds* as essentially a remake of *Platinum Blonde,* though with a quite different, and more complex, situation for the central character. See Carney, *American Vision: The Films of Frank Capra* (New York: Cambridge University Press, 1986), 273.

19. The name "Deeds" suggests both ownership (as in real estate deeds) and accomplishment (the "good deeds" he will perform in the second half of the film).

20. Charles Maland, "Capra and the Abyss: Self-Interest versus the Common Good in Depression America," in Sklar and Zagarrio, *Frank Capra,* 124.

21. The superfluity or redundancy of language can be seen even in the name of the law firm "Cedar, Cedar, Cedar, and Budington"; Deeds makes a joking reference to this early in the film when he suggests that "Budington must feel like an awful stranger."

22. Leland Poague, *Another Frank Capra* (New York: Cambridge University Press, 1994), 109.

23. Quoted in McBride, *Frank Capra,* 350.

## CHAPTER 4

1. As Brian Henderson suggests, the bank scene "reiterate[s] the social distance between the former lovers and hence reminds the viewer that Jean feels hurt and cheapened." See Henderson, ed., *Five Screenplays of Preston Sturges* (Berkeley: University of California Press, 1985), 345. This scene might have provided additional motivation for Jean's revenge, but it would have gone against the more comic tone of the rest of the film. The final filmed version of *The Lady Eve,* as opposed to the screenplay, appears to deemphasize Jean's class identification: for example, the line "I need him like Dempsey needed Firpo," with its reference to a contemporary prize-fight, is changed to the more generic "I need him like the axe needs the turkey." It would seem that at least part of the original revenge motive was based on social class. It was prompted, as the screenplay makes clear, by Jean's feeling that she wasn't deemed "good enough" for Charles, in both moral and socioeconomic terms.

2. Diane Jacobs, *Christmas in July: The Life and Art of Preston Sturges* (Berkeley: University of California Press, 1992), 91–92.

3. Another satirical scene involving the relationship between the American upper class and the British aristocracy is that in which the Pikes' English butler and the French chef attempt to prepare a cake with the appropriate design for the "Sidwich" family from Burke's Peerage. As the butler reads the lengthy and arcane description, the chef tries to put the design on the cake with a squirtgun. Finally, he gives up in disgust and slams down the squirtgun, shooting cream

onto the butler's face. The Pike household, despite its upper-class pretensions, is clearly not up to the demands of entertaining aristocracy.

4. Brian Henderson, "Cartoon and Narrative," in Andrew Horton, ed., *Comedy/Cinema/Theory* (Berkeley: University of California Press, 1991), 166.

5. Rowe, *The Unruly Woman*, 167.

6. This exchange fits a pattern of Charles misunderstanding Jean, or Jean/Eve deliberately misunderstanding Charles in order to mock him. At one point, Charles suggests that her father's cardplaying is "uneven." When Jean ironically comments that he is "more uneven sometimes than others," Charles obtusely retorts, "that's what makes him uneven, of course." In the proposal scene with Eve, Charles declares that "lots of men are more careful in choosing a tailor than they are in choosing a wife." Eve replies: "That's probably why they look so funny." Charles, in his gently pedantic manner, corrects her: "No, dear, they're *more* careful in choosing a tailor than in choosing a wife."

7. The parallel is made explicit when Charles tells Muggsy to take flowers from him to Jean: "It's your funeral," Muggsy replies.

8. In this respect *The Lady Eve* appears to be a rewriting of *Remember the Night*, the melodramatic romantic comedy written by Sturges and directed by Mitchell Leisen the previous year. In that film the female protagonist, also played by Stanwyck, is a compulsive thief from a lower-class background who is "reformed" when she falls in love with a prosecuting attorney played by Fred MacMurray.

9. Todd McCarthy gives the consensus view when he claims that "*Ball of Fire* doesn't rate with Hawks's best comedies of the period, *Bringing Up Baby* and *His Girl Friday*, although it remains utterly charming for the brash cleverness of the dialogue, the heartwarming geniality of the professors, and the expert comic playing of Cooper and Stanwyck." See Todd McCarthy, *Howard Hawks: The Grey Fox of Hollywood* (New York: Grove Press, 1997), 327. James Harvey, in a rather strange omission, does not even mention the film in his *Romantic Comedy*, though he discusses every other Hawks comedy. Audiences, however, appear to have embraced *Ball of Fire*, which earned $2.2 million at the box office to land in the top twenty-five films of the year. *Bringing Up Baby*, by contrast, was a major box-office disappointment, with combined domestic and overseas revenues of just $1.1 million, not even enough to recoup its cost.

10. "Match Boogie" is sung *sotto voce* and played with a pair of matches on a matchbox instead of drums.

11. The name "Sugarpuss" suggests both the sexual and vocal parts of the anatomy.

12. According to McCarthy, Potts's speeches were so pedantic and complicated that Cooper complained to Hawks about the difficulty of speaking the dialogue (325).

13. Both Ginger Rogers and Carole Lombard rejected the role of Sugarpuss, and Jean Arthur, Lucille Ball, and Betty Field were all considered before the final decision was made to cast Stanwyck.

14. Ed Sikov includes *Christmas in July, The Lady Eve, The Palm Beach Story*, and *Unfaithfully Yours* in the "Selected Filmography" of *Screwball*. Sturges's other comedies of the 1940s – *Hail the Conquering Hero, Sullivan's Travels, The Miracle of Morgan's Creek*, and *Mad Wednesday* – all contain elements of screwball comedy, though none conforms to the screwball genre as it is generally defined.

15. The first Tom and Jerry cartoons were released in 1941, the same year in which *The Palm Beach Story* was written and filmed.

16. According to Brian Henderson, Sturges was forced to cut a number of lines that equated John D. Hackensacker too openly with the Rockefeller family. See Brian Henderson, ed. *Four More Screenplays of Preston Sturges* (Berkeley: University of California Press, 1995), 64. Nevertheless, the film makes obvious reference to John D. Rockefeller's "legendary tightness," including his habit of only tipping a dime.

17. This is not surprising, since the film was based on a play, *A Cup of Coffee,* written by Sturges in the early 1930s.

18. *Four More Screenplays,* 46. The type-casting of Claudette Colbert as Gerry also plays with her screen persona, further suggesting that Sturges is parodying aspects of the 1930s screwball comedy rather than merely trying to re-create the genre. Colbert had made a specialty of golddigger roles in the 1930s, from the stenographer who makes a play for an English duke in *The Gilded Lily* (1935), to the secretary who takes over the boss's business in *She Married Her Boss* (1935), to the shopgirl who attracts two rival suitors in an Alpine resort in *I Met Him in Paris* (1937), to the impoverished daughter of a French aristocrat who marries a rich American in Lubitsch's *Bluebeard's Eighth Wife* (1938), to the golddigging American showgirl in Mitchell Leisen's *Midnight* (1939).

19. The frequent reference to the $99,000 figure throughout the film makes it seem all the more absurd, rendering it less a real amount of money than an abstraction. As Hackensacker puts it, "Ninety-nine thousand dollars isn't a small amount … on the other hand it isn't large." The comedy is enhanced by the fact that Gerry has to ask for the money twice: Once as a payoff for her "husband" and once to help her "brother" build his airport. On the second occasion, she tries to disguise the duplication by asking for "about a hundred thousand dollars," leaving the audience to wonder where the $99,000 figure came from in the first place.

20. John D. is not only far wealthier than Hopsie Pike, but he is also further removed from the origins of his wealth. It was his grandfather (John D. Hackensacker I) and not his father who made the original family fortune. John D. himself confesses to this fact in his conversation with Gerry: "I'm not my grandfather of course … he's dead anyway. I'm John D. the Third." So unoriginal is John D. that he uses his grandfather's yacht and follows his habit of writing his accounts in a notebook. In the case of the grandfather, this habit was presumably attached to some actual thriftiness, but for the current John D. it has become simply a personality tick with no real significance.

21. Quoted in Ray Cywinski, *Preston Sturges: A Guide to References and Sources* (Boston: G. K. Hall, 1984).

22. The scene receives another level of irony from the fact that Vallee, who sings the song in the film as Hackensacker, had in fact written and successfully recorded the same song, "Goodnight, Sweetheart." See *Four More Screenplays,* 78–79.

23. It was the film's treatment of marriage and divorce that offended the censors from the Hays Office. Although the picture was finally approved with only relatively minor changes, there was a good deal of correspondence between the censors and Struges concerning details of the script, particularly those involving sexual innuendo.

24. Given the similarity of the word to the German word for "cut," it may also be a private joke, making Toto a comic stand-in for the director himself.

25. In fact, John D. appears to confuse his own categories. In the same speech to Gerry, he bemoans the death of chivalry but also claims that "the days of serfdom" are over. Torn between aristocratic values and what he believes to be democratic sensibilities, his class attitudes remain ambivalent.

26. The theme of children and of John D.'s possible inability to father any recurs throughout the film. When John D. declares that he will finance Tom's airport, even if Tom is Gerry's husband, the Princess jokingly says, "You might have little airports some day." Of course, John D. is not alone in his failure to reproduce: Tom and Gerry are childless after five years of marriage, and the Princess has no children from any of her marriages.

27. This fact was of more than merely theoretical interest to Sturges, who had at one time married into the wealthy Hutton family, with disastrous consequences.

28. The unenthusiastic critical reception of *The Palm Beach Story* suggests that reviewers and audiences may not have been prepared for the film's ambiguously cynical tone. As Diane Jacobs suggests, critics "either missed or were unconvinced by the sober undertones" of the film. Bosley Crowther, for example, wrote that Sturges had abandoned the "harsh reality" of *Sullivan's Travels* to make "hey-hey films." Other critics wrote of the film's "airy nothings of matrimonial contentions" (Archer Winsten) and called it "not as completely satisfying a film entertainment as other Sturges pictures" (Kate Cameron). See Jacobs, *Christmas in July*, 289. If my reading of the film as a parody of the screwball genre is accurate, the film is *intentionally* unsatisfying, and its reality is even harsher than that of *Sullivan's Travels*, since no redemptive ending is possible in *The Palm Beach Story* as it was in that film. Duane Byrge and Robert Miller at least hint at an interpretation of the film as parody rather than as traditional screwball comedy in their reading of the ending. See Byrge and Miller, *The Screwball Comedy Films: A History and Filmography, 1934–1942* (Jefferson, NC: McFarland, 1991), 132–33.

29. Similarly, *Sullivan's Travels* can be seen in part as a parody of *It Happened One Night*: both films have cross-country journey plots in which the upper-class character is forced to cross class barriers in the path to self-discovery. The social critique is more trenchant in *Sullivan's Travels* than in Capra's film. Where Ellie Andrews is able to make the class switch that is required of her, the gap between Sullivan and "real" poverty is shown as too absolute to cross, as Sullivan comes to realize at the end of the film. *It Happened One Night* follows a fairly conventional plot of romantic comedy in terms of plot and characterization, but *Sullivan's Travels* is distanced from the romance plot by what Brian Henderson has called its "more externalized … cartoonized version of romance" ("Cartoon and Narrative," 169).

30. *Pursuits of Happiness*, 153.

31. Compare, for example, the tasteful sailing yacht built by Dexter for Tracy in *The Philadelphia Story* (the "True Love"), with the ostentatious power yacht owned by John D. in *The Palm Beach Story*.

32. In part, it is the increasingly cartoonlike quality of Sturges's later films that militates against any direct social statement. Sturges dropped the class theme from his original idea for *The Miracle of Morgan's Creek*, conceived in the late 1930s, which involved a small-town girl seduced by a banker's son. In the film, Trudy

becomes pregnant during a one-night stand with a soldier who goes off to war the following day.

**CHAPTER 5**

1. Ed Sikov, *Laughing Hysterically: American Screen Comedy in the 1950s* (New York: Columbia University Press, 1994), 76.
2. While the hyperbolic performances of Monroe and Russell may be read as a carnivalesque subversion of dominant or patriarchal norms, the film certainly does not seek to overturn the dominant social ideology in any fundamental way. Nor is Monroe's Lorelei intended as parody, though Frank Tashlin would use Jayne Mansfield to parody *Monroe's* performances later in the decade. Rather than a satire or parody of stereotypical gender and class relations, the film functions as a rather straightforward exaggeration of them: the avaricious blonde wants men for their money; the wholesome brunette wants them for love and sex. Hawks himself described the film as a "fairy tale" and rejected the ironic reversal of the original screenplay, in which Lorelei ends up marrying for love and Dorothy for money. See Noel Simsolo, *Howard Hawks* (Paris: Edilig, 1984), 124.
3. Marianne Conroy, "'No Sin in Lookin' Prosperous': Gender, Race, and the Class Formations of Middlebrow Taste in Douglas Sirk's *Imitation of Life*," in David James and Rick Berg, eds., *The Hidden Foundation: Cinema and the Question of Class* (Minneapolis: University of Minnesota Press, 1996), 115–16.
4. C. Wright Mills, *White Collar: The American Middle Classes* (New York: Oxford University Press, 1951), 75.
5. Ibid., 76. On the changing distribution of incomes, see Mills, *White Collar*, 72–73. Whereas in the mid-1930s the median income of white-collar employees was over 50% higher than that of urban wage-workers, by the postwar era (1948) that difference had fallen to only about 20%, with the lower echelons of the white-collar spectrum actually earning about the same as skilled workers and foremen. This trend continued throughout the 1950s. By 1957, such "blue-collar" jobs as bricklayer, steelworker, electrician, and construction worker were more highly paid than such "limited-success" white-collar professions as schoolteacher, airline agent, IRS agent, and bank clerk. See Vance Packard, *The Status Seekers: An Exploration of Class Behavior in America and the Hidden Barriers That Affect You, Your Community, Your Future* (New York: D. McKay, 1959), 102–3.
6. Mills, *White Collar*, 73.
7. Esther Milner, *The Failure of Success: The Middle-Class Crisis* (St. Louis, MO: Warren G. Green, 1955), 13.
8. Stephen Harvey, *Directed by Vincente Minnelli* (New York: Museum of Modern Art/Harper and Row, 1989), 160.
9. Packard, *The Failure of Success*, 313–15.
10. Harvey, *Directed by Vincente Minnelli*, 166.
11. Ibid., 26.
12. The epitome of the smoothly masculine Hollywood actor of which Randall plays the nervous antithesis, Peck was also the star of *The Man in the Grey Flannel Suit*, the 1956 picture depicting the life of a Madison Avenue executive. Rock's "pipe troubles" signal a physical and possible sexual inadequacy as well as a lack of the success drive.

13. Cynthia Fuchs, "Split Screens: Framing and Passing in *Pillow Talk*," in Joel Foreman, ed., *The Other Fifties: Interrogating Midcentury American Icons* (Urbana: University of Illinois Press, 1997), 240.
14. Frank Krutnik, "Jerry Lewis: The Deformation of the Comic," *Film Quarterly* 48.1 (1994): 14.
15. Scott Bukatman, "Paralysis in Motion: Jerry Lewis's Life as a Man," in Andrew Horton, ed., *Comedy/Cinema/Theory* (Berkeley and Los Angeles: University of California Press, 1991), 204. In the 1996 remake of the film, with Eddie Murphy in the Lewis role, ethnicity is more overtly marked. Both of the characters portrayed by Murphy, the shy and overweight Professor Klump and the handsome and oversexed Buddy Love, are African-American, and various aspects of black American culture are satirized in the film. The film seems to elide the question of race at the very moment it marks it. The caricatures of black culture represented by Klump (the overweight momma's boy) and Love (the obnoxiously flashy and testosterone-filled playboy) could be seen as racist depictions of cultural stereotypes. Yet although nearly everyone else at the small college where Klump works is white, Murphy's race is never explicitly mentioned. Instead, another form of prejudice, against "fat" people, substitutes for the unspoken racial prejudice. The overweight black man is an acceptable butt of humor in the 1990s, just as the nerdy intellectual Jewish man was an acceptable target in the 1960s.
16. Robert Liebman, "Rabbis or Rakes, Schlemiels or Supermen? Jewish Identity in Charles Chaplin, Jerry Lewis, and Woody Allen," *Literature/Film Quarterly* 12.3 (1984): 196.
17. Ibid., 196.
18. *The Delicate Delinquent* comes the closest of any Lewis film to dealing with real social issues. On one level a parody of the juvenile delinquency "social problem" film of the 1950s, it is also the highly sentimentalized story of Sidney Pythias, a janitor from the slums who is mistaken for a gang member and given a chance to become a police officer despite his obvious unsuitability for the profession. Unfortunately, the film never decides what it wants to be, failing either to sustain its parody or to achieve any meaningful social comment.
19. Bukatman, "Paralysis in Motion," 200.
20. Lewis's tendency to play multiple roles in his films, such as the five characters he portrays in *Three on a Couch* (1966) and the three in *The Big Mouth* (1967), can be read simply as a promotional ploy meant to exploit Lewis's comic versatility, but they also point to the fracturing of a unified social self.

**CHAPTER 6**
1. Allen's use of parody can be contrasted with that of a more mainstream comic filmmaker like Mel Brooks. As Mark Siegal has suggested, Brooks makes light of various film genres, adopting parody as a means of "spoofing" genres like the western *(Blazing Saddles)*, the psychological thriller *(High Anxiety)*, the Broadway musical *(The Producers)*, or the horror film *(Young Frankenstein)*. Allen, on the other hand, is a "serious parodist," in whose work "parody can be a tool to stretch artistic forms to their logical (or illogical) limits in order to test the extent of their viability." See "Ozymandius Melancholia: The Nature of Parody in Woody Allen's *Stardust Memories*," in *Literature/Film Quarterly* 13.2 (1985): 77.

2. Ruth Perlmutter places Allen in the tradition of what she calls "immigrant culture-shock comics," film comedians who use comic motifs—including vulgar taste, aggression, antisocial behavior, confusion of genre registers, and formal dislocations—in order to suggest that "the crisis of the maker and the spectator of comedy is also the crisis of Jewishness and American culture." See "Woody Allen's *Zelig:* An American Jewish Parody," in Andrew Horton, ed., *Comedy/Cinema/Theory* (Berkeley: University of California Press, 1991), 215. Like Chaplin and the Marx Brothers before him, Allen uses such "culture-shock" tactics to combine elements of both parody and satire, utilizing all the means at his disposal to challenge the patterns and assumptions of the dominant culture.

3. Jameson's reading of postmodern film is concerned primarily with its use of a mode of historical "nostalgia" as a form of historical pastiche or "blank parody." See *Postmodernism, or, The Cultural Logic of Late Capitalism* (Durham, NC: Duke University Press, 1992).

4. Graham McGann, *Woody Allen: New Yorker* (Cambridge, MA: Polity Press, 1990), 3, 54.

5. Allen himself felt these insecurities acutely, as indicated by his numerous jokes about his failure to finish college and his distrust of academic intellectuals.

6. Allen describes it as "a very Jewish neighborhood" and describes his family background as "very ethnic, lower-middle-class." See Robert Benayoun, *Woody Allen, Beyond Words,* trans. Alexander Walker (New York: Harmony Books, 1986), 158–59.

7. Gerald Mast, "Woody Allen: The Neurotic Jew as American Clown," in Sarah Cohen, ed., *Jewish Wry: Essays on Jewish Humor* (Bloomington: Indiana University Press, 1987), 126.

8. Eric Lax, *Woody Allen: A Biography* (New York: Knopf, 1991), 165.

9. Allen's anachronistic use of his persona in order to emphasize his misfit status is in fact a common device in his earlier films. In *Sleeper,* Miles Monroe is a 1970s character (owner of the Happy Carrot health food restaurant) who wakes up two hundred years later in a "cosmic screw-up" and is forced to become an outlaw in order to escape a police state. In *Love and Death,* Boris is an equally striking misfit in the nineteenth-century Christian society of Napoleonic Russia. These anachronistic encounters between the contemporary Allen figure and societies of the past and future function as allegories of his encounters with his own world. In many respects, it is society that is insane and the Allen character – despite his many neuroses — who is relatively sane or rational.

10. Maurice Yacowar, *Loser Take All: The Comic Art of Woody Allen* (New York: Imgar, 1979), 122.

11. Mellish's outsider status in the film is literalized by visual gags as well. In one scene, when Mellish attempts to ask an attractive secretary for a date, he pulls the doorknob off before opening the door to enter her room and absurdly continues to hold the knob throughout the scene.

12. Allen's San Marcos is even more dystopic than the Marx Brothers' Freedonia. Known primarily for its large population of locusts and the number of hernias its citizens suffer, the country has little to offer the United States in exchange for military or economic aid.

13. Yale's last name, "Pollack," may also denote the pretentiousness of the art world through its resemblance to the abstract expressionist painter Jackson Pollock.
14. At the end of the film, Ike will compose his own list of favorite things, as if needing to have the final say on cultural value. Significantly, Ike's list is far less pretentious than Yale and Mary's, including popular culture (Groucho Marx, Willie Mays, Marlon Brando, and Frank Sinatra) as well as traditional high culture (Flaubert, Cézanne, and Mozart).
15. *Subversive Pleasures,* 216.
16. Quoted in Perlmutter, "Woody Allen's *Zelig,*" 214.
17. Richard Feldstein, "The Dissolution of the Self in *Zelig,*" *Literature/Film Quarterly* 13.3 (1985): 158.
18. See the analysis of the film in Christopher Knight, "Woody Allen's *Hannah and Her Sisters:* Domesticity and Its Discontents," *Literature/Film Quaterly* 24.4 (1996).

## CHAPTER 7

1. David Harvey, *The Condition of Postmodernity: An Enquiry into the Origins of Cultural Change* (Oxford and Cambridge, MA: Blackwell, 1989), 332.
2. According to a study published in the *Journal of Advertising Research* (J. Burnett and A. Bush, 1986), while only 14% of the baby-boom generation (those born from 1946 to 1964) can be counted as actual yuppies, nearly 50% can be defined as "psychographic yuppies" who follow the tastes and attitudes established by the yuppies themselves.
3. The cadre of young, sophisticated, upwardly mobile urban professionals portrayed in Woody Allen's films of the 1970s such as *Play It Again, Sam, Annie Hall,* and *Manhattan* can be labeled "proto-yuppies," a socioeconomically ambitious generation whose tastes, values, and participation in what Christopher Lasch called "the culture of narcissism" anticipate the yuppie culture of the Reagan years. As Douglas Brode has observed, Allen's films function at least in part as critiques of the culture of narcissism, whether it is Alvy Singer sneezing away hundreds of dollars worth of cocaine in *Annie Hall,* or Isaac Davis rejecting the superficial and narcissistic lifestyle of his friends in *Manhattan.* See *Woody Allen: His Films and Career* (Secaucus, NJ: Citadel Press, 1985), 23.
4. Douglas Kellner and Michael Ryan, *Camera Politica: The Politics and Ideology of Contemporary Hollywood Film* (Bloomington: Indiana University Press, 1988), 120.
5. While I consider *Beverly Hills Cop* and other Eddie Murphy comedies *(48 Hours, Trading Places, Coming to America)* to be more mainstream in their orientation than the films I treat in this chapter, they are of some interest in terms of the intersecting presentation of class and racial issues they provide. The idealized image of racial harmony projected by these films – and the reconciliation of both racial and class difference found in these comedies as well as those of Richard Pryor – may contain a certain degree of "counter ideological potential," as Ryan and Kellner suggest, but the films are essentially conservative in their treatment of both race and class, ignoring, as Ryan and Kellner also observe, "the increasingly brutal reality of life for blacks in a situation of recession and conservative economic retrenchment" (126). The success of such

black comedians as Pryor and Murphy can be seen as a generally positive development within American culture, but it must be recognized as at least somewhat problematic that the most celebrated black performers of the era were both comedians whose work (in films by white directors) contained little subversive potential and was in fact "well suited to the active forgetfulness of significant social issues underway at the time" (128).

6. Jeff Evans, "Comic Rhetoric in *Raising Arizona*," *Studies in American Humor* 4.3 (1996): 39.

7. The comic treatment of the unsuccessful but dogged career criminal also owes something to Woody Allen's *Take the Money and Run.*

8. Much of the irony is produced by the use of Hi's voiceover narrative, which offers a laconic summary of events. After describing his job "drilling holes in sheet metal," Hi observes that "mostways the job was a lot like prison." After receiving his "paycheck at the end of every week," we see Hi scowling at the amount that is deducted for taxes.

9. A further ironic commentary on the babies as commodified "excess" is provided by the conversation Nathan is having with one of his subordinates as Hi is upstairs trying to take a baby. Apparently, the warehouse has received eight hundred leaf tables with no chairs, which will be impossible to sell.

10. Most of Tom's forcefully expressed opinions are based less on real knowledge than on glib party talk and a course or two at Princeton, where he is in his freshman year. When another young woman in the group, Audrey Rouget, tells him of her admiration for the work of Jane Austen, he dismisses Austen without having read any of her novels.

11. Both audiences and critics found the film's comedy too dark, and despite a successful opening weekend of $20 million at the box office, the film only grossed about $60 million domestically, making it a commercial failure by the standards of Carrey's other films.

12. Michael Ferraro, "Global Village Idiot," *American Cinematographer* 77.7 (1996): 77. *The Cable Guy* can be contrasted with a film like Woody Allen's *Take the Money and Run,* which is a pure parody: we never think of Virgil Starkwell as a real criminal or have the sense that this is a real crime film.

13. Mark Poster, *The Mode of Information: Poststructuralism and Social Context* (Cambridge and Oxford: Polity Press/Basil Blackwell, 1990), 63.

14. See Jean Baudrillard, *Simulations,* trans. Paul Moss et al. (New York: Semiotext (e), 1992).